/

A GUIDE TO BIRD WATCHING

A Guide to BIRD WATCHING

By

JOSEPH J. HICKEY

With Illustrations by Francis Lee Jaques and
Bird Tracks by Charles A. Urner

DOVER PUBLICATIONS, INC., NEW YORK

International Standard Book Number: 0-486-21596-2
Library of Congress Catalog Card Number: 74-18718

Manufactured in the United States of America
Dover Publications, Inc.
180 Varick Street
New York, N.Y. 10014

TO
PEGGY

Foreword

Since Joseph J. Hickey's book appeared two decades ago
many new discoveries about birds have come to light, vast
strides have been made in the ornithological sciences, notably
ethology, and recent techniques and improvements in avian
photography, ocular equipment, sound recording, use of radar
in migration studies, widespread use of mist nets in banding,
and numerous other advances have occurred or been developed.
Despite this, *A Guide to Bird Watching* is remarkably modern
in its approach and extremely informative to the layman and
professional, to the neophyte and advanced student.

Hickey's style is such that the reader will want to finish the
book at a single sitting, and yet this volume is so packed with
interesting facts that it is extremely valuable as a reference
work. This book guides the bird watcher from the beginning
stages of field identification and listing, as well as the when,
where, and how of watching birds, to more advanced phases
of field work and ornithological endeavors for both amateurs
and professionals-to-be. That the author has succeeded in doing
this admirably is evident in his six chapters. The appendices
are in reality more than the heading implies. They are chapters
in themselves, replete with fascinating data.

The character of the book reflects the author himself. His
enthusiasm in his writing is contagious. However, the outstanding quality of the book is the author's ability to stimulate
and encourage the beginner to advance beyond the mere identification and listing stage, although no one more than Hickey
himself realizes that these are basic essentials for further
development in bird watching.

Hickey's ability as a teacher is renowned. During his earlier amateur days in New York City he was actively occupied in the business world with ornithology as an avocation pursued only on weekends and vacations. His election as president of the Linnaean Society of New York was fortunate indeed for the membership. His guidance inspired amateurs, particularly the younger observers, to engage in many worthwhile ornithological projects. When he left the New York area not long afterward, to the keen disappointment of all concerned, he took up residence in Madison, Wisconsin. There he joined the ranks of professional ornithologists and accepted a teaching position. Hickey is now a professor at the University of Wisconsin, where for many years he has distinguished himself in the fields of conservation and wildlife management. His services to ornithology and his numerous publications resulted in his election in 1954 as a Fellow of the American Ornithologists' Union. His success as professional instructor at a leading educational institution in developing graduate and undergraduate students alike is as remarkable as his earlier success as an amateur "instructor" at Linnaean Society meetings years ago. In both instances Hickey stimulated interest not only in various bird studies, but also in publication of findings and observations.

It is hoped that the suggested references updating Hickey's still very useful Appendix D, "An Annotated List of Bird Books," will be helpful to the reader. These references are considered representative of the various topics outlined below. Due to space limitations it has been necessary to omit many important regional works, such as all state lists with the exception of our two new states, Alaska and Hawaii, and all monographs on single species, of which there are now multitudes. Reviews of these may be found in the periodicals listed below. Since interest in tropical birds, and to a lesser extent arctic birds, has increased greatly in recent years, they are included, with emphasis on North America. New books on world birds are treated here, as well as a number of recent works of general interest. No attempt is made to annotate this list. Only the author, title, publisher, and date of publication are included. Where color plates are an important feature of a book, this is indicated with an asterisk.

JOHN L. BULL
Former President,
Linnaean Society of New York

New York City
August 1962

SUGGESTED REFERENCES
(Revised 1974)

An interesting reprint, "On the Building of a Basic Ornithological Library," can be obtained for $1.25 by writing *American Birds,* 950 Third Avenue, New York, N.Y. 10022.

Field Identification

* *A Field Guide to the Birds*—Roger T. Peterson (1947, second rev. ed.), Houghton Mifflin, Boston.
* *A Field Guide to Western Birds*—Roger T. Peterson (1961, second rev. ed.), Houghton Mifflin, Boston. Includes Hawaiian birds.
* *A Field Guide to the Birds of Britain and Europe*—Roger T. Peterson, Guy Mountfort, and P. A. D. Hollom (1966, second rev. ed.), Collins, London, and Houghton Mifflin, Boston.
* *Audubon Bird Guide, Eastern Land Birds*—Richard H. Pough—paintings by Don R. Eckelberry (1946), Doubleday, New York.
* *Audubon Water Bird Guide*—Richard H. Pough—paintings by Don Eckelberry (1957), Doubelday, New York.
* *Audubon Western Bird Guide*—Richard H. Pough—paintings by Don R. Eckelberry (1957), Doubleday, New York.
* *Birds of the West Indies*—James Bond—paintings by Don R. Eckelberry (1961), Houghton Mifflin, Boston.
* *The Birds of Trinidad and Tobago*—G. A. C. Herklots (1961), Collins, London.
* *A Field Guide to the Birds of Texas*—Roger T. Peterson (1960), Houghton Mifflin, Boston.

* *Birds of North America*—Chandler S. Robbins, Bertel Bruun, and H. S. Zim (1966), Golden Press, New York.
* *A Field Guide to Mexican Birds and Adjacent Central America*—Roger T. Peterson and Edward L. Chaliff (1973), Houghton Mifflin, Boston.
* *Birds of Europe*—Bertel Bruun and Arthur Singer (1971), McGraw-Hill, New York.

Distribution, World   .

* *Living Birds of the World*—E. Thomas Gilliard—color photos (1958), Doubleday, New York.
* *Birds of the World*—Oliver L. Austin, Jr.—paintings by Arthur Singer (1961), Golden Press, New York.
  Extinct and Vanishing Birds of the World—James C. Greenway, Jr. (1958), American Committee for International Wild Life Protection, New York. (Dover reprint.)
  Birds Around the World: A Geographical Look at Evolution and Birds— Dean Amadon (1966), Natural History Press, Garden City, N.Y.

Distribution, Regional

* *Land Birds of America*—Robert C. Murphy and Dean Amadon—color photos (1953), McGraw-Hill, New York.
* *American Water and Game Birds*—Austin L. Rand—color photos (1956), E. P. Dutton, New York.
  Arctic Birds of Canada—L. L. Snyder (1957), University of Toronto Press.
* *The Birds of Greenland*—Finn Salomonsen—paintings by Gitz-Johansen (1950), Munksgaard, Copenhagen.
* *Mexican Birds: First Impressions*—George M. Sutton (1951), University of Oklahoma Press, Norman, Okla.
* *Birds of the Caribbean*—Robert P. Allen—color photos (1961), Viking Press, New York.
  The Birds of Canada—W. Earl Godfrey (1967), National Museum of Canada, Ottawa.

The *American Birds* reprint mentioned at the beginning of this bibliography contains a good selection of regional bird books.

Check-Lists

Check-List of Birds of the World—James L. Peters (15 volumes with two gaps, 1931–68)—edited by Raymond A. Paynter, Jr., Ernst Mayr, and James C. Greenway, Jr.), Harvard University Press, Cambridge, Mass.

Check-List of North American Birds—(1957), fifth ed.), American Ornithologists' Union, Smithsonian Institution, Washington.

Check-List of Birds of the West Indies—James Bond (1956, fourth ed.), Academy of Natural Sciences, Philadelphia.

* *Distributional Check-List of the Birds of Mexico*—Herbert Friedmann, Ludlow Griscom, and Robert T. Moore—edited by Alden H. Miller, (1950, part 1; 1957, part 2), Cooper Ornithological Society, c/o Museum of Vertebrate Zoology, Berkeley, Calif.

The Species of Middle American Birds—Eugene Eisenmann (1955), Linnaean Society of New York, c/o American Museum of Natural History, New York.

Special Groups

* *The Waterfowl of the World*—Jean Delacour—paintings by Peter Scott (1954, vol. 1; 1956, vol. 2; 1959, vol. 3), Country Life, London.

Sea-Birds—James Fisher and R. M. Lockley (1954), Houghton Mifflin, Boston.

A Gathering of Shore Birds—Henry M. Hall—edited by Roland C. Clement (1960), Devin-Adair, New York.

* *The Warblers of America*—Ludlow Griscom, Alexander Sprunt, Jr., and others—paintings by John H. Dick (1957), Devin-Adair, New York.

* *Hummingbirds*—Crawford H. Greenewalt—color photos by the author (1960), American Museum of Natural History, New York.

Eagles, Hawks and Falcons of the World—Leslie Brown and Dean Amadon (2 vols., 1968), McGraw-Hill, New York.

Owls of the World—John A. Burton (1973), E. P. Dutton, New York.

Pigeons and Doves of the World—Derek Goodwin (1967), British Museum (Natural History), London.

Waterfowl: Their Biology and Natural History—Paul A. Johnsgard (1968), University of Nebraska Press, Lincoln.

Handbook of Waterfowl Behavior—Paul A. Johnsgard (1965), Cornell University Press, Ithaca.

Cranes of the World—Lawrence Walkinshaw (1973), Winchester Press, New York.

Life History

Life Histories of North American Birds—Arthur C. Bent, Smithsonian Institution, Washington. (For other listings see Appendix D.) (Dover reprints.)
  Jays, Crows, and Titmice (1946).
  Nuthatches, Wrens, Thrashers, and Their Allies (1948).
  Thrushes, Kinglets, and Their Allies (1949).
  Wagtails, Shrikes, Vireos, and Their Allies (1950).
  Wood Warblers (1953).
  Blackbirds, Orioles, Tanagers, and Their Allies (1958).
  Cardinals, Grosbeaks, Buntings, Towhees, Finches, Sparrows, and Their Allies (3 vols. 1968).

* *Life Histories of Central American Birds*—Alexander Skutch —paintings by Don R. Eckelberry (1954, vol. 1; 1960, vol. 2), Cooper Ornithological Society, c/o Museum of Vertebrate Zoology, Berkeley, Calif.

* *Handbook of North American Birds: Loons to Flamingos*— edited by Ralph S. Palmer—paintings by Robert M. Mengel and Roger T. Peterson (1962, vol. 1), Yale University Press, New Haven.

The Handbook of British Birds— H. F. Witherby, F. C. R. Jourdain, N. F. Ticehurst, and B. W. Tucker, 5 vols. (1943–1944, rev. ed.), Witherby, London.

Birds of the Soviet Union—edited by G. P. Demet'ev and N. A. Gladkov (6-vol. translation 1966–68), U.S. Department of Commerce, Springfield, Va.

Handbuch der Vögel Mitteleuropas—Kurt M. Bauer, Urs N. Glutz von Blotzheim, and Einhard Bezzell (a series of volumes beginning in 1966), Akademische Verlagsgesellschaft, Frankfurt-am-Main.

Voice

A Guide to Bird Songs—Aretas A. Saunders (1951, rev. ed.), Doubleday, New York.

Bird Song: The Biology of Vocal Communication and Expression in Birds—W. H. Thorpe (1961), Cambridge University Press, London.

A Study of Bird Song—Edward A. Armstrong (1963), Oxford University Press, London. (Dover reprint).

Bird Song: Acoustics and Physiology—Crawford H. Greenewalt (1968), Smithsonian Institution, Washington.

Bird Watching

Watching Birds—James Fisher (1951), Penguin Books, London.

The Animal in Its World—Niko Tinbergen (1972), Harvard University Press, Cambridge, Mass.

The Life of the Robin—David Lack (fourth ed., 1965), Witherby, London.

Photography

Hunting with the Camera—edited by Allan D. Cruickshank (1957), Harper & Row, New York.

General

A Guide to Bird Finding East of the Mississippi—Olin S. Pettingill, Jr. (1951), Oxford University Press, New York.

A Guide to Bird Finding West of the Mississippi—Olin S. Pettingill, Jr. (1953), Oxford University Press, New York.

Animal Dispersion in Relation to Social Behaviour—V. C. Wynne-Edwards (1962), Oliver & Boyd, Edinburgh.

Parental Care and Its Evolution in Birds—S. C. Kendeigh (1952), University of Illinois Press, Urbana, Illinois.

The Natural Regulation of Animal Numbers—David Lack (1954), Oxford University Press, London.

The Herring Gull's World—Niko Tinbergen (1953), Collins, London.

Fundamentals of Ecology—E. P. Odum (1953), W. B. Saunders, Philadelphia.

The Migration of Birds—Frederick C. Lincoln (1952, rev. ed.), Doubleday, New York.

A Laboratory and Field Manual of Ornithology—Olin S. Pettingill, Jr. (1956, third ed.), Burgess, Minneapolis.

An Introduction to Ornithology—George J. Wallace (1955), Macmillan, New York.

Bird—Lois and Louis Darling (1962), Houghton Mifflin, Boston.

Instructions to Young Ornithologists—Museum Press, London.

Bird Biology—J.D. MacDonald (1959, no. 1).

Fundamentals of Ornithology—Josselyn Van Tyne and Andrew J. Berger (1959), Wiley, New York. (Dover reprint.)

Bird Behaviour—Derek Goodwin (1961, no. 2).

The Birds—Oskar and Patharina Heinroth (1958), University of Michigan Press, Ann Arbor, Mich.

Systematics and the Origin of Species—Ernst Mayr (1942), Columbia University Press, New York. (Dover reprint.)

Methods and Principles of Systematic Zoology—E. Mayr, E. G. Linsley, and R. L. Usinger (1953), McGraw-Hill, New York.

Social Behaviour in Animals—Niko Tinbergen (1953), Wiley, New York.

Bird Life—Niko Tinbergen (1954), Oxford University Press, London.

The Flight of Birds—John H. Storer (1948), Cranbrook Institute of Science, Bloomfield Hills, Mich.

Bird Study—Andrew J. Berger (1961), Wiley, New York. (Dover reprint.)

A New Dictionary of Birds—A. Landsborough Thomson (1964), McGraw-Hill, New York.

The World of Birds—James Fisher and Roger T. Peterson (1964), Doubleday, Garden City, New York.

The Birds—Roger T. Peterson and the Editors of *Life* (1963), Time, Inc., New York.

Avian Biology—edited by Donald S. Farner and James R. King (various volumes starting in 1971), Academic Press, New York.

Breeding Biology of Birds—edited by Donald S. Farner (1973), National Academy of Sciences, Washington.

The Life of Birds—Joel Carl Welty (1962), W. B. Saunders, Philadelphia.

The Migrations of Birds—Jean Dorst (1962), Houghton Mifflin, Boston.

Bird Display and Behaviour. An Introduction to the Study of Bird Psychology—Edward A. Armstrong (1947), Lindsay Drummond Limited, London. (Dover reprint.)

Ecology—Robert E. Ricklefs (1973), Chiron Press, Portland, Ore.

Population Studies of Birds—David Lack (paperback ed., 1969), Clarendon Press, Oxford.

Classification

A Classification for the Birds of the World—Alexander Wetmore (1960), Smithsonian Institution, Washington.

A Classification of Recent Birds—Ernst Mayr and Dean Amadon (1953), American Museum of Natural History, New York.

Families of Birds—Oliver L. Austin, Jr. (1971), Golden Press, New York.

Species Taxa of North American Birds—Ernst Mayr and Lester L. Short (1970), Nuttall Ornithological Club.

Taxonomy and Distribution

(The first two following references are continuations of these great works.)

Catalogue of Birds of the Americas—Charles E. Hellmayr and Boardman Conover (1948, part 1, nos. 2 and 3; 1949, part 1, no. 4), Chicago Natural History Museum.

The Birds of North and Middle America—Robert Ridgway and Herbert Friedman (1946, part 10; 1950, part 11), Smithsonian Institution, Washington.

The Birds of the Palearctic Fauna—Charles Vaurie (*Passeriformes*, 1959; *Non-Passeriformes*, 1965), Witherby, London.

Periodicals

Auk (quarterly), American Ornithologists' Union, P.O. Box 23447, Anchorage, Ky. 40223.

Condor (bi-monthly), Cooper Ornithological Society, Box 622, Route 4, Edgewater, Md., 21307.

Wilson Bulletin (quarterly), Wilson Ornithological Society, 2140 Lewis Drive, Lakewood, Ohio 44107.

Bird-Banding (quarterly), Northeastern Bird-Banding Association. Mrs. J. R. Downs, S. Londonderry, Vt. 05155.

Canadian Field-Naturalist (bi-monthly), Ottawa Field-Naturalists' Club, Box 3264, Postal Station C, Ottawa K1Y 4J5, Canada.

American Birds (bi-monthly), National Audubon Society, 950 Third Avenue, New York, New York 10022.

British Birds (monthly), MacMillan Journals Ltd., 4 Little Essex St., London WC2R 3LF, England.

Ibis (quarterly), British Ornithologists' Union 24–28 Oval Road, London NW1 7DX, England.

Bird Study (quarterly), British Trust for Ornithology, Beech Grove, Tring, England.

The Living Bird (annual), Cornell Laboratory of Ornithology, Ithaca, New York 14850.

Preface

Bird watching embraces individual enterprise on the one hand, collective effort on the other. Above all else, it is marked by a ready exchange of experience, by a high regard for truth, and by a conviction that wild birds express the most spectacular development of nature. These characteristics form the basis of the present volume. Many of the propositions derive from a common fund of bird-lore that is hard to acknowledge fully.

The desire to keep the text original and to avoid unnecessary repetition of material in other bird books has led to two decisions in the method of treatment. No attempt has been made to summarize the literature of bird watching and to fill the pages with pertinent references. That has already been done by James Fisher in his admirable *Birds as Animals*. No special consideration has been given to the fascinating subject of bird behavior. This has just been covered in the second volume of Margaret Nice's scholarly *Life-History Studies of the Song Sparrow*. Both these books are described in the appendix.

I should like to express my sincere thanks to the following persons, whose help in so many places has made this book possible:

For unpublished field notes: Allan D. Cruickshank and Roger T. Peterson of the National Audubon Society; C. L. Broley of Delta, Ontario, and Tampa, Florida; the late Albert A. Cross of Huntington, Massachusetts; Dr. John T. Emlen, Jr., of the University of California; Dr. Ernst Mayr of the American Museum of Natural History; and, through his wife, the late Charles A. Urner of Elizabeth, New Jersey.

For bibliographical help and assistance of many kinds: Dr. Arthur A. Allen of Cornell University; Miss May Thacher Cooke, Frederick C. Lincoln, and James O. Stevenson of the United States Fish and

Wildlife Service; Mrs. Richard J. Dillon, Jr., of Flushing, New York;
Joseph A. Hagar of the Massachusetts Department of Conservation;
Dr. Jean M. Linsdale of the University of California; Roy Latham
of Orient, New York; Robert A. McCabe and Dr. Banner B. Morgan
of the University of Wisconsin; C. Russell Mason of the Massachusetts Audubon Society; Mrs. Margaret M. Nice of Chicago, Illinois;
Julian K. Potter of Collingswood, New Jersey; Richard H. Pough
of the National Audubon Society; Dr. A. W. Schorger of Madison,
Wisconsin; and Dr. C. Brooke Worth of Swarthmore College.

For a critical reading of the main part of the manuscript: Professor Aldo Leopold of the University of Wisconsin; Dr. Ernst Mayr
of the American Museum of Natural History; and William Vogt of
Washington, D. C.

I also want to acknowledge my very great debt to Ernst Mayr
and the late Charles A. Urner, with whom I have had many stimulating discussions on bird watching; and to the staff members of the
American Museum of Natural History—James P. Chapin, the late
Jonathan Dwight, Ludlow Griscom, and John T. Nichols—who years
ago so generously encouraged a boy at the threshold of bird study.
The inspiration for many ideas in this volume undoubtedly stems
from these men, and from my companions in the Linnaean Society
of New York who, like me, used these ideas to enrich their observations of birds in the wild.

William Vogt first suggested that I write this book; Aldo Leopold
gave me the opportunity to finish it. From the beginning, preparation of the *Guide* has been facilitated at every turn by the devoted
assistance of my wife. To her constant and much-appreciated en-
couragement, I owe completion of the manuscript.

This book is for the old as well as for the young. Beginners in bird
study will find their own problems discussed in the opening chapters. In the later pages they will learn of the many methods by
which they can in time explore the mysteries of bird life. More experienced naturalists may skip the first chapter if they wish; the
remaining pages discuss bird study in progressively increasing detail and with a continuous development of ideas. In a very real
sense, this book has been written for the bird clubs scattered all
over our continent. Nearly all of them are purely amateur organiza-

tions, headed by officers who seldom receive recognition for their continuously unselfish work. It is my hope that their programs and activities will derive some inspiration from these pages.

                                                                    J. J. H.

Department of Wildlife Ecology
University of Wisconsin
Madison, Wisconsin

Contents

Some Examples and Results of Bird Watching

A GUIDE TO BIRD WATCHING

CHAPTER ONE

How to Begin Bird Study

BIRD WATCHING is old enough to have stood the test of time, young enough to lie within the age of exploration. By some, it is regarded as a mild paralysis of the central nervous system, which can be cured only by rising at dawn and sitting in a bog. Others regard it as a harmless occupation of children, into which maiden aunts may sometimes relapse. The truth is that it is anything you care to make it. It is unquestionably a hobby that can be thoroughly enjoyed for an entire lifetime. It can be taken up at any age, by the active as well as by the convalescent. To both old and young it yields the same high measure of interest. It is packed with drama because it centers on the annual miracle of creation. It is rich in movement, since birds are among the greatest travelers on our planet. It combines the visual and the auditory, for there are beautifully plumaged birds and equally stirring singers. Most of all, its essence lies in the unknown. Birds travel to the ends of the earth and back, we know not exactly how. Much of their everyday life is still unrecorded. Countless new channels of knowledge still await exploration by enterprising bird students.

The riches offered by a lifelong hobby are not something to be lightly cast aside. They are reflected in health, in recreation, and in a peace of mind beyond the price of money. It is the chief purpose of this book to show how bird watching can be made to last a lifetime, and to yield to the very end the same full measure of enjoyment.

In meeting a spectacular bird for the first time, every tyro naturalist experiences much of the same tingling delight that undoubtedly came to Audubon when he found some species new to science. The living bird is a creature of light and shadow, a picture of color tones changing with each movement, and a shy treasure, which, unlike a stamp, cannot be viewed at will. Each species offers a new glimpse of creation, each carries its own reward. This reward of discovery is a memorable series of sensations in which surprise, tension, and elation often follow one another in quick succession. If you have never encountered it, visit the rich woodland of some valley at dawn when birds are reaching the climax of their spring migration. It is then that the variety is greatest, for half the bird population of a continent is rushing northward to perform its annual nesting ritual. Trees encompass a veritable cauldron of sound. Hundreds of birds are in full song, while countless others show themselves in the homely but necessary business of feeding.

Bird watching today is not the groping, bewildering hobby it was only a few decades ago. Details of birds' plumages once required years of study; today they are captured for us in the beautifully colored plates of nearly a dozen fine bird books. One of these should form the cornerstone of every student's library. Their relative merits and their availability are discussed in the appendix. Both Canada and the United States have been particularly fortunate in possessing painters who have specialized in bird portraits. Where once it was necessary to shoot a bird in order to examine its plumage, a colored plate can now be studied and the needed information readily acquired.

How Birds Are Named

Retaining the names of the various birds remains, unhappily, a business for which there are few short cuts. Birds have at least two names. One is the scientific name, a more or less carefully worked out binomial or trinomial of Latin or Greek derivation. It is used by scientists both to identify the species and, if possible, to express its relation to other birds. Ordinarily, *this is a name that you can skip*. It does help, however, when you are checking up on a bird, to learn if it possesses some close relatives in your region. A fine explanation of how scientific names are given to birds may be found in the introductory pages of Dr. Chapman's *Handbook of Birds of Eastern North America*. This is a standard reference book, which many public libraries possess. For a literal translation of the scientific name of each species, the curious-minded are referred to Elliott Coues' *Key to North American Birds* or Elon H. Eaton's two-volumed *Birds of New York*. All of these books are described in the appendix.

Besides its scientific name, every bird in our country also has a common or popular name. Since people in various regions often make up their own names for birds, reason is maintained in the bird world by acceptance among authors of the popular name adopted by the American Ornithologists' Union. This is the ranking body of birdmen in North America. Largely due to its influence, a certain bird illustrated in the textbook is called a Cooper's hawk. Farmers in your region, never having heard of Cooper, much less of the A.O.U., doubtless have their own name for the bird—perhaps 'chicken hawk' or 'blue darter.' Generally speaking, then, local names of birds often persist, but bird books are happily standardized, and these official names are the ones to learn. About the easiest way to do this is to pore through the illustrated pages of a reference book until the figures on each plate can be recognized at will.

Many bird names are often associated with the places where they were first recognized by scientists. These are not easy to retain. There is nothing in the name 'Philadelphia vireo' to suggest whether that bird is red or blue, pink or black. Actually it is nothing but a green and greenish yellow. The Cape May warbler is even worse. George Ord first found it at Cape May at the southern tip of New Jersey. Since this species has a normal migration route to and from Canada that is well in from the ocean beach, it was not recorded again at Cape May for the next hundred years.

Sometimes birds are named after their discoverers. Lincoln's sparrow comes down to us because young Thomas Lincoln, in accompanying Audubon to Labrador, collected the only new species on that trip. The famed Lewis and Clark expedition returned with a rich harvest of data on natural history. Hence, Clark's nutcracker is named to honor Captain William Clark and Lewis's woodpecker pays tribute to Captain Meriwether Lewis. Famous scientists are also frequently honored. Swainson's hawk is named after William Swainson, the brilliant British ornithologist; Nelson's sparrow is after Dr. E. W. Nelson, a noted chief of the old United States Biological Survey; and Baird's sparrow is after Professor S. F. Baird, a famous secretary of the Smithsonian Institution and founder of the United States National Museum. Once a young army lieutenant named a bird after a great United States general, and so we now have Scott's oriole. Birds have been named after beautiful women, too. Anna's hummingbird honors a now-forgotten Duchess of Rivoli, and Zenaida dove pays tribute to the eldest daughter of a onetime king of Spain. Sisters, brothers, and wives have also come in for their share. Even little girls have captured the fancy of naturalists, for Dr. J. G. Cooper named Lucy's warbler after the 13-year-old daughter of a colleague.

How to Learn Bird Names

If these names seem hard to remember, they are more than balanced by those of birds like the black-throated green warbler, the scarlet tanager, and the white-throated sparrow. Then there are the marsh hawk, the chimney swift, the barn swallow, and a host of others. Names like these mean much more to the beginner. Use of the others, however conceived in error some may be, has now been sanctioned by many decades of established usage.

Not many years ago, Professor Samuel Eliot (perhaps thinking of beginners for the next thousand years) bravely suggested new names for some of the more mistitled species. The northern water-thrush, which isn't a thrush at all, he said could be called 'bogbird.' Geographic names, Professor Eliot continued, should be reserved for geographic races. The Tennessee warbler, which does not breed in Tennessee, could be called the 'aspen warbler.' The Canada warbler would never object to being called the 'neck-laced warbler.' And the Acadian flycatcher, which has never even been seen in

Acadia, might well be called the 'green flycatcher.' To veteran ornithologists who had long since forgotten their own unhappy introduction to avian nomenclature, these revolutionary ideas fell on deaf ears. Apparently the growing pains of an ornithologist are forgotten after thumbing through a favorite bird book for a quarter or half a century.

One short cut for the beginner is the practical one of learning at first only those birds that can reasonably be expected to occur in a given local region. To ascertain the distribution of these, the observer can consult Peterson's field guides, Chapman's handbook, or the standard regional books described in the appendix of the present volume. Once the first bird book has been acquired, underline or check the names of birds likely to be encountered. Such a procedure can save a great deal of confusion for those just starting bird study. There is no sense in a Texas bird student worrying about field marks of the rhinoceros auklet, which breeds on northern Pacific islands and is limited in distribution to the Pacific Ocean.

If one is still distracted with the multiplicity of bird names and often confused by species that look very much alike, a simple solution is to work out a series of private and temporary names for harder species. The two water-thrushes, for instance, could almost pass for twins. One has a yellow line over the eye, the other a white one. Many observers can never remember which has which. Try privately calling one the 'white Louisiana' for a while, and the other the 'yellow northern.' In a surprisingly short time, a once-vexing personal problem will have been permanently settled. This trick can be extended to many other species—horned larks, shrikes, cormorants, and so on.

How to Identify Birds in the Field

In mastering the names of birds, the beginner soon meets the problem of learning to separate the creatures in the field. For ordinary birds about the garden, colored plates are completely adequate. Quick short cuts to identification are superbly summarized in two field guides by Roger Tory Peterson. These are more fully described in the appendix. They tend to emphasize how birds look at a distance, and often show how they look when in flight. Before

1930 this information had never been reduced to diagrams, and to retain a mental picture of much of it required years of study in the field. Today the flight patterns of two dozen ducks can be memorized in an hour. Thousands of people, once overwhelmed with the task of identifying birds at great range, can now do so with considerable certainty. Thus, the pleasures of bird watching have been increased and a new lode of migration data made accessible to many.

The fun of identifying birds in the field normally runs through three stages. In the first, only the common birds are identified and only those that are near. Gradually, an acquaintanceship with their habits, their postures, and their manners of flight makes possible the identification of birds at increasingly greater distances. In the second stage, the student is able to identify correctly birds at considerable distances, often with the aid of but one or two field marks. This is an uneven stage, for familiarity does not extend to all species with the same degree. Learning the tricks of shape and flight comes only with experience in the field and no amount of book study can be substituted for it. Books, of course, help. The field guides may point out that the ruddy duck has a 'buzzy' flight, but this must be seen to be understood. In the third stage, the student has acquired a practical knowledge of bird songs. He knows not only those of the robin and song sparrow, but also those of the countless migrants that pause for but a brief time in his region. This is the stage that the beginner feels is nearly impossible of attainment, at least as far as he himself is concerned. He is sure of this because he is always forgetting bird songs, and because each spring he must learn those of the migrants all over again.

There is, of course, no short cut to mastery of stage 1, but stage 2 can more quickly be reached by getting into the field with sympathetic and more experienced companions. To the beginner, a large bird wheeling overhead represents just another question mark in his notebook. If the same bird is identified as a golden eagle by his associate, the field marks can be studied with more appreciation. A lot of birds are never seen well, and to the novice they are just so many lost opportunities.

The art of identifying birds in the field is still subject to certain limitations. Theoretically, almost every species can be identified in life—providing that it is observed at close range, at leisure, and in good light. In practice this is often impossible, and at the present time a small number of birds can be identified only in the hand. These include females and immatures of the European and American widgeon (baldpate), the European and green-winged teal, greater and lesser scaup, and American and king eiders among the waterfowl. It seems likewise impossible to separate in the field birds like Xantus's and Craveri's murrelets, rock and willow ptarmigans in the brown plumage, and Wright's and Hammond's flycatchers. Unless they are singing, it is similarly almost impossible to separate the least, Acadian, and alder flycatchers. Many other birds can be identified in the field only by the most experienced observers favored by fine opportunities. These include such birds as the black gyrfalcon (which often resembles a very dark young duck hawk) and the eskimo curlew (now practically extinct but somewhat similar to young Hudsonian curlews).

Many students seem to feel, however, that unless they have identified every single bird seen on every single field trip, they cannot join the ranks of the experts. This not only ignores the fact that certain species can be identified only in the hand, but it also implies that birds are co-operative creatures with a special sympathy for members of the local Audubon society. Occasionally this is almost so. I can recall a tired white-crowned sparrow that mistook for shrubbery a large party of bird watchers out on a wide, expansive mud flat on Long Island. Dropping down from a considerable height, the bird alighted in the 'shrubbery.' For several minutes this shrubbery was even more confused than the bird.

Not infrequently, however, birds are shy or seen under particularly difficult circumstances. The shy ones can, with patience, finally be 'captured' with binoculars. (Once I had to wait a month to see well a pair of Bell's vireos that I knew were nesting in a black locust plantation.) Some birds, which are not seen until they are flying directly away from the observer, are virtually impossible to identify—owls, for instance, flushed too easily in a dense woodland. Sometimes birds are misidentified because of tricky lighting effects that are ever present in nature. White may appear to be yellow, blues may appear to be black. Hence, it is advisable to view a perplexing bird in as many lights and from as many angles as possible. It is always with a chuckle that I recall a bird that Robert P. Allen and I saw dash into a large bush on a New Jersey salt marsh only a few years ago. With our glasses we noticed that it had a green back and stripes on the throat. 'A European species,' we whispered to each other, 'or at least one from the Northwest.' It was a shy migrant and it did not feel safe on a salt marsh. After a full five minutes we finally saw it well. It was a robin. The green back was purely an illusion.

There are many other illusions ready to trap the unwary student. This is especially true when birds are identified at great range and only one field mark is noted. Once, two other bird students and I spent a quiet half hour watching a distant wader on a river in Virginia. It was, we felt sure, a white ibis or a little blue heron in the white immature plumage. Very, very slowly it approached us. It was a harmless tin can slowly bobbing in the stream, shining brightly in the sunlight.

Snap identifications often lead to surprising errors. There was the screech owl that turned out to be an old rag hanging in a hemlock. Another was the bluebird spotted on a far-off sand dune along the ocean side of Long Island. When approached, this remarkable bird was recognized as a discarded and entirely innocent-looking Bromo Seltzer bottle. These examples are errors that were detected, and one wonders how many others unconsciously have been entered into students' notebooks.

In the long run, expertness in field identification depends on continuous practice. It is aided by good field companions and by the study of bird skins in museum collections. It is not the goal of bird watching but rather a useful tool. However surprising it may seem, the richest opportunities to explore the mysteries of bird life exist among common species of birds and not among migration rarities. To the beginner, this is perhaps the hardest lesson to learn. As subsequent chapters will show, this is the first principle of modern bird watching.

How to Learn Bird Songs

As in the case of field identification, the learning of bird songs can be expedited with the help of an experienced colleague. Songs are best learned by comparing the song of one species with the song of another. This comparison is not normally attained by a tense half hour's search for a small warbler high up in the canopy of a dense woods. Rather it is achieved by hearing the somewhat similar songs of different species in as short a time as possible.

The help of a veteran naturalist is especially useful in learning the calls of marsh birds, like the rails. Many of these put forth their best vocal efforts when it is dark and the birds are almost impossible to see. Marsh sounds often puzzle the keenest listeners, as Julian K. Potter once pointed out in *Audubon Magazine*.

Late in April, Mr. Potter reported, the familiar voice of a friend over the phone told him that a strange winnowing note had been heard on the river marshes near Palmyra, New Jersey. A rail was suggested. But which rail?

The following night an ornithological conference was held on the road beside the marsh. The mysterious note was heard again.

'It must be a rail! What else could it be?' the three experts concluded. In due time, the customary complication of wartime bird watching developed. An officer of the law appeared.

'What are you doing here?' he asked the suspects.

'We are ornithologists,' they answered.

The law greeted this statement blankly.

'We are bird cranks,' was the next admission.

An even blanker look followed.

'We are listening for rails,' they explained.

Now the officer was interested. 'Didn't know they called at night,' he ventured.

'Listen!'

The officer listened. The strange winnowing note floated across the marsh.

'Rails?! Rails?!' he exploded. 'That is a jacksnipe!'

A jacksnipe it was, giving his spring aerial performance. 'Can anyone,' concludes Mr. Potter, 'imagine a more humiliating experi-

ence than having the "village cop" tell ornithologists "what bird
is that?"'

Most observers do not realize that the learning of bird songs
depends on more than a good teacher. Birds sing in a great many
frequencies and to few ears does the same bird sound exactly
alike. For this reason, it is well to take a series of notes on bird
songs. What do they sound like? An excellent plan is to make notes
right on the spot in a rough kind of musical shorthand. Thus (to
me), Bell's vireo sounds like

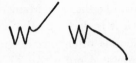

queedle queedle quee, queedle queedle qua

Notes like these provide a useful source of personal data for the
following year when a new song season is starting.

Some bird students claim that putting words to a bird's song
never makes sense to them. Others, including myself, have found
words occasionally helpful in learning bird songs. Many of these
ditties, like the chestnut-sided warbler's *I wish to see Miss Beecher,*
are found in Peterson's field guides. Bird songs do vary, of course,
but no more, I sometimes think, than the acuity of the human ear.
Some persons have ears that are especially sensitive to high frequencies, such as those found in the songs of certain sparrows
and warblers. Others are better able to hear the low frequencies,
like those present in the calls of many owls. As a general rule,
sensitivity to bird song is largely a matter of practice. One so
consistently concentrates on bird songs that insect sounds are unconsciously 'screened out,' and the ear automatically registers what
the observer wants to hear.

Some very revealing stories have been told about the decreasing
abilities of naturalists to hear various bird songs and call notes.
W. E. Saunders, the well-known Canadian ornithologist, reports
that the loss of hearing due to age can be measured ornithologically
with almost uncanny accuracy. At the age of 60, he lost the tiny
lisp-notes of the golden-crowned kinglet and the brown creeper at

almost exactly the same time. At 65 he lost the notes of the cedar
waxwing, at 67 the song of the black and white warbler, at 68
those of the bay-breasted, blackburnian, and Cape May. Other
songs appeared distorted, shortened, new, and strange as time
went on. Under such circumstances, some of the satisfactions of
observing birds are undoubtedly lost, but one's zest for bird watching seems in no way diminished. James L. Edwards, one of the
most competent naturalists I know, has been completely unable to
hear any of the high frequencies for years.

Perhaps the greatest difficulty connected with learning songs of
migrant birds lies in the relatively short time during which it is
possible to hear these birds each year. They seldom or never sing
in the fall, and during the spring they may be present but a few
weeks. During these two or three weeks, migrating birds generally
sing only for perhaps two hours after dawn. Hence, if the observer is afield but once a week, he may only hear a given species
sing a relatively few times each year. Many enterprising observers
get around this by taking a daily 45-minute pre-breakfast walk in
some near-by woodland, from May 1st to 20th. In the larger cities,
like Boston, Chicago, New York, and Philadelphia, dozens of businessmen do this in the more wooded parks and cemeteries. Other
observers try to spend their vacations among some more northern
mountains in June. Here they find migrants from back home now
settled down for the breeding season, and both birds and their
songs can be studied at leisure.

Other short cuts to learning bird songs can be found by study
of Aretas A. Saunders' *A Guide to Bird Songs*. This is essentially
limited, however, to birds of the northeastern states. A very valuable aid may also be found in an album of 6 double-disc recordings put out by the Albert R. Brand Bird Song Foundation. These
reproduce the songs of 72 different species which, in spite of enormous difficulties, were actually recorded in the field.

As a general rule, all males of a given species sing pretty much
alike, but the more elaborate songsters often have individual variations that are both interesting and delightful. Some species have
two or more songs. Others sing somewhat differently on their breeding grounds than they do on migration. Sometimes a few birds in

a certain locality have a local 'dialect.' Birds belonging to the same species will sing slightly differently in different regions. Yellow-throats are especially noticeable in this connection. In other species, dialectic songs have been noticed in fairly small localities. This is an aspect of bird life on which careful note-taking by bird watchers will be sure to shed more light, for birds have a vocabulary fully as interesting as their plumage but not nearly so well known.

How to Acquire a Good Field Glass

To identify many birds in the field, it is absolutely necessary to possess a pair of binoculars—the one expensive item in the bird student's equipment. Old opera glasses may do at first, but within a relatively short time, the beginner will appreciate the increased opportunities that come with the use of standard field binoculars. To many, the purchase of a pair of binoculars is a compromise between the glasses' performance and limitations of the pocketbook. The price of a field glass is naturally based on the materials and workmanship required to manufacture it. Some glasses can withstand more rough handling than others. In prismatic glasses, this rough usage often throws the glasses out of alignment. In effect, both barrels are then not directed toward the same point; to compensate for this, eyes are strained, with ultimately unhappy results. More than any other class of users, bird students handle their binoculars to a point bordering on sheer negligence.

A good glass can last a lifetime. The lens should always be dusted with soft brushes or cleaning papers. Scratches on the lens may reduce the amount of light on the image. Binoculars suspended by long straps from the neck swing in a wide radius when the observer is bending over. This is an invitation to chipping, denting, and jarring shocks against fences and trees, which may put the glasses out of alignment. The shorter the strap, the less chance of damage.

In acquiring a glass for bird watching, there are five essentials to consider in addition to price: magnification, illumination, field, weight, and durability. As a general rule, when one of the first four elements is emphasized by the manufacturer, certain advantages among the others are sacrificed. Thus, 12-power glasses are heavier than 6-power glasses, and the image appears brightly illuminated in a smaller field. Two pairs of 8-power binoculars may vary widely in their characteristics: one may be heavy, with fine light and a field of, say, 140 yards at 1000 yards' range; the other 8-power glass may be less heavy. This may be owing to the use of new light-weight alloys in its manufacture (a 'light-weight glass'), or it may simply be correlated with a more restricted field and less light on the image.

It is hard to recommend the best binoculars for a bird student, for the very reason that they are as personal as eyeglasses. Some men have strong arms and wrists, and to them weight is of no consideration. Others do most of their birding on the seashore, where birds are often seen at great distances; they want magnification. People who spend lots of time on boats prefer large fields of vision. As a general rule, however, it can be said that light-weight 7's or 8's represent a good all-round pair of binoculars and, taking second-hand prices into consideration, fairly adequate glasses start in around $25, and really adequate ones range anywhere from $50 to $100. The particular model that represents the best dollar-for-dollar buy varies every five years or so, as new improvements are perfected and manufacturers jockey for supremacy. Some years ago, Zeiss 8-power Deltrintems were considered the last word in superb workmanship and general all-round usage. I think they still are. Some people then began buying Le Maire 9's; today many have swung to the Bausch and Lomb 7's and 9's.

For bird watching it seems best to avoid purchasing binoculars for which each eyepiece must be focused separately. From watching a warbler at 15 yards' range, you may turn in a flash to a large hawk wheeling 200 yards overhead. In frequent situations of this kind, only exceptionally skilled hands can avoid the fumbling attempts to focus individual eyepieces. It is also advisable to avoid getting a glass that has a small field. This means that at 1000 yards' range, you have a field of, say, 90 yards instead of, say, 130. This is extremely important when you are following with the glass a speeding flock of ducks or shore birds, or trying to locate a nervous kinglet in a tree.

To those specialists who have frequent opportunities to observe ducks from a car, the Bausch and Lomb spotting telescope is an auxiliary glass of considerable value. These telescopes, which are set at a magnification of 20 power, are sold with simple attachments by which they can be fixed to the window of a car. This is a de luxe way of observing birds at great distances, but the birds cannot be followed in flight. It is, of course, impossible during times of war to purchase new spotting scopes and other equipment from manufacturers of optical goods.

Before leaving the subject of binoculars, it should be emphasized that most beginners worry along on 4-power and 6-power binoculars very nicely. As a boy, I had a marvelous time without realizing that glasses were used for anything outside the opera. Accompanied by two kindred spirits, I would simply climb a giant maple in those days and wait for the high-feeding warblers to flit in the branches before our very faces. The subsequent gift of a 2-power opera glass seems, at this distance, practically the turning point in our lives. After all, 2-power just about doubles one's potentialities.

How to Meet Other Bird Students

Certain practical advantages of having an experienced field companion have already been mentioned. The pleasures of meeting a kindred spirit are much more subjective but they are nonetheless real and they often ripen into lifelong friendships. In grade school it never occurred to my chums or to me that bird books were written for anyone other than boys, and that grown men and women liked to watch flickers and killdeers just the way we did. Our beloved scoutmaster, the Reverend Basil Hall, had given some of us a helping hand, but bird study still seemed like a boys' game. It was an almost stupefying shock when Richard A. Herbert and I, aged 14, quite by accident found an elegantly dressed gentleman watching a chickadee one February day in New York City's Bronx Park. Charles Johnston, who looked not unlike Charles Evans Hughes to us, had been a distinguished member of the British Civil Service in India. He was kindly and apparently ready to answer questions. He answered them for two full hours, probably with no little amusement. The decades between us seemed to vanish and from that point on, our bird study took on dignity and purpose. He helped us many times more in the years that followed.

I tell this story to illustrate how an interest in ornithology can span any barrier, and how people of widely diverse cultures can rapidly find a common bond of understanding. There are several ways to get in touch with other bird students. One is to attend meetings. Bird clubs and societies in our country vary considerably in their composition, in their programs, and in the help they can give the beginning bird student. Some hold frequent meetings, others run field trips, and many issue local publications for their

A second way to meet other bird students is through the medium of *The Auk*. This is the national quarterly devoted to ornithology and published by the American Ornithologists' Union. The Union is composed of both professional and amateur bird people from all over the United States and Canada. Anyone can join as an associate member and so receive *The Auk*. In its pages, the A.O.U. periodically publishes a complete membership list. This gives the addresses of all the prominent birdmen in North America and thus enables the beginner to communicate with authorities near his home or near places he intends to visit. A bird student need feel no compunction about writing a stranger for advice, or to ask for companionship on some convenient field trip. The four-day annual meetings of the A.O.U. are theoretically devoted to a reading of learned papers about bird life, but actually they resemble college reunions in both spirit and function. Open to nonmembers and guests, they require only a willingness to talk (or listen to talk) about birds for four days in a row. Every bird watcher will profit by occasionally spending a part of his vacation at one of these conventions, which are held in a different city each year.

Especially progressive and alert is the Wilson Ornithological Club, which holds annual meetings in the Middlewest. These are similar to those of the A.O.U. but are smaller in scale. This society's publication, *The Wilson Bulletin*, also contains, from time to time, a list of members and their addresses.

Another source of contact among bird students is *Audubon Magazine*, publication of the National Audubon Society. *Audubon Magazine* is a bimonthly emphasizing problems in wildlife conservation and featuring articles on birdlore. In one of its regular departments, 'The Season,' may be found accounts of migration and significant bird observations in various sections of the United States. In its annual 'Christmas Bird Count' over 2000 bird students submit lists of birds seen in their local regions. Should you find a bird list published for some locality near yours, you can readily obtain the address of the observer by writing to the editor of this publication. Annual meetings of the National Audubon Society are held in New York City each fall. These include field trips to Cape May, New Jersey, and Montauk Point, Long Island, and a two-day program devoted to reports, discussions of bird conservation, and motion pictures of wildlife.

Although composed almost entirely of adults, most of these organizations are only too happy to welcome youngsters. Despite its somewhat terrifying name, the A.O.U. will accept applications for associate membership from small boys as well as elderly gentlemen. Veteran naturalists are usually glad to take a youthful bird student along on their field trips, although they generally are averse to taking along a crowd.

Where and When to Look for Birds

Generally speaking, swampy woodlands often possess the richest bird life. This is especially true if they are not heavily grazed. Many songbirds show a marked attraction for water; stream borders and springs may play a considerable part in their lives. Dry oak woods tend to have a limited bird population, especially if they are overgrazed or frequented by too many people. Factors affecting the density of bird life will be discussed in a later chapter. Here we are concerned with the personal problem that many beginners face: 'How can I add more species to my own list of birds seen and identified?'

In general, this can be accomplished in point of time and in point of space. In the first instance, one must need take to the field in all seasons, in summer and winter, in spring and in fall. Each season not only has its own birds, but the panorama of bird life may change markedly from month to month. Some persons insist on birding during every single week end of the year. They probably miss very little. However, I can remember one year when I saw about 250 species by birding only on alternate Sundays in the New York City region and by taking a two-weeks' vacation in Maine. To see a wide variety of bird life, it is necessary to be afield not only frequently but also at the right time of day. This is not important during the winter season or when one is looking for ducks and shore birds; but it is particularly necessary during the breeding season and during the warbler migrations of both spring and fall. Many birds are then most conspicuous before 7 A.M. and they are often markedly less active by 11. As far as listing species is concerned, a brief walk after these hours is often a waste of time. Marsh birds, like the bitterns, gallinules, and rails, are best heard right after dawn. Ducks and shore birds can usually be sought at any time; on the seacoast, however, the tide may affect their daily movements.

In point of space, it is not necessary to walk vast distances in order to see a wide variety of birds. On the contrary, students with this in mind should visit a wide variety of habitats. These may include cultivated fields, farm buildings, orchards, ungrazed wood lots, stream borders, springs, cattail swamps, sedge marshes, conifer groves, sandy fields, cliffs, bogs, golf courses, air ports, cemeteries, and so on. To locate all of these in one region is often no easy matter. Some observers obtain topographic maps of their county and systematically explore every swamp and bog that has been mapped. Others, living in mountainous regions that possess a zonal type of bird life dependent on altitude, just as systematically explore the high mountain tops for the rarer species. Those living near the seacoasts lead a particularly varied existence, for within relatively short distances access can be gained to a vast number of marine and fresh-water habitats. It was in such circumstances in New Jersey, along a route worked out by Charles A. Urner, that I once observed 160 kinds of birds on a single day in May. Longer lists, based on equally exhausting trips, are occasionally reported.

By and large, the search for new habitats is no easy matter and is best undertaken with the advice of some older persons who need not necessarily be ornithologists but who do know the local region. In a few states, it is now possible to consult recently compiled land-cover maps. These give not only the sites of bogs and marshes, but the kinds of timber as well, whether the trees are young or very old, and the approximate density of each stand.

How to Take Notes and Keep Records

All bird watchers worthy of the name take some sort of notes. At first these may be simple annotations in the margins of a bird book, giving the place and date that a certain species was seen. Not infrequently this information can be used in later years when some attempt is made to see if the bird 'came back.' Additional notes on what kind of habitat the bird was using are often of help. Thus, if a saw-whet owl was found in young pine trees, a search of other such pines might be fruitful.

Most observers like to keep lists for each trip. In time these can be used to review and compare the ornithological merits of various localities, as well as the relative abundance of birds at different seasons. They make interesting rereading and recall exciting birds that were seen in the past.

There are several ways to keep 'daily lists.' Each system is useful but many that are recommended take no account of the small amount of time that the average bird student has for writing up his field work. The simplest way of keeping daily lists is to carry a field card giving a list of the birds seen in your locality. Many bird clubs publish such cards and sell them at cost, usually one or two cents apiece. On a long trip in May, when many birds are seen, cards like these save much writing in the field. They can be filed in order, classified according to locality, or the information can be transferred to a journal.

Most cards are so closely printed that there is barely room for a check mark or a number and almost no space left for additional notes. As a rule, I am always suspicious of birdmen who rely solely on cards. Bird watching involves more than a mere date, a few check marks, and some rough numbers. Small pocket-sized field notebooks are actually indispensable for the careful bird watcher; what to record in them will be the subject of later chapters.

Home journals for the keeping of permanent records vary widely according to the amount of time available for them. Some, like Thoreau and Brewster, choose to enter their notes in diary fashion.

These can always be indexed at the end of the year or the end of the volume. Many professional ornithologists favor a permanent index-card system. Notes can then be kept under species headings and cross-referenced for subject matter, i.e. nests, courtship displays, roosts, and so on. For those who cannot find time for elaborate journal keeping, it is best to take careful notes in the field, on one side of the notebook paper only. If this is done in indelible pencil or ink, the material can be quickly scissored out and pasted under appropriate headings in loose-leaf journals or on index cards. An inexpensive record book is published by the National Audubon Society. This is a loose-leaf affair into which one can readily transcribe from field cards numbers of birds observed on a given trip. Audubon record books are compiled for various sections of the country.

The equipment of the novice bird student is thus seen to comprise a set of colored plates, a field guide, a pair of binoculars, and a notebook. Armed with these, he can begin to explore the bird world. He needs no hunting license to take to the field, no card of introduction to meet a fellow enthusiast in the next county or in the next state. He should, however, have patience and perseverance, for he stands on the threshold of an absorbing hobby that can last him a lifetime. To the ornithologist, no corner of the earth is dull, no season is without its compensations.

CHAPTER TWO

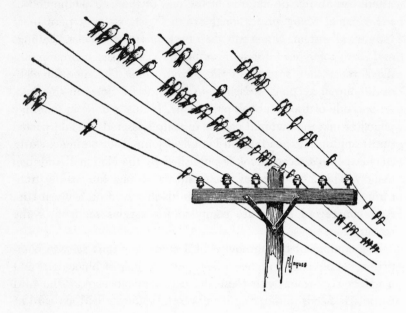

The Lure of Migration Watching

FEW MYSTERIES in nature can so capture man's imagination as bird migration. I can still recall the group of migration watchers that, as a boy, I self-consciously encountered for the first time in a New York City park. Among them were a quiet electrical engineer, a scholarly church organist, an excitable lawyer, a nervous advertising man, a taciturn botanist, a retired member of the British Civil Service, and an amiable 80-year-old veteran of the Civil War who would not brook assistance in climbing a fence. We lived a life of mingled awe and excitement—awe because we were constantly seeing birds in the process of moving from Central and South America to the cool northern forests of New England and Canada, excitement because the park was sometimes spilling over with bird life or brightened here and there with birds that we had never before seen. As a group, we were no different than scores of others scattered throughout the United States and Canada, drawn together by the lure of migration watching.

The more migration is studied, the more apparent it is that in their annual movements birds outstrip the human race. With no calendar to guide them, they set forth each year for their northern breeding grounds at much the same time. Annually they cross great seas without a compass. Nightly they speed through the pathless dark, sometimes alone, more often in loose flocks. After thousands of miles of travel, they arrive on their nesting grounds with little evidence of weariness or fatigue.

Migration is now regarded by scientists as an inherited rhythm of behavior that was adopted by birds in ancient times. The young of a few species actually accompany their parents south, but they are the exceptions, never the rule. Many young birds start south weeks before the adults. Today their behavior is felt to be regulated both internally and externally—internally by changes in their glandular system, externally by such factors as temperature and changing hours of daylight. The exact interrelationship of these is by no means settled.

The great popularity of migration watching has resulted in the publication of an enormous quantity of somewhat isolated facts. Speaking conservatively, I would estimate the number of published items about migrating birds in the United States at not less than 750,000. Such a mass of information would seem to signify that very little is left to explore in this branch of natural history. Such a conclusion is, I think, far from true.

Once in a great while, for example, birds are observed migrating in the wrong direction. Almost nothing about this is known in North America but every observer should be on the watch for it. Such a migration was recorded on the morning of May 12, 1937, by Harrison F. Lewis on Pelee Island, almost midway in Lake Erie between the shores of Ontario and Ohio. Thirty-five species were actually seen to strike out southward over the water in the face of a southerly surface wind and in spite of a fairly high temperature. Flocks of cedar waxwings, pine siskins, and goldfinches made this unusual journey, as well as large numbers of wood warblers, like the myrtle, black-throated green, blackburnian, and the chestnut-sided. Under ordinary circumstances it is rather difficult to ascertain definitely that reverse migration is taking place. Observers who can watch migrants at concentration places on islands and peninsulas have the best opportunity to throw light on this phenomenon which today is scarcely understood and seldom recognized.

The great mass of published information has, I believe, dulled many of us to the opportunities for individual initiative that are still available. Probably the most spectacular successes in migration studies will, in the future, be scored by bird banders, but a great deal of interesting and unusual information can still be furnished by field workers who clearly recognize the glaring gaps in our knowledge of bird migration.

The Need for Daily Observations

To bird watchers, the most absorbing phenomena about migrating birds have been the dates of their arrival. Every bird club emphasizes this kind of note-taking, and the first recorded bluebird outranks all other bluebirds in the dignity and admiration with which it is regarded. The next hundred bluebirds are just so many birds, but it is on them that the spotlight of bird watching is now centering.

For well over half a century, migration watching has been more or less encouraged in our country by what is now the Department of the Interior's Fish and Wildlife Service. Migratory birds are the special wards of the Federal Government, since they cross state and international boundaries, help agriculture in some regions, injure it occasionally in others. They provide food and sport, and are the basis for a considerable industry. Over 2,000,000 migration records are now on file with the Service in the Department of the Interior, and it is safe to say that, in every populated region of the United States, the first-arrival dates for most species are well explored and recorded.

It is now well known, for instance, that the first spring migrants vary widely in their arrival dates from year to year. From 1923 to 1927, I saw my first migrant robins around New York City on March 11, March 12 and March 15, January 30 and February 26. As spring progresses, birds arrive with more and more regularity.

Going through my notebook for an extreme example, I notice that on successive years my first redstarts were seen on May 1, May 1, May 2, May 2, May 1, May 10, and May 6. Variations of this sort depend not only on the weather that birds encounter but also on the success of the observer in making daily trips afield.

Some years ago members of the Linnaean Society of New York assiduously set out to determine the period of maximum abundance for each migrant passing through the New York City region. In

TABLE 1

HOW RED-WINGS ONCE ARRIVED AT ITHACA, NEW YORK

Careful watching will often disclose that many birds of the same species arrive in spring in distinctly different groups. So much attention has been given to merely the first arrivals that reports like the following are still very rare in America. These observations were made by Arthur A. Allen in 1911.

(1) vagrant birds . . . . February 25–March 4
(2) migrant adult males, which went on north . . . . March 13–April 21
(3) resident adult males . . . . March 25–April 10
(4) migrant females and immature males . . . . March 29–April 24
(5) resident adult females . . . . April 10–May 1
(6) resident immature males . . . . May 6–June 1
(7) resident immature females . . . . May 10–June 11

Compiled from Abstracts of the Proceedings
of the Linnaean Society of New York. 1914.

the case of a large number of species, the Society found, this period was invariably fixed on a week end. Most of the members being businessmen, the persistent week-end character of their observations had naturally affected the data.

It can be said with some certainty that, given a little guidance and the right equipment, the average school boy with only a limited experience with birds could produce more new facts on local bird migration in a single season than the average expert does in a decade of Sunday field trips. It is the school boy's free time that is the envy of the expert. For years I have encountered boys who regularly found migrants earlier than more matured ornithologists. Their powers of observation were not yet fully developed and they were without motor cars, but they did make *daily* observations. Birds ordinarily do not wait until Sunday to migrate.

Of actual importance to ornithology, however, is not the date on which the first robin arrived, but rather the dates on which subsequent robins appeared. Practically nothing about them has ever been recorded! This holds not only for the robin but for the majority of our other common birds as well. If all the first-arrival dates for the next fifty years went unreported, ornithology would profit by the experience rather than lose.

Migration Studies on Small Areas

The most useful form of migration watching consists, in its simplest form, of carefully kept records on a single species. Observations should be daily in character, if possible, but those made every other day might do. Many birds can be seen on the way to school or to one's place of business. Cruises on such a regularly traversed route have far greater value than random trips into the country. Assume that the first robin has been recorded. How many more are present? Are they all males? Are they present in the same places on subsequent days? Does the population build up gradually or in jerky fashion? When do the female robins arrive? Do they come singly or in groups?

During the spring of 1942, it seemed quite obvious to me that local robins arrived in southwestern Wisconsin in March and that small flocks of more northern birds passed through weeks later in April. Resident robins were easily distinguished because they tended to separate themselves during the day and to sing advertising songs in defense of their territories. Migrant robins remained in small flocks of 8 or 10 birds. They did not sing and they were gone in a day or two.

It should be stressed that migration watching, even within small areas, can yield extremely interesting information—always provided the observer is willing to check carefully the common species, which, for decades now, have been virtually disregarded. A small but interesting example of this is illustrated by counts of purple martins given in Table 2.

Up to the present, many bird books have been content to give the first date on which a migratory species has been known to arrive and the last date on which it has been seen on its way north. This is scarcely the fault of the authors, but rather a reflection on the loose kind of migration watching in America. To the

TABLE 2

ARRIVAL OF PURPLE MARTINS AT RYE, NEW YORK, IN 1937

One of the chief tasks of migration watching now lies in counts of a single species on small regularly traversed areas. The late flight of female martins shown here was *completely* unrecorded in one of the regions most intensively worked for birds in America. It was discovered by Michael Oboiko and Allan D. Cruickshank in the course of careful periodic counts at a colony of this well-known species.

Date	Males	Females and Immatures	Total
April 6	2	1	3
April 11	9	4	13
April 20	31	15	46
April 24	36	15	51
April 29	36	15	51
May 9	36	16	52
May 16	36	16	52
May 23	47	33	80
May 30	42	37	79

Reprinted from *Proceedings of the Linnaean Society of New York*. 1941.

beginner this is frequently a serious handicap, for he often has no way of knowing the normal period of maximum abundance for a given species. Such information can only come with repeated counting and more or less daily observations.

Migration Routes

Another important gap in our present knowledge of bird migration involves the regular use of local routes by migrants. Opportunities for exploration along these lines tend to vary with the physiography of each region. Around New York City, where much of my own field work has been done, at least 8 local routes are readily discernible and many more await recognition or evaluation.

It is well to appreciate the present state of our knowledge on this subject. It is known, for instance, that many species migrate along a very broad front. With slight changes in wind conditions, their course deviates and their numbers in a given locality may vary accordingly from one year to another.

In some regions the same species tend to follow available landmarks, and local concentrations of birds may occur as a result. Coasts, rivers, and ridges are the places to watch in this connection. The birds' local use of each should be carefully noticed and mapped

in every regional bird book. Up to the present, only the main outlines have been blocked in, but ridges can be compared and contrasted with each other and the preferences for each river valley
determined. Coastal observations may occasionally uncover unexpected flight lines. I once heard Charles A. Urner report that along
the ocean beaches of New Jersey, many species followed the shore
line north past Barnegat and then cut northeast across the ocean.
These birds were presumably by-passing the whole of western
Long Island.

Whenever a flock of migrating birds is seen overhead, the direction of travel can be noted, the altitudes approximated, the hour
recorded, and notes taken on weather conditions. Even if the birds
can only be identified as 'ducks,' this information is worth preserving. Filed in a separate place among one's records, the data can
eventually be published as a useful contribution to local ornithology.
In the case of certain species, the accumulation of such regional
material may help complete our continental picture of bird migration.

Mapping the nocturnal migrants is obviously not so easy. Not
many years ago, I enjoyed a mellow April evening with two friends
atop the Palisades along the lower part of the Hudson River near
New York City. Hundreds of scaups began flying over our heads
at 5:44 P.M. Leaving Long Island Sound, a few miles eastward,
the birds were headed in a west-northwest direction over New
Jersey's hills—supposedly for the Finger Lakes. They were still passing over at 6:43 when visibility ceased. While we were marveling
at this flight line, also being used by canvas-backs, other species
were moving directly north up the river on a highway of their own.
These included 2 female sparrow hawks, an apparently transient
duck hawk, and 8 great blue herons that came out of the southwest
before turning north.

Many weak flyers take their chances with the owls, by migrating
at night, rather than with the diurnal hawks. During May, August,
and September, the calls of these birds as they speed overhead is as
dramatic as any one aspect in bird life. Certain calls are special
ones used by some species only at night. As far as I can tell, several
of these have yet to be identified. Most warblers call a colorless *zip*

as they keep in touch with their fellows. No one has yet made nightly counts throughout a full migration season on the number of birds passing overhead. This is perhaps a job for some night watchman or someone suffering from insomnia. Counts for, say, 60 minutes at the same time every night could be made even in the center of a city, and could probably show the peaks of migration.

One of the most fertile fields for exploration in bird migration lies in the movements of pelagic birds, which ordinarily remain well out to sea. Fairly definite highways, for instance, seem to exist only a few miles off the coast, used apparently by shore birds and particularly by ducks. Somewhere offshore, too, are often found thousands of tiny phalaropes and great flocks of shearwaters, according to season. Observation of pelagic birds can often be effectively increased by baiting. Several techniques are available. The oldest in point of use seems to be that discovered by the famous bird collector, Rollo H. Beck. This consists in heating animal fats or oils and then laying a slick along about two miles of sea. In the southern Pacific, this procedure would often bring into close range numbers of albatrosses and small petrels that previously were completely out of sight. Another bait, which I have seen Ludlow Griscom use off Cape Cod, consists of a smelly mixture of one gallon of halibut oil and two large boxes of puffed wheat which are first mixed in a bucket. When this is slowly thrown on the sea in very small cupfuls, a long oily slick is formed on the ocean, attracting shearwaters, petrels, and phalaropes, if they are anywhere near. They can thus be lured close to the boat and readily identified; some petrels have even been netted and banded. Another bait, originally perfected by Major Allan Brooks in New Zealand, is thought to have application for albatrosses off the Pacific coast. Ten to twenty pounds of suet are first chopped into small bits about one-quarter inch square. On leaving port, handfuls of these are continuously tossed astern to lure gulls offshore. The presence of the gulls eventually attracts albatrosses to the boat.

In recent years, migration watching has not been well organized in North America, owing mainly, I think, to the pressing need with which the United States Fish and Wildlife Service has had to concentrate on rescuing our waterfowl population from disaster. A number of co-operators still send records to the Division of Migratory Birds (some have done so for over 50 years), but their observations undoubtedly reflect uneven opportunities for field work. No efforts are being made to solicit the co-operation of lighthouse keepers and, in the more underpopulated regions, only an ele-

TABLE 3

A MODERN MIGRATION TABLE

By far the most exact information on migration now comes from bird banders. This unique table, from Margaret Nice's work on the song sparrow, shows how individuals of this species varied in their arrival each spring at Columbus, Ohio. This pioneering piece of field work was based on daily censuses and mapping of a bird population that had been marked with colored bands.

Field number of individual	Sex	1930	1931	1932	1933	1934	1935
2M	male	Feb. 26	Mar. 20	Mar. 1	Mar. 8		
10M	male *	Mar. 15	Apr. 3–5	Mar. 26	Mar. 18	Mar. 16	
K14	female *	Apr. 8	Apr. 3–5	Mar. 29			
23M	male		Apr. 3–5	Mar. 21	Mar. 18		
68M	male		Mar. 26	Feb. 27	Mar. 1		
K58	female		Mar. 24	Mar. 3	Mar. 14		
70M	male		Feb. 28	Feb. 26	Mar. 2		
115M	male			Feb. 26	Feb. 24	Mar. 17	
123M	male			Mar. 5	Mar. 16	Mar. 18	
K90	female			Mar. 30	Mar. 15	Mar. 18	
111M	male *			Feb. 27	Mar. 15	Mar. 28	Mar. 17
K131	female *			Apr. 18	Mar. 23		Apr. 3
K165	female				Apr. 22	Mar. 17	Mar. 19–20
average for birds cited here		Mar. 20	Mar. 13	Mar. 15	Mar. 19		

* = first-year bird

Condensed from *Transactions of the Linnaean Society of New York*. 1937.

mentary knowledge of the local avifauna is now available. Much of this basic work could be undertaken by ambitious bird clubs. Observations in Nova Scotia and Newfoundland would help to fill out our picture of what is being recorded on both Cape Cod and Long Island. In *Audubon Magazine,* migration watchers can regularly find something of interest in 'The Season,' especially since it has been summarized by Ludlow Griscom. Here, however, facts are often reported only because they were easy to record and coverage is lacking for such large sections of the country as the Rocky Mountains, the Southwest, and the lower Mississippi valley, where bird migration is still being studied by only a mere handful of people.

Ordinarily birds migrate along fairly broad paths, but this is not universal. James L. Edwards once described to me an interesting experience he had while waiting for hawks on a ridge in New Jersey. During frequent lulls, when no raptores were overhead, he began to notice that ruby-throated hummingbirds were passing by with an unusual degree of regularity. Once attention was focused on them, it became readily evident that these tiny birds were repeatedly following an extremely narrow path perfectly invisible to man, along the side of the ridge. Every hummingbird followed this line with meticulous accuracy.

Hawk Flights

It is now generally accepted that birds do not migrate at great heights. Not infrequently, however, some hawks pass over beyond the limit of human vision. Everyone who has watched a trained falcon perched on an outdoor block is impressed with this phenomenon. Suddenly the falcon will cock its head and intently peer at some distant point in the sky. Turning its head slowly, it follows an invisible hawk that the average naturalist would invariably miss. In northern New Jersey, members of the Urner Ornithological Club found their migration studies of hawks along the ridges hampered by this very obstacle. They surmounted it by team work, observers lying flat on their backs and studying the sky with binoculars. In the fall of 1942, this enterprising group of field workers observed a total of 5000 hawks on migration.

For many years I have wanted to determine some basis for estimating the height at which birds are flying. When a bald eagle is seen as a speck in the heavens, who can tell how far up it is soaring? I doubt if anyone can in flat country. If a flock of geese goes over, so high as to be almost invisible, who can estimate their height? Facts like these can be (and have been) measured with instruments called theodolites. They might even be determined by experiments in which stuffed specimens are sent aloft in balloons. Fantastic? Of course. Yet European observers can now tell at what heights the outline of a buzzard's wings is still visible and at what height this bird becomes a speck in the sky. So far, the vaunted ingenuity of Americans has not been exercised in this direction.

William Vogt points out to me that the popular use of the airplane after the war is bound to offer a new opportunity to explore bird migration. More records can be kept on the heights at which birds fly, their air speeds, and their use of wind currents. Aviation meteorologists, possessing exact knowledge of wind directions and velocities aloft, can also furnish information in a way that was seldom before possible.

An extremely interesting migration route is now being worked out for many of our eastern hawks. For years, so-called sportsmen annually slaughtered thousands of these birds on certain ridges in Pennsylvania and New Jersey. Finally, conservationists went to work. The slaughter was stopped. Under the energetic leadership of Mrs. Rosalie Edge, a unique sanctuary for hawks was established at Hawk Mountain, Pennsylvania. Bird students began to take up the gunners' old stands. Facts were fitted together. A series of well-established flight lines is now known to exist from the Mt. Tom range in western Massachusetts well into eastern Pennsylvania. In time, our knowledge of these routes will be extended. Thousands of hawks use them every fall, but the routes that many of them follow upon leaving Pennsylvania are as yet unknown.

Watching hawk flights is now a unique American institution. To take a position of vantage along a flight line at the right season is to learn the field marks of hawks at a rate that might ordinarily encompass months or even years. One of the best points is at the now-famous Hawk Mountain Sanctuary, at Drehersville, Pennsylvania. This has been visited by thousands of bird watchers from all over the continent, and special excursion trains have actually been run to it from Philadelphia. Here one sits atop a ridge, and hawks can be well seen as they pass fairly close to the observer.

According to Maurice Broun, who annually serves as curator and guide at Hawk Mountain, the big broad-wing flights occur between September 10 and 26 (once 4078 in one day), and red-tail concentrations have been seen between October 30 and November 12 (twice averaging over 230 per day). Bald eagles go south early in September, golden eagles from early October until the end of the migration. Since the broad-wings winter throughout Central America (even to Venezuela and Peru), the further tracing of their main flight through the southern states should be one of the most exciting problems in field ornithology. Following the golden eagles

TABLE 4

THE AUTUMNAL MIGRATION AT HAWK MOUNTAIN

Some of the best migration watching in America is now being carried out by Maurice Broun for the Hawk Mountain Sanctuary Association at Drehersville, Pennsylvania, where hawks were once slaughtered in enormous numbers. The figures below are the result of his daily counts of the birds following a single ridge.

Species	1934	1935	1936	1937	1938	1939	1940	1941
Turkey vulture	166	374	87	44	60	146	150	182
Goshawk	123	293	177	49	9	26	11	21
Sharp-shinned hawk	1,913	4,237	4,486	4,817	3,113	8,529	2,407	3,909
Cooper's hawk	333	553	474	492	204	590	166	416
Red-tailed hawk	5,609	4,024	3,177	4,978	2,230	6,496	4,725	4,700
Red-shouldered hawk	90	181	153	163	143	314	149	198
Broad-winged hawk	2,026	5,459	7,509	4,500	10,761	5,736	3,159	5,170
Rough-legged hawk	20	9	9	4	.....	8	4	2
Golden eagle	39	66	54	73	31	83	72	55
Bald eagle	52	67	70	38	37	64	38	50
Marsh hawk	105	153	149	160	189	273	161	254
Osprey	31	169	205	201	124	174	91	201
White gyrfalcon	2	...	...	...	...	...	...	...
Black gyrfalcon	...	...	1	...	...	...	1	...
Duck hawk	25	14	36	41	24	38	25	44
Pigeon hawk	19	20	34	10	12	43	11	35
Sparrow hawk	13	123	102	141	87	184	60	196
Unidentified	208	23	11	8	...	...	7	38
Totals	10,776	15,765	16,734	15,719	17,024	22,704	11,237	15,471

Reprinted from *Annual Reports* of the Hawk Mountain Sanctuary Association.

north and south should also be interesting, for no one knows where the 'eastern' population breeds or winters. Hawk migration exists along the ridges in the spring, but the fall flights are by far the most spectacular and most studied.

Another important migration route for hawks in the eastern states lies along the Atlantic coast. This route has never been carefully mapped, although many pertinent notes have already been made by migration watchers. Near the Connecticut-Rhode Island

line many birds cross to Fisher's Island and thence to the tip of
Long Island. Some migrants then move westward along the outer
islands making up the ocean beach. Others follow farther inland
parallel to the bays. Still others, I suspect, perhaps strike out over
the ocean for a more southern point along the coast.

At Cape May Point, the southern tip of New Jersey, a combination of factors contributes to some of the most amazing spectacles
of autumnal bird migration in America. In this locality, according
to Robert P. Allen and Roger T. Peterson, most of the hawks seem
to arrive on or shortly after northwest winds. Here, during the fall
of 1935, Peterson and W. J. Rusling identified over 11,000 hawks.
About 8200 were sharp-shinned hawks, 840 were Cooper's hawks,
777 were sparrow hawks, 706 were ospreys, 402 were pigeon hawks,
367 were broad-wings, and 274 were marsh hawks. This migration
begins in late August and continues until the middle of November.
It is characterized by lulls and heavy flights that flood the countryside with all kinds of birds, and on one occasion (October 21, 1932)
Allen recorded 4562 hawks. Cape May Point is the only place in
the United States that I know of where coveys of bob-whites have
been observed on migration. The great land-bird flights on this
coast have been found by members of the Delaware Valley
Ornithological Club to continue southward to definite points on
Cape Charles (Virginia) but their progress across Chesapeake Bay
has not yet, I believe, been actually mapped. Great concentrations
of migratory birds are also known to occur at Whitefish Point
(Michigan), which extends into Lake Superior, and at Point Pelee
(Ontario), which juts out into Lake Erie. Opportunities to discover similar concentration points undoubtedly are limited by local
topography.

Dispersal Movements

Typical migration might be said to represent an annual rhythm
by means of which birds leave and return to their nesting localities.
In some instances, the birds may merely move down a mountain-
side to a warmer and more favorable climate on the slopes below.
Other species may move only a few hundred miles, or as many as
ten thousand. What is often erroneously called migration occurs in

certain species after the young are fledged. These youngsters may disperse in every direction, except possibly out to sea. Herring gulls do this to some extent, black-crowned night herons even more so. Young little blue herons and American egrets, which add so much to many of our landscapes each summer, are also examples.

Another and more important kind of dispersion takes place when birds like the snowy owl and the crossbills descend upon the temperate regions in considerable numbers. These invasions apparently are due to scarcity of the birds' food in the North. During the winters of 1876-7 and 1926-7, great flights of snowies occurred in the northern United States. Lesser flights took place during at least 12 other winters. These occasions were thrilling for bird students, but were not untouched with sadness. The fearlessness with which these splendid birds perched in the open made them picturesque figures in the field of one's binoculars, but perfect targets for gunners as well. In the 1901-2 flight, for instance, J. H. Fleming estimated that at least a thousand were shot in Ontario alone. In the 1926-7 invasion, I would guess that not more than 20 per cent of the birds that reached Long Island ever returned to their homes in the Arctic.

The crossbills have an equally interesting history, which has been summarized by Ludlow Griscom. Red crossbills arrived in eastern Massachusetts in June 1868, bred there late the following September, and left for unknown parts late in October. They were abundant in Massachusetts again in 1870-71 and in southern New England and lower New York during the fall of 1874. In the spring of 1875, some bred near New York City and late that summer others nested in eastern Massachusetts. Flights again occurred in 1878-9 and 1882-3. In the latter year a casual breeding bird was reported from Long Island late in April. Thus runs the history of this amazing species. In some years it reached Virginia, and from 1886 to 1887 it was even abundant in South Carolina. Some crossbills go east and west in search of an adequate food supply, for a bird banded at Milton, Massachusetts, on May 12, 1932, was found dead two years later at Bemidiji, Minnesota. Other birds that intermittently leave their usual quarters in Canada and the Far North include glaucous and Iceland gulls, goshawks, the redpolls, the pine and evening grosbeaks, and the handsome bohemian waxwings.

Still another kind of dispersal takes place when birds are caught up by the currents of a hurricane. About three or four of these great storms occur every year in the West Indies from August to October, much of them spinning out to sea and dissipating themselves in a northeasterly course over the Atlantic. A few, however, sometimes travel along or near the coast line, and occasionally sweep southern sea birds far to the north. In this way, black skimmers have from time to time appeared in New England. Similarly, in the fall of 1928, numbers of sooty terns (mostly dead) were found on Long Island. Hurricanes have also carried man-o'-war-birds north from the tropics and such 'freaks' from southern seas as the black-capped petrel. One of the most impressive of these storms was the terrific hurricane that smashed Long Island and New England in September 1938. This deposited the yellow-billed tropic-bird (from the West Indies, perhaps) in at least three places in Vermont; oceanic birds like the greater and Cory's shearwaters were dropped inland in Massachusetts; pelagic Wilson's petrels were blown as far as Montreal and subsequently recorded on Lake Ontario.

Although migrating birds arrive at their destinations pretty much on schedule, many are sometimes driven far out to sea where they perish. Tales of birds alighting in an exhausted condition on oceanic vessels are fairly common. Undoubtedly, an occasional land bird succeeds in crossing the ocean in this manner. For instance, C. A. Alford found four greenfinches seeking the sanctuary of the S. S. *Alaunia* one October day off the British Isles. After a short time one bird disappeared, but the other three refused to leave the steamer. They remained on it until Newfoundland was sighted—the only greenfinches ever recorded for North America. (The record, mentioned in *British Birds,* is still unrecognized by the A.O.U.)

A number of other European species have been reported in the United States, but most of these migrants appear to be purely accidental visitors. Among them have been six kinds of shore birds (woodcock, curlew, whimbrel, bar-tailed godwit, dunlin, and ruff), four species of waterfowl (rufous-crested duck, sheld-duck, ruddy

sheldrake, and barnacle goose), a falcon (the kestrel), a land rail
(the corn crake), and some oceanic birds (Madeira petrel and
Manx and Mediterranean shearwaters). Many others have occurred
in Greenland and Labrador. The Cory's shearwater, an offshore sea
bird, occurs regularly off our Atlantic coast each autumn. Occasionally Mediterranean shearwaters are reported by collectors.

Since 1930, several more European birds have been regularly
recorded in our northeastern states. Among these are the curlew
sandpiper, the European widgeon (known to breed in Greenland),
the little gull and the European teal (both known to nest in Iceland), and the black-headed gull. One accidental species occasionally reaches us from abroad in straggling numbers—the lapwing.
The last trans-Atlantic flight of these handsome crested plovers was
largely due to a freak gale that averaged 55 miles per hour across
almost the entire Atlantic. According to H. F. Witherby, the eminent English ornithologist, these plovers must have left the British
coast shortly after dusk on December 19, 1927 (7 P.M. Greenwich
time). With an air speed of their own rated at 45 miles per hour,
the birds rode the gale at a total speed of 100 miles per hour. They
were actually seen in Newfoundland in small flocks on December
20 at 3 P.M.—24 hours after their approximate departure; and estimates of 500 and 1000 birds were made on the following day.
This great storm is also believed to have brought to North America
at least one European snipe, one European jacksnipe, and two
European coots. Another storm, on November 19, 1932, swept
thousands of dovekies inland to destruction.

Several shore birds do, however, make long sustained flights annually across the ocean. Among these is the bristle-thighed curlew,
which breeds in western Alaska and is known to winter on islands
of the South Pacific from Hawaii to New Caledonia. The much-
quoted flight line of the golden plover runs nonstop from berry-
laden Labrador, over or past Nova Scotia and across the sea to the
Lesser Antilles and South America. Persistent barometric pressures,
known to all aviators as 'the Bermuda high,' may, as Captain Neil
McMillan points out, explain why these birds have a tail wind for
their journey each autumn and why they cannot come back the
same way each spring.

Are birds exhausted by long flights? Under ordinary conditions they are not. Very obviously, long flights over water would never have evolved unless the birds found these to be successful. So vigorous are the tiny flyers entering the United States through Florida that in one particular year, Professor Cooke estimated, between one and two dozen species passed on northward nonstop at least to Georgia.

Dispersal is thus seen to be periodic, as in the snowy owl and goshawk; annual as in the case of young herring gulls and American egrets; irregular or accidental in many other species. To the scientist the first two types are more important and full accounts of them may be found in several bird books, such as Frederick C. Lincoln's volume on bird migration and James Fisher's useful booklet on *Watching Birds* (see appendix).

No account of accidental dispersion is complete, I think, without some mention of the historic bird that once swam across the Atlantic Ocean. The story is told (as I recall) by E. M. Nicholson, now secretary of the British Trust for Ornithology, and an author of several fine books on bird watching. During a heavy storm some years ago in the North Sea, Mr. Nicholson reports, a Norwegian sailing vessel lost one of its masts. When the wreckage was cleared away, a small crippled gull was found to be following the ship. For some reason the bird, which was probably a kittiwake, could not fly. It was fairly tame and the sailors fed it every day. In this way, the two cripples crossed the Atlantic, the little gull swimming after the half-wrecked vessel. Off Newfoundland, however, it eventually deserted the Norwegians. I should too, I think, if I had lived on spoiled oleomargarine for three-and-a-half months.

Migrational Homing

Everyone has heard about the marvelous homing ability of homing pigeons. Relatively few are aware, however, of the homing ability of wild birds. Between the racing pigeon and the wild species there is hardly any comparison. The pigeon is a mere novice.

Among wild birds, migrational homing behavior may be considered first, as it is known in adult birds and has been observed among young that have not yet nested. Homing has been defined as the ability of animals to return great distances over a route, part of which is entirely unknown or without landmarks. Migrating birds have this ability to a very great degree. The Greenland wheatear, which breeds in the Canadian Arctic, annually migrates to West Africa through the British Isles. Many other striking examples could be quoted. Bird banders have also proved beyond all doubt that once migratory birds have nested in a definite locality they will return to breed there as long as they live. There appear to be only a few exceptions to this important rule. Some ducks, for instance, pair on their wintering grounds. The male may have come from central Alberta, the female from the coast of British Columbia. Obviously both cannot return home and still remain mated. It is said that the female always wins.

Do young birds have this homing ability too? It seems quite apparent that they do, although some aspects of the question are still unsettled. Many young birds migrate south before their parents. If their species is known to winter regularly only in southern California, the young birds do not, for example, winter in Florida instead. Birds never make that mistake, no matter how young.

In only a few species do the young birds accompany their parents south. Whooping cranes do this, often traveling from Canada to Texas in what are evidently family flocks. Geese are said to be another example. In some species, young and adults may winter in separate regions. During the winter the herring gulls of Boston harbor are mostly adult; those on the Texas coast are for the most part first-year birds.

Some uncertainty still surrounds the question where birds nest for the first time. Do they return to breed in the locality of their birth? Or is the selection of their first nest site fortuitous—'anywhere,' as one authority has postulated, 'within the natural range of the species'? The answers to these questions must rest upon the efforts of bird banders. Up to the present, however, only a few banders have provided any satisfactory information on this subject. In Holland, H. N. Kluijver once found that 44 per cent of the surviving nestling starlings that he banded returned to nest in the locality of their birth. Similarly, in Ohio, Margaret Nice concluded that 50 to 60 per cent of her fledgling song sparrows that survived returned to their birthplace. Unfortunately, many other banders never succeed in retrapping any number of their banded fledglings.

It is now clear that one important reason for this failure is the terrific mortality suffered by young birds in their first year. Among songbirds this loss may amount to 75 per cent; in game birds it may be even higher. Another reason is said to be the failure of bird banders to search the surrounding countryside for banded birds. One of Mrs. Nice's song sparrows settled down about one mile from its birthplace, although most of her fledgling returns were between 100 and 500 yards from the original point of banding. Just how far the bander is supposed to search is hard to say.

If young birds scatter and nest almost anywhere within the breeding range of their species, the follow-up activities of bird banders would have to be Herculean. Some years ago, it occurred to me that the banding records reported *only* by laymen might answer this question. With this in mind, and with the kind permission of Frederick C. Lincoln, I began a search of the banding files of the United States Fish and Wildlife Service. Eventually the robin proved to be the species I wanted. Fledglings had been banded by the thousands (I never did learn how many). Sixty-one had been reported in some subsequent breeding season (mid-April to mid-July) by ordinary citizens who had no connection with the banding program. Some of the robins had been killed by cars; others had caught themselves on strings; still others had fallen victims to cats. They, one could say, were a random sample of a normal robin population. Probably in the smaller villages where a bander resided, his activities might have stimulated more people to report the band numbers on dead birds. (In large towns and suburban areas his work might be cloaked in anonymity.) This would tend somewhat to increase the percentage of returns made by the robins to the place of their birth. It would not, I think, affect reports a few miles away.

Even with this bias kept in mind, the accompanying table suggests a marked tendency for robins to return to the region of their birth. Although the banders did not separate the nestlings according to first, second, and third broods, some clue to this is furnished by the banding dates. These dates do not suggest that birds in the first brood settle farther away than fledglings raised in subsequent broods. Another interesting thing about these banding records concerned the birds reported at some distances from their birthplace. All of them were somewhere *south* of their original home. Without

TABLE 5

DO YOUNG BIRDS RETURN TO THEIR BIRTHPLACE?

Scientists are not in complete agreement on this question, owing largely to a lack of concrete facts on the subject. Here are the distances at which 61 robins probably nested from their birthplace. They are based on birds banded as fledglings and reported as dead or injured in some subsequent breeding season.

	Dates birds were banded					
	May		*June*		*July*		*Approximate density*
Zone of recovery	1–15	16–31	1–15	16–30	1–15	*Total*	*of recoveries*
Same community	6	6	12	4	5	33	40 birds per square mile
1–10 miles away	..	4	2	3	3	12	1 bird per 6 square miles
11–50 miles away	..	..	5	2	..	7	1 bird per 270 square miles
51–100 miles away	..	1	2	1	..	4	1 bird per 1470 square miles
101–200 miles away	..	..	1	1	1	3	1 bird per 7800 square miles
201–300 miles away	..	..	1	..	..	1	1 bird per 39,000 square miles
301–400 miles away	..	..	..	..	..	0	
401–500 miles away	..	..	1	..	..	1	1 bird per 70,000 square miles
	6	11	24	11	9	61	

Compiled from banding files of the Fish and Wildlife Service. 1940.

speculating why this happened, the fact does have some significance.

Experimental Homing

Homing experiments offer special opportunities for bird watchers to explore the mysteries of migration. Some experiments deal with adults, others concern young birds. Nearly all require considerable co-operation and organization.

Granted that migratory birds are able to follow the routes of their ancestors, can they also return home over paths completely outside the range of their species? In the early part of this century, two pioneering Americans, John B. Watson and Karl S. Lashley, attempted to answer this question. Capturing five tropical noddy and sooty terns on their nests off the tip of Florida, the young men marked their birds with artists' oils and arranged for their release off the capes of Hatteras, a thousand miles north and far outside the normal range of these species. Three birds promptly returned, two sooty terns making the journey in only five days.

Other homing experiments proved to Watson and Lashley that about 50 per cent of these birds could return from other points of the compass. Some were undoubtedly weakened by captivity, while others were suspected of following the coast. Many years later, the subject attracted the attention of German ornithologists. Using starlings, Dr. Rüppell proved that even this small species could return from any direction and with no previous knowledge of the country. Here, the absence of prominent landmarks made no difference. When sea birds were released in Italy and Switzerland, R. M. Lockley was later able to prove, they could return to their Welsh island on a straight line, and sometimes in a surprisingly short period.

Even the much maligned cowbird has been found to be an excellent homer. Once in the middle of April one of these birds was trapped by William I. Lyon and banded at Waukegan, Illinois. Shipping the bird westward, Mr. Lyon had it released at Denver, Colorado, on April 28. Twenty-five days later it was back in Waukegan. Sent eastward and released at Quebec on May 26, it eventually got back to Illinois and was present in Mr. Lyon's banding trap the following March. Other cowbirds, Mr. Lyon found, could return from equally remote places.

Waterfowl are no less competent. Some years ago, E. A. McIlhenny captured pintails wintering in Louisiana and shipped them to distant points all over the United States. In succeeding winters, he reported, 7 returned from their point of release near Washington, D. C., 5 returned from Cape Cod, 2 from western Montana, 15 from California, and 4 from eastern Oregon.

Today the most interesting migrational homing experiments are those designed to shed light on how the homing instinct is transmitted from old to young. Mallard eggs were once shipped from England, where the species is completely sedentary, to Finland where mallards are definitely migratory. Sixty-two young birds hatched and were successfully banded. About the middle of October all but six of the Finnish birds left for southern regions; a month later these six and all the young English birds finally departed. Three of the latter were subsequently shot in Yugoslavia, one in southern France, and seven others were reported from less distant localities. None returned to England. In the following summer more than half of the English mallards returned to breed in their Finnish birthplace.

This fascinating project would at first seem to show that these young birds had no hereditary knowledge of their ancestors' home. Mallards in England must have a dormant migratory instinct of some kind, for how could the young English birds have migrated north again to their foster homeland? What would have happened if the eggs of a highly migratory group of birds had been used instead? Some inkling is given by the story of some sheldrake eggs that were once taken from the island of Sylt in the North Sea and hatched in Switzerland, where the species is practically unknown except as a very rare straggler. Out of the 17 young that hatched, one was shot that October in the Baltic—only 120 miles from the parental nesting site. Was this a coincidence, as W. B. Alexander once asked, or do migratory birds have an inherited memory of their ancestral home?

The answer will be found in careful experiments worked out on a continental basis. Waterfowl are easily shot and yield a high percentage of recoveries. But these records tend to become bunched in hunting seasons when the birds are already on migration. Besides, ducks tend to pair on their wintering grounds, which introduces a further complication. Perhaps a more suitable species would be the herring gull, which nests on the Pacific coast, the Great Lakes, and the Atlantic seaboard. Suppose a mass exchange of fresh gull eggs between two of these regions was carried out over a period of years. Would the birds hatched from Great Lakes eggs remain, say, on the Pacific coast, or would they eventually return to the home of their parents? What would happen if follow-up experiments could be conducted with young birds, well grown but still unable to fly? Would they behave the same as birds hatched from transported eggs? Would there be any difference between very young birds and older fledglings transported just before they were ready to fly? No one, I think, can at this time be sure of just what would happen.

The opportunities for gathering eggs (or young) obviously vary from species to species, challenging bird clubs and students to con- centrated co-ordinated effort. Usually the transportation costs for eggs is small. An air-mail shipment of 72 snowy egret eggs from Florida to Long Island once cost the Linnaean Society of New York about $10. (Most of the eggs failed to hatch in this experiment and four young nestlings died after a week. We were inclined to be- lieve that their white down failed to release the normal feeding behavior patterns of the black-crowned night herons selected as their foster parents.)

This last experiment closely paralleled others made in England, where gray herons failed to rear young from eggs of the stork shipped from the continent. Other possibilities along similar lines can still be successfully explored. Some years ago 260 eggs of the common gull were sent over 300 miles to a black-headed gull colony in Rossitten, Germany. Here, 79 young were fledged by their foster parents. Although the heavy vegetation at Rossitten was not at all adapted to their nesting needs, two pairs of these 'trans- planted' birds eventually returned and successfully raised their own young in the vicinity.

Some Homing Theories

The ability of wild birds to return over an unknown course is so far without adequate explanation. There are many theories and even the most fantastic ones are gradually being subjected to study.

Something of the history of these was reviewed not long ago by Ernst Mayr. One of the oldest and most widely accepted theories has held that homing was simply a matter of memory and random searching—when a bird is on familiar ground, it follows the known landmarks; on unfamiliar ground, it wanders about and eventually, by trial and error, picks out something familiar in the landscape. When birds were released in homing experiments, however, they almost invariably set right out in the proper direction. Proof that this theory was worthless came when it developed that birds re- leased 500 miles from home took only 5 times longer to return than others with only 100 miles to go. If random searching were the answer, this distance would always increase geometrically instead of algebraically, as it does in nature. During the course of experiments abroad, homing birds were picked up dead—almost exactly on the theoretical straight line to their nesting localities.

Another explanation offered for homing has given the birds a marvelous ability to retrace the exact journey on which they had just been taken. The most striking proof against retracing, writes Dr. Mayr, is the triangle experiment. Suppose we have the three towns A, B, and C forming the corners of an equilateral triangle. We take 20 starlings from A and transport them to B; then we retain 10 at B, and carry the remaining 10 to C. We now release the 20 birds at the same moment. According to the retracing theory, it should take the C starlings just twice as long as the B birds to get home to A, because they would have to fly via B. 'Actual experiments, carried out in Germany, have shown that the B and C starlings arrived home at the same time,' Dr. Mayr reports, 'thus upsetting a very fine theory.'

Still another explanation of homing similarly assumes that birds have extraordinary organs that register every turn on the road of transport. In addition, this third theory credits the bird with always knowing its geographic position in regard to its nesting locality. To check this idea, scientists shipped two cages of starlings from a German village to Berlin, over 90 miles away. Both cages were darkened, but one was mounted on the revolving disc of a phonograph and rotated during the entire journey. Of these birds, 50 to 60 per cent returned home—so well, in fact, that they even bettered the record of birds that had not been subjected to this unusual treatment.

Another of the striking experiments carried out by Dr. Rüppell in Germany involved the shipment of starlings by airplane to England, Sweden and other points in Germany, some more than 400 miles distant. Of these nesting birds, 52 out of 97 were known to return to their home localities. Moreover, the best percentage of return (75.9 per cent) was obtained by birds sent the greatest distances.

It has also been suggested that birds are sensitive to terrestrial magnetism. It is argued that each part of the earth has its own magnetic field. A bird might be able to detect this through its ears and so recognize whether its home lay to the north or to the south. A few years ago Polish investigators shipped storks to various parts of Europe. Some birds had magnets attached to their heads; others, serving as 'controls,' carried unmagnetized weights. In spite of storms, a few birds managed to return. The head magnet had failed to impair homing ability.

Homing today remains as much of a baffling mystery as it ever was, puzzling both biologist and bird watcher alike. The search for the mechanism of homing is, however, no more knotty than many other studies that scientists have successfully completed. Homing is now so well established in migratory birds that haphazard experiments with adults in the future can only be regarded as stunts. Nesting birds, it is now known, will return vast distances. Wintering birds are not so responsive. (They may have homing *ability*, but very little *urge* to use it outside the nesting season.) I do not think it is up to bird watchers to establish records along these lines, but they can regard the homing of young birds as their own problem. Here we are still faced with fundamental questions. Are migratory routes to a wintering ground a matter of inherited knowledge in all species? Is the recognition of a specific home locality inherited, or is just the homing ability inherited? Do young birds memorize something about their home while they are still nestlings or just after they have left their parents?

Carefully planned shipments of eggs and young will, I think, furnish the answers to many of these questions. Plans should be worked out according to local opportunities; many might be carried out by local bird clubs. Only careful attention to details will insure success in such matters. Among these details, I would include the following:

1. The help of bird students in distant regions must naturally be enlisted. If the names of such persons are not known in the area to which the eggs or birds are to be shipped, assistance might be secured from the nearest bird club (a useful index for Canada and the United States appears in the appendix). Help can also be

solicited by writing to the editor of one of the bird magazines, like *The Auk, The Wilson Bulletin, The Condor,* or *Bird-Banding.*

2. The greatest care must be used to select a species that will yield banding recoveries. Ducks, herons, gulls, terns, crows, and sparrow hawks are all satisfactory in this respect, although their availability is often markedly limited in some regions.

3. When a large number of subjects cannot be secured in a single year, the project should be put on an annual basis until the number of recoveries is large enough to be significant.

4. Due recognition should be given to controls. Thus, the shipment of crow eggs from Maine to Ohio would prove nothing if no information was available on the normal migration of birds raised in both these regions.

5. No attempt should be made to raise young outside the known breeding range (past or present) of their species.

6. Whenever migratory birds are shipped across a state line, they are subject to a federal law called the Lacey Act. In such cases, it is necessary to describe the project in detail and send this information to the Chief, Fish and Wildlife Service, Department of the Interior, Washington, D. C. When such studies are properly organized and one of the experimenters already possesses the necessary banding permits, no difficulty will be experienced in getting permission to carry out projects of this kind.

7. Great care should be exercised in obtaining fresh eggs. It seems advisable to ship these by plane. Nestlings used in homing experiments should, of course, be well grown.

8. In some cases the services of a state game farm might be enlisted in hatching the eggs. In others, local zoos might be encouraged to rear young birds. All such birds should be ringed with aluminum bands of the United States Fish and Wildlife Service. Certain colonial species, like the gulls and terns, might be further marked with colored celluloid bands if follow-up observations are planned at key nesting colonies concerned in the study.

Co-operative studies in bird migration are by no means confined to experiments in homing. An equally interesting series of projects awaits those who would like to map the weekly progress of migratory species as they traverse the length of our continent during a given season. This method of summarizing continental observations might well be taken up by bird watchers who, through some unfortunate circumstance, are no longer able to get into the field. All sorts of birds lend themselves to this type of investigation, but no more than 40 species have, I think, been so studied on our continent. Bullock's oriole would be an easy bird to map in the West, the Baltimore oriole a parallel bird in the East. Many other species that are commonly observed on village streets, in gardens, and in suburban areas might be chosen. The bird clubs indexed in the appendix of this book could be circularized in this connection. Not all of them might accurately report when the very first chimney swift arrived in their locality from South America, but they could check to observe when the swifts became common and so furnish information on this species' progress from Mexico to Canada. The postage involved in inquiries of this kind is small. It could well be carried by bird clubs anxious to have their own committees on bird migration fill in the many gaps still existing in our knowledge of this subject.

The exploration of bird migration today is obviously a many-sided one. Many observations are still needed at lighthouses and islands off the coast. Daily observations correlated with weather data at the point where migrants start their daily or nightly flight are still needed to show which species move only with favorable weather and which migrate with little regard to wind and temperature. In many regions only the vaguest correlations have been made between the exact development of local vegetation and the spring arrival of the main body of each species.

Migration watching is thus a branch of natural history in which scientific research is still fun. Narrowed down to simple rarity chasing, it is an exciting sport that in time dulls the appetite and eventually suffers from the law of diminishing returns. Within the last twenty years, I have seen many people drop bird study; they had seen 'all that there was to be seen' in bird life and there was nothing more to be discovered. I think of them as belonging to those ancient orchard sitters to whom a falling apple was simply a

knock on the head. In migration watching, each of us has a chance
to follow in the path of Newton, to observe the wonders of creation
as they are expressed in the most common phenomena, and to explore nature as assiduously as Wilson and Audubon—and with no
less profit.

CHAPTER THREE

Adventures in Bird Counting

COUNTING BIRDS is a relatively recent innovation. However surprising this may seem at first, it is but a normal step in the evolution of our study of bird life. Consider the enormous difficulties that faced the bird student in 1800. No bird books had yet been printed in America. Such pictures as existed were crude and of little help to the beginner. Field glasses were unknown. Each bird had to be shot and its plumage carefully compared with those of species already described. Ranges meant very little; only their roughest outlines had yet been charted. The Mississippi and the West were still in the hands of Frenchmen, Spaniards, and the Indians. On each field trip, the naturalist collected one or two dozen specimens and then spent the rest of the day (or night) skinning them.

As ornithology gradually grew up, the field glass slowly began to replace the gun. This significant change has occurred within the last fifty years. The new epoch in bird study can be said to have come of age in 1900, when Dr. Frank M. Chapman inaugurated the annual Christmas Bird Census in *Bird-Lore.* Some 27 persons took part in that first count; today over 2000 do so.

Only a few statistics on birds come down to us from the early ornithologists. Back in 1806, Alexander Wilson, the Scotch poet, master weaver, and itinerant peddler who is the father of American bird study, made a conservative estimate of a pigeon flock in Kentucky. The birds, he decided, totaled 2,230,272,000 individuals. A few years later, Audubon tried to estimate another flock. These passenger pigeons, only a small part of a three days' flight, he calculated at 1,115,136,000 birds. 'Large flocks' were mentioned now and then in early accounts of the country, but who can say today what Audubon considered to be 'large'? This early lack of actual statistics on bird life is a serious handicap to all sorts of people today. Conservationists wish they could know exactly how large were the numbers of ducks in, say, 1850, 1875, and 1900. Ornithologists would like to know more about the mechanics of primitive wildlife populations. The status of many birds has changed in the course of a century, a fact attested to by every Pigeon Island, Pigeon Mountain, and Pigeon Creek on our maps. Rare indeed is the bird student who has not wondered what kind of wildlife once thronged his favorite bird-watching area.

Although this numerical concept of bird life fascinates both beginner and expert, a great many observers are still unaware of its place in their own field work. Many still write 'common' or 'abundant' in their notes on the more numerous species. What 'common' or 'abundant' will mean to bird watchers of future generations can only be conjectured. Every beginner thus has a superb opportunity to work out a rather exact picture of the bird life of his region. In this respect he is almost certain to be a pioneer, for at the present time less than half a dozen county lists in the entire United States have given detailed numbers on local birds.

Common Errors in Estimating Birds

Counting birds has been largely neglected because it seems to consume time, and because it does require note-taking on the spot. To the beginner there is always the chance of some strange species hiding in a distant tree, and common birds are lucky to receive a check mark on the field card as he walks along in anticipation of the rarity. Sometimes these everyday species are given a nod of recognition by an 'estimate' such as 100, 1000, or 5000. After several years of systematically checking many 'experts' with whom I am acquainted, I am convinced that the estimate is all too frequently subject to wide margins of error. This conviction has been driven home time and again along the eastern seaboard where numbers of birds are relatively large at certain seasons.

When a big flock of birds is seen, the observer tends to under-estimate the total number present if the species is small in size. Small sandpipers densely packed on the beach are commonly noted in this manner. On one occasion I can remember when '2000 or 3000' was the figure ventured. A few minutes' counting disclosed that 8000 was more nearly right. A quite opposite optical illusion takes place when individual birds of a flock are large in size. Five hundred Canada geese or cormorants can fill quite a sizable piece of landscape, and only the most wary observers can avoid estimat-ing 'several thousand' present. I remember an estimated report of 25,000 herring gulls along a certain section of Long Island. Several friends and I had been intensively watching these birds for weeks. Over a much greater area, perhaps 10,000 birds were actually present. Those making the estimate had undoubtedly seen only some fraction of this number.

Many bird students seem to feel that if they make their estimate quite conservative, they are contributing something valuable to our knowledge of bird life. This type of reasoning is perhaps com-mendable, but the reported number may be so low as to be un-scientific. Not only has the observer lost the opportunity of learn-ing the true status of many species, but he has also missed one of the most interesting aspects of contemporary bird watching.

It is a common practice among migration watchers to note in their journals only birds they have actually seen. Very often, how-ever, they can roughly calculate the total number really present. If red-throated loons are found to be following the ocean beach at a rate of five birds per ten-minute period, it is not necessary to spend the entire day counting them from the top of a sand dune. Brief counts can be scattered throughout the morning and afternoon. The average of these can then be used to calculate the total flight for whatever hours it lasted. The total number of loons is then apt to be impressive, and is also likely to convey a far better picture of the day's migration along the ocean shore.

At no other place have I been overwhelmed by the sheer numbers of birds as at Cape May Point, New Jersey. All previous experiences with migrants left me totally unprepared for the vast panorama of bird life that my first autumn dawn there unfolded. Scores of robins were sweeping past, flocks of meadowlarks crossing high over the pine and holly woodland, smaller birds everywhere in the trees. Every few minutes a sharp-shinned hawk would dart by, sometimes pursuing a flicker. It was the myrtle warblers, though, that stunned my imagination. For almost two hours, they were constantly moving through marsh and woodland, and at every point along a half mile of road small flocks were constantly crossing. According to published records, 3000 is the maximum number of myrtle warblers reported at Cape May on one day by one observer. I feel sure that, during a big flight, to count or estimate the total number of birds in this area is a larger task than one man can handle. Perhaps a team of keen-eyed bird watchers from a near-by bird club, strung out along that half mile of road, could settle the question whether these great flights involve 3000 birds, or 10,000, or 50,000, or 100,000.

On some occasions it is virtually impossible to make any reasonable estimate of the numbers of wild birds present in a given locality. Lee Jaques has consistently refused to set for me any number on the multitudes of snow and blue geese that make southwestern Minnesota one of the most spectacular places for migrating waterfowl each spring. On the Sabine National Wildlife Refuge, where these two species winter in Louisiana, the Fish and Wildlife Service meets with similar difficulties. During the winter of 1939-40, for instance, the Service merely reported that 'on several areas closely packed flocks extended one mile long and three hundred yards wide.'

Communal Bird Roosts

The communal bird roost is one of the most exciting places for the bird watcher to spend the closing hours of a field trip. Here he can often see great numbers of birds and experience some of the same thrills that come to the migration watcher at Cape May or at some concentration spot of the waterfowl. Sometimes the birds are in small groups that can be readily counted. At other times they are massed in great flocks that perform amazing gyrations in the sky, like some spectral cloud of smoke which can change its shape in an instant. Watching a huge flock prepare to enter a roost is to see a surge of life that no camera can capture and few writers can describe in its entirety. It is often half hidden by growing darkness and nearly always accompanied by sounds of a mighty fluttering of wings that fill one's mind with dull echoes of pandemonium.

To count birds approaching a communal roost requires skill, but it is a skill more easily attained than in ordinary bird watching. It is the alternate counting of large and small birds that so often is the pitfall of migration watchers. Roosts are usually limited to one or but a few species, and as a result the confusion caused by birds of different sizes is often lacking. With practice the observer becomes able to estimate flocks of 100 or more birds with considerable accuracy and great rapidity. Care should be taken to select the most advantageous spot for watching the flight, such as some elevated or open space that will permit most of the counting to be carried out with the unaided eye. In the course of one afternoon or evening, thousands of birds may be recorded with confidence and an accurate picture of local bird life thus made available.

Sometimes an estimate of the size of a roost has been calculated at a point adjacent to the roosting site. In England, for instance, starlings often settle in great masses on a few fields just before they enter the reeds, brush, or trees for the night. The probable number of birds per square yard is first carefully fixed and the acreage then determined for those fields that are literally black with resting birds. As many as 500,000 starlings are thus said to use a single communal roost each night during the winter period.

This method of calculating numbers of birds was once used by Dr. C. W. Townsend, the eminent New England naturalist, to estimate a flock of 28,800 herring gulls resting on a sand bar in Massachusetts.

Scores of observations are still needed on flocks of many species where the birds were actually counted and the area they occupied carefully paced off and reported. Additional notes on what the birds were doing (preening, sleeping, feeding) would then enable us to learn the characteristics of flock areas for each species. This kind of bird watching involves common species, and long experience in the field is of no great advantage to the observer.

To locate a communal bird roost is a feat which undoubtedly varies from one region to another. In my own experience I have found it fairly easy. Available roads are a great help, and an automobile virtually a necessity. I like this aspect of bird watching because it is best undertaken late in the afternoon, when the law of diminishing returns has affected other observations. Besides this, tracing the birds in the morning has its own difficulties. Not only do I like to stay in bed, but grackles have actually been seen foraging in village streets while the electric lights were still burning. In setting out to find a roost, the student should look for flight lines. If the roost is small or far away, these may be traversed by but a few birds. As the lines of flight converge nearer the roost, the numbers of birds are naturally larger, reaching into hundreds or even thousands.

How can a flight line be readily identified? Perhaps the most notable aspect of a large roost is the *regularity* with which each line of flight is often used. Night after night, birds may cross the same meadows, cut past the same buildings, alight in the same trees and bushes. This rule holds well for starlings and blackbirds, but not for crows and herring gulls. A second characteristic is the *directness* of the birds' flight. Even swallows, which feed on their way to the roost, tend to show this. A final clue is the *time* of the birds' departure for the roost—late in the afternoon or evening. Some species differ widely in their roosting time, however, and details that are true for one do not always hold for the others.

Crows are especially interesting birds to follow to a roost, and

their nightly gatherings near the roosting site are among the greatest wildlife spectacles which still persist in the heavily inhabited
states east of the Mississippi. These hardy foragers finish feeding
much earlier than most birds in my experience, and small groups
of crows flying high at 2:30 or 3 o'clock on a winter afternoon can
be regarded with suspicion in this connection. When a few arrows
indicating the birds' direction of flight are drawn on a map, the
site of the roost can be roughly located. Only in two states (California and New York) has the location of such sites been mapped
assiduously, and in both cases by the same observer, John T. Emlen,
Jr. According to Dr. Emlen, these birds can range daily as far as
35 miles, although 15 to 20 miles is the more usual limit. The feeding areas about the roost do not change appreciably from one year
to another, and one roost in New York was found to be in use for
over 125 years.

Like the rooks of Europe, crows apparently proceed to their
roosts in a rather leisurely manner. Not long ago Dr. Emlen sent
me a number of interesting facts for those students who would
like to count these birds. Flight lines toward the roost, he wrote,
will vary somewhat from day to day. On cloudy and midwinter
afternoons some crows have been known to leave as early as 1 P.M.
Early arrivals may pass right over the roost to join the great throngs
in some field a mile or two beyond. The final assembly point may
be anywhere from fifty yards to a half mile or more from the actual
roosting site. Here nearly all the crows, except very late arrivals,
gather together. They may choose a field for this, a grove of trees,
a beach, a sandy island, or even ice, the assembly point changing
from day to day, apparently at random. As darkness settles they
adjourn to their roost.

Crows have many variations in the ritual of their afternoon as-
semblies, Dr. Emlen added. Sometimes they may have three distinct assembling grounds from which they pour into the roost as
darkness falls. Three days later the same birds may have four as-
semblies and then drift into the roost for an hour after darkness,
'like columns of smoke from smoldering grasses.'

Somewhat in contrast to the crow is the afternoon flight of the
herring gull. On cold, cloudy days it may be quite direct, with

birds passing over low in V-shaped flocks, like so many geese. Their direction is then readily ascertainable. On warm days the birds may often be found riding thermals (rising masses of warm air). At such times they may circle high in the heavens, endlessly and with all the grace of buzzards. On these occasions even the dullest observer is impressed with the birds' great beauty, but their leisurely soaring does not readily indicate the direction of their destination. To the uninitiated, herring gulls are often deceptive birds to follow. Around New York City, for instance, there is often a marked mid-day flight of birds intent on bathing in fresh water.

Later in the afternoon they wend their way to a preening site. This is not long after the crows have left their feeding grounds. A preening site may be a parade ground, a golf course, a great macadam parking field, a sand bar, a long fish pier, or an unfrequented part of the beach. Here the gulls preen and even nap. They may be a half mile from their nightly sleeping place or several miles from it. Careful counts at preening sites are always interesting but the vicissitudes of feeding vary, and some birds may be still greedily foraging on one day when ordinarily they might be loafing on a preening site with their fellows. Their final site may not be reached until long after dark, when they move to an island, a sand bar, a marsh, the beach, or—when the land is unsafe—some sheltered body of water.

The great increase of herring gulls in recent years renders careful counts of these birds of considerable interest. They are gradually extending their range southward along the Atlantic coast and are frequently reported to be driving terns from their nesting sites. Indeed, federal authorities for some years have attempted to control their numbers by pricking thousands of their eggs. (In Holland, the eggs are shaken to destroy the embryo; in Canada, they are often eaten.) If northern cities ever universally install a system of incineration plants and sewage disposal units, bird watchers may find themselves counting a somewhat decreasing gull population.

To locate a roost of little blue herons and American egrets is to experience one of the great thrills of August bird watching in the North. What the still larger ones are like in the South I can only conjecture. My first experience with a white-heron roost occurred in 1930 when a particularly large movement of these birds reached a peak in northern New Jersey late in August. Together with the late Charles A. Urner, I crossed the ill-scented Newark meadows to a locust grove that Charlie had been regularly watching. At about a half hour before sunset the first egrets appeared, following

TABLE 6

HERON ROOSTS OFTEN YIELD EXCITING MOMENTS IN BIRD COUNTING

Of all communal roosting sites, those of the 'white herons' are among the least studied, although these birds have few peers in beauty of plumage and grace of movement. Here are the total counts for 12 evenings made by Charles A. Urner at Newark, New Jersey, in August and September. A count of 554 birds was once reported as the maximum flight on a single evening.

Minutes in relation to sunset	LITTLE BLUE HERON		AMERICAN EGRET
	Total arrivals	Per cent	
80–98 before	15	.7	..
70–80 "	56	2.5	..
60–70 "	36	1.6	..
50–60 "	88	3.9	⎧ 30
40–50 "	120	5.4	⎨
30–40 "	192	8.5	⎩
20–30 "	318	14.2	64
10–20 "	554	24.7	37
0–10 "	399	17.8	35
0–10 after	328	14.6	10
10–20 "	133	5.9	16
20–35 "	3	.2	..

From *Cassinia.* 1929-30.

a creek that led from tidal flats to the trees where we were stationed. They never crossed the meadows directly, my companion pointed out. Even though the herons had to go three sides around a square, they always followed the water. The early herons approached at some height, their great white forms catching the fading rays of the tired sun. Once over the grove, each dropped with a breath-taking combination of dive and sideslip. The late birds came in low when it was nearly dark. Their wings beating slowly, their white plumage still immaculate in that muddy marshland, they seemed more like ghostly phantoms in the dusk than weary birds in search of a tree's protection. Sunset, cloudy weather, tide, and lateness of the season all seem to affect the arrival of these birds at a roosting site, Mr. Urner subsequently reported, but their exact role has yet to be determined.

Of all the communal roosting birds, starlings are by far the most persistently ignored by American bird watchers. To many die-hards (and I am one of them) the species is still an alien, noisy and belligerent. Yet the aerial evolutions of a great flock in summer compel the admiration of the most reluctant. One of my most exciting bird-watching memories goes back some two decades to an afternoon when Dick Herbert and I watched a great mass of these birds expertly outflying a hawk. Twisting and turning in the sky, they would churn above their pursuer and sideslip in perfect precision—as though they had been drilling for weeks on such a maneuver. On another occasion, I was attempting to count the great numbers that nightly come to roost on the ledges of New York's Metropolitan Museum of Art. It was exciting enough at first, when scores of birds approached from Long Island and cut around the skyscrapers. As the magnitude of the flight built up, however, I realized that my place of observation was too low and its view too broken by tall buildings. At the peak of the flight, clouds of birds descended, like so many flakes of black wind-driven snow.

TABLE 7

STARLING FLIGHT LINES DO NOT ALWAYS LEAD TO THE SAME ROOST

Flight lines to roosts are often quite conspicuous, although some lines may cross one another and birds occasionally are seen going in nearly opposite directions to one another. These complexities make the mapping of communal roosts one of the most engaging diversions of bird watching. This table summarizes counts made by the writer at a small starling roost in a school tower at Bronx, New York, on February 16, 1936. Over one-third of the birds reaching the roost either paused briefly or went on to some other site.

| | Direction of arrival | | | | Direction of departure | | | | Remained |
Time	E&SE	N&NE	W&NW	Total	E&SE	S	W	Total	at roost
4:20–29	..	29	18	47	3	5	..	8	39
4:30–39	12	91	29	132	5	30	2	37	95
4:40–49	3	117	54	174	28	46	..	74	100
4:50–59	5	87	64	156	18	43	..	61	95
5:00–10	..	34	21	55	10	17	..	27	28
Total	20	358	186	564	64	141	2	207	357

My counting degenerated to guessing, and I turned homeward somewhat awed and with a new respect for *Sturnus vulgaris*. Some years later, on December 5, 1938, Roger T. Peterson and Samuel C. Harriot estimated this roost at approximately 38,000 birds. Six days later they made a second count. Their total this time was 24,700.

Starling counts are important for several reasons. Primarily, of course, they provide a record of contemporary bird life. Then too, the exotic nature of the starling's origin on our continent makes the record of their increase especially interesting. Abroad, the species is definitely known to have changed considerably in numbers. According to B. J. Marples, the birds were once so common in England that a reward for their heads was offered in 1564. About 1850 or so, they were rather rare in the British Isles, but around 1885 they began to spread in numbers. Starlings are now so common in England that the filth of a communal roost is often said to drive out other birds and animals. Some roosts in Europe are known to have been in use with only short breaks for periods as long as 135 and 180 years.

Counting starlings is usually a fairly easy matter—if one has a clear view of the birds' approach to the roosting site. The starling uses an exceedingly regular flight line, although the height of the birds varies considerably with wind conditions, the hour of the day, and the degree of cloudiness. In late summer and early fall, reeds and trees are commonly used, but with the approach of winter more sheltered places are taken. In many cities, towers and ledges of public buildings are then occupied, although individual birds may here and there occupy old woodpecker holes and similar crannies. Winter starlings were found by E. R. Kalmbach to use identical perches night after night, and I believe that in general this is true.

In the northern part of New York City, where Ernst Mayr and I once surveyed the starling population, two major winter roosts were found to contain 3000 or more birds, while scattered minor roosts served as many as 700 individuals. The presence of these smaller roosts was often quite apparent, and at one point I found birds moving in 4 different directions (see cut). Flight lines to the major roosts in this region were clearly discernible at least 6 miles away.

In the British Isles, starlings are reported to forage quite commonly as far as 12 to 20 miles from their roost site, and 30 miles is the longest authenticated flight line reported by Marples. The

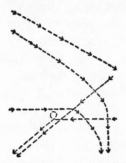

mapping of such foraging areas about large starling roosts has seldom been undertaken, and I know of none that has been published in America. Indeed, many of the bird books in the East scarcely mention the migratory habits of this species. One ornate regional book omits the bird entirely! When so many birds winter in numbers, this information is not easy to discover, but systematic counting at large city roosts offers an excellent opportunity for this kind of exploration.

TABLE 8

COUNTS AT STARLING ROOSTS MAY DISCLOSE MIGRATION PEAKS

The migration of starlings is seldom recognized in regions where these birds breed in numbers. The following counts, taken mostly by Ernst Mayr at a winter roost, show a peak in both spring and fall populations. These birds slept on the ledges of General U. S. Grant's tomb in New York City. They were counted as they flew in late in the afternoon.

August 31	1	February 9	2,705	April 27	1,947
September 21	25	February 20	2,794	May 8	840
October 21	3,399	March 3	2,564	May 18	656
November 30	13,401	March 8	3,012	June 1	98
December 22	5,761	March 25	5,897	July 13	10
February 5	3,496	April 15	3,557	August 17	1

Some of the most exciting moments in bird counting occur at blackbird roosts, especially when starlings are also present and the numbers of local birds have not yet been depleted by migration.

My first experience at one of these sites occurred some years ago on Long Island. On a Sunday afternoon in January, Bob Allen, the Cruickshanks, and I set out to find a large communal roost somewhere east of Amityville. Mrs. Allen, who is making a life-long study of the behavior of naturalists, agreed to go along. Our first clues were starlings flying along Merrick Road on the south shore of the island. After a few miles our birds stopped in some trees. Others joined them, but the entire company left shortly. We pressed on for almost 15 miles. As we neared East Islip the stop-offs became longer, the flocks larger, the confusion greater. Red-wings, bronzed grackles, cowbirds, and starlings were everywhere—flying from trees to adjoining fields, from the fields back to the trees. The bedlam sounded like a swamp in spring rather than a crossroad in the dead of winter. Birds began drifting to the south and we started off in pursuit. Our road turned and twisted. We lost the birds. For some minutes there ensued some frantic driving as we tried to re-establish contact. Far out near the ocean we at last found them—dropping into a huge bed of reed-like phragmites. Our wanderings on the road had taken time, and it was getting dark now. Birds were pouring into the reeds in a steady stream. Finally, a mighty roar of bird wings came out of the west, and a long mass of birds as large as a great dirigible approached the roost. Twisting somewhat as it reached the site, this incredible flock began to rain thousands of birds into the reeds. This was the climax of the flight. The cries of the birds in the enveloping darkness, the sight of such innumerable numbers and—most of all—the beating of countless wings in that mighty mass all left the naturalists in a state of high excitement. Even Mrs. Allen smiled with satisfaction—although no one actually learned whether she was pleased with the birds or the opportunity she had had in observing what makes ornithologists the people they are.

On such occasions it is, of course, impossible to count birds. Subsequent field work by Allan Cruickshank led him to estimate this roost at 90,000 birds, about 15,000 of which he believed were blackbirds and the remainder starlings. In northeastern New Jersey, a much larger roost has been a subject of considerable interest in recent years. Counts by local observers point to 250,000 being present, but no one is willing to quote even a tentative figure without considerable study. In Minnesota, my wife and I once found a summer roost that lent itself fairly readily to counting. The birds here approached a cattail swamp in a long line, stretching as far west as the eye could see. Estimating by 10's and 20's as the birds went over, we found they averaged about 600 per minute. This

TABLE 9

BIRDS DO NOT ALWAYS ROOST AT THE SAME HOUR

Each species has its own roosting time, but this tends to vary with the time of year and the degree of cloudiness on a given day. The following counts were made by Dr. Witmer Stone in 1913 at a summer roost of purple grackles in Philadelphia. Counts like these are still uncommon in bird watching.

Time	July 22	July 23	July 24	July 25	July 26
6:15 p.m.			3	4	
6:20			3	2	
6:25			218	9	16
6:30	15		102	11	25
6:35	123		41	108	115
6:40	125	11	15	576	70
6:45	205	433	1	87	141
6:50	137	248		42	311
6:55	23	52		2	4
7:00	103				
7:05	75				
7:10	2				
Total	808	744	383	841	682

From *Cassinia*. 1912.

early-season roost probably involved 20,000 birds. Under such conditions one observer is needed to handle the counting, and an assistant is necessary to record the time and to write down the estimates as each hundred is called out.

Probably the best field work so far completed on blackbird roosts has been published by the Delaware Valley Ornithological Club. At the close of the nesting season, the DVOC found, smaller roosts begin to combine into larger roosts. At one site some 3000 grackles were present, along with 2000 cowbirds, and 2500 robins, the three species tending to arrive in that order. Ordinarily the birds have preliminary and final gathering places, but in a heavy rainstorm they do not attempt to fly a great distance. In the city of Philadelphia, a grackle roost was once found by C. J. Peck to be in use throughout the year. Peck's interesting summary of this site, condensed from a report in *Cassinia,* follows:

January. Lowest numbers; about 400 to 500 birds present throughout the month; roost deserted on a few very severe nights.

February. No change for the first three weeks; migration then begins; probably 5000 birds present on last few days of the month.

March. Numbers increase rapidly throughout the month, reach 20,000 to 25,000.

April. A drop in numbers sets in about April 15 and continues in a steady decline throughout the next two weeks.

May. 2000 to 3000 birds always present.

June. Same as in May, but with very few females; toward the end of the month, males come in with young birds.

July. Most birds coming in as family groups; birds feed on the way; flight lines not yet apparent.

August. Large flocks now come in from considerable distances; numbers greatly increased; routes well defined.

September and *October.* Period of maximum abundance; flights begin at 5:30 P.M.; from 25,000 to 50,000 present.

November. Marked drop in numbers takes place in two or three nights about the middle of the month.

December. Probably 800 to 1000 birds present; but roost may occasionally be deserted as in January.

The possibilities of counting birds at communal roosts obviously differ from one section of the country to the other. Starlings are present in the East, the tricolored red-wings in the Far West. Great robin roosts are to be found in the more southern states, although smaller roosts are also present in the North. On the sea coasts, curlew flight lines are often well marked and frequently present the amusing spectacle of southbound migrants flying north each night. Hudsonian curlews are easily counted, and Irving Kassoy, Richard Herbert and I once noted 1500 coming in to spend the night on a mud flat at Cobb Island, Virginia. Undoubtedly larger concentrations occur at the peak of migration. Tree swallows also roost in great concentrations, but I have found them hard to count. As many as 10,000 birds resting and preening on telephone wires have been carefully estimated by Dr. Stone at Cape May. Chimney swifts are still another species that can occasionally be counted. In my own experience, roosts with more than 500 swifts tax the eyes of the observer and probably weaken his efficiency, but banders have been able to trap several thousands in a single chimney. A good deal of work still remains to be carried out on the time of day when birds enter their roosts and how this is correlated with light. This aspect of bird behavior has been admirably summarized for the student in Mrs. Nice's monograph on the song sparrow (see appendix).

An Adventure with Hawks

Counting hawks on a well-known migration flight line ranks among the finest amenities of bird watching. Not all of its aspects are ornithological. The views from a ridge top in the Appalachians mask the hustling world in a hazy peacefulness, while the autumnal landscape blushes at the flight of chlorophyll. Sometimes a few hawks lazily ride the air currents. If they are absent for the day, it does not seem to matter.

Some years ago, Joseph A. Hagar, the state ornithologist of Massachusetts, invited me to join a party of ornithologists and witness part of the fall hawk migration at Mt. Tom. Previous observations had led him to believe that many hawks crossed the Connecticut valley at this point as they followed the ridges toward Hawk Mountain in Pennsylvania. This was an interesting discovery. Mr. Hagar had, in fact, written an article on the subject, and newspapers all over his state had been quick to pick up the story.

As the week end of September 18-19 approached, one rainy day followed another. It didn't look like hawk weather to me. In New York on Friday morning a telegram from Mr. Hagar did little to clarify the situation. 'Hawk prospects only fair but come if you think advisable.' An unpleasant rain was falling in the city. Somewhat apprehensively I consulted with R. H. Pough.

A good authority on bird migration always consults a weather map in such cases, and to Mr. Pough's practiced eye the latest map told quite a story. A low-pressure area was just going out to sea, and a high-pressure area was centered near Pittsburgh. The forecast called for gentle, shifting northwesterly winds, with clear skies, and cool weather.

'There should be a big flight of broad-wings very soon,' Dick decided, 'but you may be a day or two ahead of it at Mt. Tom.' Never having seen more than 50 hawks on one field trip, I took the next train for Massachusetts.

At Northampton, Mr. Hagar met me. He had been watching for hawks for days. On Wednesday, 14 had passed over, 43 flew over on Thursday, none had been seen on Friday. From Cambridge, Mr. Peters had wired that he was indisposed; from Taunton, Mr. Bent had reported that he could not make the trip. Mr. Hagar still believed in Mt. Tom, although his faith was now somewhat on the conservative side. He too had been studying the weather maps, and he too had decided that the date of a good broad-winged hawk flight was only a matter of some days. Right then and there I would have settled for 100 birds.

Saturday turned out to be a clear bright morning, with a gentle wind from the north-northeast. By eight o'clock Mr. Hagar and I were atop the fire tower that straddled the ridge. Within a few minutes Mr. and Mrs. Harrington, from near-by Greenfield, joined us. They had read an article about hawks at Mt. Tom, and this was their fourth attempt to see them. Not long afterward an elderly man named J. E. Bliss climbed the steep steps to our platform. Hawk counting was new to him, too, and the article in the newspaper had aroused his curiosity. Mr. Hagar's reputation as a journalist seemed to be considerable; it looked to me as though his reputation as an ornithologist was now at stake. Perhaps I should let him tell the rest of the story, as he once described it in the *Bulletin of the Massachusetts Audubon Society.*

The ground mist rose quickly from the valley floor, streamed along the flanks of the hills, and disappeared, revealing Mt. Monadnock on the horizon. The first bird was an osprey at 8:50, followed by another at 9:18. At 9:30 two broad-wings went by—straggling sharp-shins and a sparrow hawk—a red-shoulder—one of the local duck hawks. At 10:12 four broad-wings—at 10:40 nine more together. Getting better all the time, but too slowly. Three more Springfield people were watching from the ground by now—they too had 'read an article in the paper,' and when John Slattery of Holyoke stuck his head up through the hole in the floor of the tower and said that *he* had 'read an article,' he was somewhat set back for a moment by the general laughter, but we soon explained the joke. Eight more broad-wings at 11:15—ten minutes of searching the sky on all sides—and then a general gasp of amazement, for on the east side of the tower, just across from Smith's Ferry, the air was full of broad-wings! For a moment it seemed as if they must be swallows; there couldn't be so many hawks *together*. Hawks they were, though, circling up from the background of dark woods where we could not see them so well, past the sky-line, and on up. A rapid count showed roughly 175 in three groups, swirling round and round, in and out like leaves in the fall, and in no time at all they were very high in the air and gliding off to the west perhaps a mile away from us.

Well, when the rest of us looked at Mr. Bliss we appreciated then and there that the right kind of an oldish man can get all the kick out of things that youngish ones can. Mr. Harrington was pretty pleased too. They kept telling each other that it was worth all the wait, my reputation seemed to be back on solid footing once more, and everybody felt pretty excited. As a matter of fact I soon became a little over-enthusiastic and offered the remark that we'd see a good many more before the day was over. 'When?' said everybody. 'Between three and five,' said I. That prediction gave me some bad moments later.

At noontime the others went off to eat, and when they returned Joe Hickey and I went into Northampton for dinner, stopping on the way to call Mr. Aaron C. Bagg of Holyoke. We were back at half past one, just in time to see a magnificent adult bald eagle and four broad-wings come through the river-notch between Mts. Holyoke and Nonotuck, and spiral grandly up into the sky until the larger bird was hardly a speck, and his smaller companions were lost to sight. But otherwise the going seemed pretty thin— only single sharp-shins and broad-wings at long intervals. Worse still, the wind changed to light S and SSE between two and two-thirty, and I was doubtful as to what effect that would have on the hawks. Mr. Bagg and his son came at two o'clock, and then Mr. and Mrs. Hervey Elkins of Cambridge. It got to be three o'clock, and still only scattered birds. Somewhat desperately I recalled that the farm superintendent at the Northampton Veterans' Hospital had once told me of seeing a great flight of hawks over Florence; with my glasses I searched the crest of the hills behind Westhampton, and by the greatest luck picked up a flock of sixty or so broad-wings circling for altitude, but so far away that the others scarcely found them. Four o'clock, and the Baggs decided to wait no longer. Lots of kidding about the 'three-to-five flight,' especially by Hickey, but ten minutes later he started calling me 'Doctor,' because at just five minutes past four someone had yelled, 'Look—look at the hawks!' and we had looked, and west of the tower one great flock was already well across the valley, with an eagle in its lower edge, and east of the tower an enormous flock, a perfect swarm of hawks, was circling up above the Holyoke Range. We started counting the western flock like mad, and made it 163; we turned to the eastern flock and took them as they slipped overhead and on both sides, and at 4:11 we announced the result—518 birds in sight at once. Behind them came other flocks—some large, some small, pouring across the valley over a lane that extended in width from Northampton to Holyoke. In five minutes from 4:40 to 4:45 we counted 765! Other kinds were mixed in, too—a number of red-shoulders, another eagle high overhead, some Cooper's and sharp-shins, ospreys, and marsh hawks. Not until quarter past five was there any moment when hawks were not in sight all around us, and in that hour and a quarter the total of broad-wings was better than 1800.

Our excitement all this time had been intense. I had been counting out loud at top speed, Hickey had been scanning each new group as it appeared for possible rarer species, and the rest had been moving back and forth across the platform to see the birds as they came closest. We were all too absorbed to pay much attention to the parties of ordinary sightseers who had been coming and going to the tower, but afterwards, as we laughingly talked it over, we realized that our enthusiasm had been communicated to many of the visitors, and several amusing happenings had resulted, as for instance when a large man put his head up through the hatch and shouted in stentorian tones, 'What are they—ducks?' I remember another man who leaned pensively on the rail beside me and remarked, 'I hope they keep away from my house—I left the chickens out,' whereupon Mr. Bliss took him in hand and explained that these were not 'chicken hawks,' but the most consistently harmless and often beneficial species which we have in New England. Hickey had a good story about still another visitor who stood in the corner nearest the stairs wagging a stubby forefinger and counting aloud 'fifteen, sixteen, seventeen'—doggedly doing his bit for science. Altogether, one of the most interesting and pleasant features of the day was the way everybody entered into the friendly and informal spirit of the occasion.

A rather dramatic incident concluded the flight shortly after five-fifteen, when the last large flock of some hundred-odd birds was seen circling for altitude just south of Amherst Notch. We had already noticed that when the birds circled there, they were likely to come by the tower very close, and so it was with these. In a few minutes we could see them gliding toward us, and it was apparent that the higher ones would go through the Free Orchard Notch a hundred or two feet above the tower, while the lower ones would be at our level. On they came until they almost reached us, when suddenly several of the leading lower birds partially folded their wings and pitched down into the woods below, going from sight at once beneath the leafy canopy. Others followed, one or two at a time, until twenty or more had gone into the trees all around the base of the tower, very apparently to spend the night. Time and again we could look down on them at no more than fifty or sixty yards' distance. The higher ones kept on across the Manhan valley, and presumably roosted in the hills on the other side. At 5:25 the last broad-wings were gone, and three ospreys coming by together a little later marked finis at the end of a great day. The grand total had been 13 sharp-shins, 5 Cooper's, 19 red-shoulders, 2094 broad-wings, 4 adult bald eagles, 2 marsh hawks, 11 ospreys, 1 sparrow hawk, and the local duck hawk seen three times—in all, 2152 hawks.

Changes in Local Bird Life

In comparing his own first records of local birds with those of others that have already been published, the beginner invariably reaches a very curious position. From his reading and his local list, he ceases to worry about species that occur only in the distant tropics or in other far-off regions. Not infrequently, however, he is startled to find birds that are supposed to be fairly rare in his own locality. Shall he doubt the evidence of his own eyes—or toss his new textbook into the woodpile? In the light of experience, it is best to refrain from the latter. This is especially true when one cannot yet tell at a glance the difference between a warbler and a vireo.

Books dealing chiefly with the distribution of birds in a relatively small area are not intended, as a matter of fact, to be infallible by their authors. Local lists are designed only to give the status of birds in the past and up to date of publication. The birds themselves are gradually changing in numbers. As this is being written in 1943, almost all ducks are increasing, shore birds are more than holding their own, while marsh birds (like the rails) are gradually being driven by drainage from the most densely populated parts of the country.

In addition, there appears to exist a number of unexplained fluctuations among songbird populations. Many of these have been obscured by inadequate bird counting and lack of census work in the past. Their occurrence is frequently suggested by the surprising invasions made into large regions by many species and the disappearance of other species for inexplicable reasons. In the period from about 1915 to 1925, the Acadian flycatcher practically vanished in the northeastern part of its range. Cardinals have been spreading northward over a wide range since about 1925. Lark buntings have disappeared in eastern Minnesota, where they were common some 60 years ago. Brewer's blackbirds, on the other hand, have invaded Wisconsin within the last two decades. Sixty or seventy years ago the Kentucky warbler was a common summer resident in New York's lower Hudson valley, birds arriving each spring around the end of April. At the same time, the hooded warbler was scarce and hard to record before the middle of May. Today, their positions are exactly reversed, for only the hooded is common and only the hooded can be recorded before the first of May.

Changes like these are not due to the pressure of hunting or to laws protecting birds from the millinery trade. It seems equally difficult to ascribe them to changes in the birds' environment. The dickcissel, which once bred commonly on the Atlantic coastal plain from Massachusetts to Georgia, practically disappeared from that region between 1860 and 1880. It has since been restricted principally to the Mississippi valley. Now that more and more stragglers are being found in the East (curiously enough in flocks of English sparrows), perhaps the pendulum of numbers will swing back again. Quite in contrast to this is the history of the evening grosbeak, which was first discovered in Michigan in 1823. By 1854 it was reported in winter at Toronto, by 1876 in Indiana, and by the spring of 1887 it was found in New York State. It now regularly winters in New England, and the well-known bird bander M. J. Magee has shown that these birds move east each fall through Michigan.

It is often assumed that the spread of a species into new regions is a reflection of a marked upward fluctuation in the population at the center of its distribution. This is a nice theory, but we need much more bird counting to confirm it. In England, a co-operative survey a few years ago disclosed that the spread of the great crested grebe was actually accompanied by a *decrease* in this species' total population. So little is yet known about this subject that no one can predict which species is next destined for some curious change in status. It may be a night heron or a nighthawk, a bush-tit or a bobolink. We do not know. What we do know is that a change in numbers is sure to affect common birds in many regions.

Our knowledge of these changes must inevitably rest on the careful counting of all bird life encountered. Both the scientist and the conservationist look to the bird student for this information. It consists of field notes that can be readily taken on week ends. Businessmen and school boys can each contribute to this pool of knowledge. In many respects the utility of the counting may not be discernible for years. If it cannot be published, it should, I think, be finally filed in some central library, like that of the Wilson Ornithological Club at the University of Michigan. A half century later the careful counts may be of extreme interest.

The changes of bird life in such a period remind me of Courtenay Brandreth's story of Dr. A. K. Fisher, a famed ornithologist of the old United States Biological Survey. Some years ago, Dr. Fisher visited his boyhood birding haunts at Ossining, New York. He had been gone for nearly half a century. Even the name of the town had changed (from Sing Sing). English sparrows were now everywhere. As he walked along with Mr. Brandreth, the returning native noticed hordes of starlings flying overhead. Pests like these were entirely absent in the good old days. Dr. Fisher's feeling of wretchedness mounted. Suddenly a series of raucous screeches emanated from a near-by tree. The two men turned—and a frightened parrot emerged from the foliage. This, says Mr. Brandreth, was more than

Dr. Fisher could stand. 'Courtenay,' he cried with dismay, 'what in heaven's name is this country coming to!'

Periodic Fluctuations in Bird Life

Every young naturalist is quickly impressed with the seasonal changes in the numbers of local birds. On a winter day in southern Wisconsin, 30 species seem to constitute a fairly long list to me. Yet in spring, Elton Bussewitz, Samuel Robbins, and I once recorded 140 species in the same country. In most regions contrasts like these are no longer news. Almost nothing, however, has actually been reported showing how the total number of birds changes in a given locality from one month to another. This kind of information depends on counting. Blue jays and other common birds must be counted along with the rarities.

Although birds are less conspicuous in fall than in spring, their total numbers are then considerably larger. How much larger? On this point most bird books are silent. Here and there scattered reports on individual species suggest that the fall bird population may be double that of the spring, but much more counting is still needed. There are many possibilities for careful counting throughout the year. The simplest might be the week-end counting of a single species that is known to be a permanent resident. This could be done in a given area or along the same stretch of road. Taken over a period of years, those counts can be combined with weather data to show the exact effect of ice storms and blizzards during the winter, the probable effects of excessive rains in spring, and occasionally the destruction of local habitats by fire, floods, pasturing, plowing, and logging. It is always best to standardize such counts by

1. traversing the same area;
2. getting into the field at about the same hour each day, and
3. devoting approximately the same amount of time to each census.

More ambitious counts can cover all species encountered.

In addition to their seasonal fluctuations, a number of species periodically reach a peak in numbers and then decline. These periods are measured in terms of years, rather than mere seasons. They are called cycles. Two general types are now apparent. The first of these for the most part centers around sedentary populations of birds, like the ptarmigans and the ruffed grouse. These species gradually build up in numbers until they are relatively abundant, and then rapidly or gradually become relatively scarce. In time they again reach a high peak and the whole process is repeated. This phenomenon of rhythmically changing numbers has consistently escaped the notice of ornithologists, but it is now well known to many discerning sportsmen and to many wildlife biologists specializing in upland game research.

The second type of cycle is one of dispersal. At periodic intervals many thousands of birds, like the snowy owl and the goshawk, invade southern Canada and the northern United States in a mass dispersal from their breeding grounds in the Far North. Sometimes these irruptions are extremely spectacular and the invasions may extend over an immense area. According to Professor Gross, who summarized the great autumnal flight of 1926, during that winter 2363 snowy owls were recorded from New England west to North Dakota and south to North Carolina. These, of course, represented but a small fraction of the numbers actually present. Typical invasions do not extend over such a large area nor do they involve such great numbers. The dispersal cycles that have now been reported show markedly different rhythms for the birds concerned. The approximate length of these cycles is given in Table 10.

The causes of the sedentary cycles are still unknown. Though all grouse seem to be subject to a cycle of approximately 10 years, their peaks in numbers vary slightly from one region to another. These variations themselves are subject to change. In eastern Ontario (see Table 11), the ruffed grouse peak was reached in 1875, two years after the peak in the central part of the province. In 1900, both peaks occurred at the same time. By 1913 eastern Ontario forged ahead. Eventually it dropped back. For a long time, game specialists felt that the grouse cycle was due to disease, but no disease has been found that would account for the curious cycles now known. Dispersal cycles seem to be closely connected with variations in food supply. Snowy owls, for instance, habitually feed

TABLE 10

NOT ALL WILDLIFE CYCLES ARE ALIKE

The wildlife cycles already reported differ considerably in the length of time
they involve. In some cases they may affect purely sedentary species; in others
they may cause wide dispersals into other regions. In all cases a periodic
change in numbers is involved. Lemmings occasionally disperse in spectacular
irruptions.

Approximate length of cycle	'Sedentary' cycles	'Dispersal' cycles	Source or authority
3–4 years	meadow mouse	rough-legged hawk	Elton; Speirs
3–5 years	lemming	snowy owl	Elton; Gross
4–5 years		northern shrike	Davis
5–6 years		pine grosbeak	Speirs
9–11 years	(willow) ptarmigan	goshawk	Comeau; Cabot; Speirs *
9–11 years	ruffed grouse	great horned owl	Clarke; Speirs

Compiled from various sources.

* A 7-to-10-year rhythmic invasion of goshawks is said by E. H. Forbush to
have occurred in southern New England, but a study of his data and that
quoted by Bent clearly shows a 9-to-10-year cycle instead. This is illustrated
in Table 12.

on lemmings. A decline in lemmings thus might force these birds
south for a given winter. An absence of good observers and bird
banders throughout the Far North leaves many of the exact details
of this relationship still shrouded in mystery.

For some cycles (Tables 11 and 12) the dates are occasionally
missing. Several explanations for this come to mind. It seems likely
that at least in some cases the population of the affected species
was too low to produce an *observable* fluctuation in numbers. A
rather remarkable cycle, hitherto unnoticed, seems to have existed
among eastern red crossbills. During the latter part of the last
century, these birds regularly appeared in Massachusetts almost
every four years in October and November. Their amazingly erratic
nesting behavior during other parts of their cycle has already been
mentioned. According to Ludlow Griscom, from whose monograph
the dates for the appearance of these birds are taken, no marked
autumnal flight of this race of crossbills has occurred in the United
States since 1906. I interpret this as the logical result of the logging
of the virgin coniferous forest in eastern Canada. It seems not un-

likely that these birds are now so greatly reduced in numbers that a cycle is no longer apparent.

It should also be emphasized that the intensity of cyclic dispersals varies greatly. Snowy owls can undoubtedly be seen regularly in northern New England, but only on great flights will they reach North Carolina. It is also important to remember that autumnal invasions into Chicago by, say, the goshawk need not be correlated

Table 11

HOW THE NUMBERS OF RUFFED GROUSE FLUCTUATE

Exact information on the remarkable cyclic changes in the numbers of local birds is still missing from nearly all regional bird books. This table summarizes the periodic fluctuations of ruffed grouse reported by C. H. D. Clarke for different parts of Ontario. Similar information on shrikes, rough-legged hawks, and many other birds is still wanted by scientists.

Central Ontario

Peaks	1873	1882	1893	1904–05	1915	1922–23	1932
Declines	1874	1883	1894	1906	1916	1924–25	1933–34
Minima				1907–08	1916–17	1926–27	

Eastern Ontario

Peaks	1875	1883–84	1893?	1904–05	1913	1922–23	1933–(34)
Declines	1875–76	1884–85	1895	1905–06	1914	1924–25	1934–35?
Minima	1878	1885–86	1897–98	1907	1917–18	1926?	

Reprinted from *University of Toronto Studies.* 1936.

with invasions into Pennsylvania by the same species. Such birds probably originate in different parts of Canada. Although both groups of birds may have cycles of about the same length, these cycles may be in slightly different phases.

Many other birds sometimes make mass invasions. Bohemian waxwings, evening grosbeaks, and redpolls are familiar examples. During the fall of 1941, there was an enormous irruption of the black-capped chickadee in the East. Restless flocks of these nervous birds thronged every small park on Manhattan Island from September on. Some were even reported on the gardens atop New York's skyscrapers. This flight occurred over a wide expanse and extended south to New Jersey and west as far as Ohio. It was followed by an unusual movement of Acadian chickadees through New England, the first to be recorded since 1916. ('Whenever the Acadian chicka-

TABLE 12

SOME WILDLIFE CYCLES THAT ARE KNOWN

Periodic changes in bird life have only recently been found to be rhythmic in character. Sometimes the birds make extensive fall migrations, like those shown in this table. In other cases, like that of the grouse, they affect the numbers of sedentary species. Not infrequently the peak of the cycle is missed by naturalists (note dotted lines below) and only a general increase is reported in the numbers (shown here with years enclosed in brackets).

Ruffed grouse peaks in central Ontario	Mice peaks in northern Labrador	Arctic fox peaks in Ungava	Snowy owl flights to ne. U. S.	Northern shrike flights to ne. U. S.	Horned owl peaks in Toronto	Flights of goshawks to New England	Red crossbill autumnal flights to Massachusetts	Pine grosbeak peaks in Toronto region
1873	1874 1875	(1876)	1876	....	....	....	1874	....
		(1879)	....	1878			1878	
1882		1882	1882	....			1882	....
	1888	1887	....	(1889 Toronto)	1887	(1886 Toronto)	1886	1889
		1890	1889				....	
1893		1893	1892	(1895 Toronto)		1896	1895	1895
		1897	1896		1897			
							1899	

Rough-legged hawk flights in Toronto

Approx. Cycle 9–11 years	3–4 years	3–5 years	3–5 years	4–5 years	9–11 years	9–10 years	3–4 years / 3–4 years (Griscom)	5–6 years
Clarke	Elton	Elton	mostly Gross	mostly Davis	Speirs	mostly Forbush	Speirs	Speirs
1904 1905	1904 1905	1901	1901	1900		1906	1903	1901
	1908 1909	1905	1905	1905	1907		1906	1906
	1913	1909	1909 (Toronto)	1909				
1915	1916 1917	(1913 or 14)	....	1913	1916	1916	1917	
	1920	(1917)	1917	1917			....	
1922 1923	1924 1925	(1921)	1922	1921			1926	
	1927	(1926)	1926	1926	1927	1926 1927	1930	1929
	....	1930	1930	1930			1934	1935
1932	1933 1934	1934	1934	1934	1936	1935	1937	1935
	....	....	1937	....				
			1941					

dees come down,' Roger Peterson observes to his friends, 'you can prepare yourself for a declaration of war by Congress!')

Whether these irruptions have a cyclic rhythm remains to be seen. There are at this time no continuous counts for long enough periods to show that songbirds gradually increase to peak numbers on their breeding grounds, like upland game birds, and then just as gradually decrease. Perhaps many of them periodically fluctuate in numbers without making a 'spectacle' of themselves. I have often suspected that yellow-throated vireos did this near New York City, but my counting of these birds was too casual to be of value.

It seems obvious that careful counting of all species of birds is more than ever necessary, if our regional bird books and knowledge of bird biology are some day to be complete. It is, of course, possible to carry the idea of cycles too far, and I do not want to imply that all birds or all dispersal movements are cyclic. The subject is here reviewed because so little of it is found in bird books and manuals. In part, this is due to the present failure of bird watchers to make careful counts of birds and to keep in close touch with grouse hunters, who can help estimate the relative changes in the numbers of game. A second weakness lies in the limited time that many amateur naturalists have for their field work. No one can confidently say that a snowy owl flight has occurred just because he has seen a single bird. Yet the collected impressions of many gunners have been successfully used to show the nature of a local cycle in grouse, and the collected records of one or more bird clubs have likewise been utilized to estimate the size of a shrike or snowy owl invasion. It is in this manner that co-operative studies of birds are seen to be increasingly important. They will be mentioned again in the discussion of the cyclic changes in birds' food (Chapter 4) and further reviewed in Chapter 6.

Cross-Country Cruises

Most observations by bird students are now carried out in the course of walks about the countryside. Rambling from one oasis to another is a pleasant form of exercise but its net contribution to our knowledge of bird life leaves much to be desired. Some bird watchers try to evaluate the numbers of birds seen in this manner by calculating how many were seen each hour, each three hours, and so on. These efforts deserve commendation, but up to the present I confess that they have not been very impressive. This is due in part to the individual variations in recording birds, for, as everyone knows, some men see better and walk faster than others.

Cross-country cruises have, however, been used effectively to record birds on an acreage basis. Years ago two students, A. O. Gross and H. A. Ray, did this for Professor Forbes in Illinois. The

TABLE 13

A CROSS-COUNTRY CRUISE OF THE BREEDING BIRDS OF ILLINOIS

Counting birds as one traverses the country is most effective when the counting is put on an acreage basis. Here are the results of a pioneer census undertaken by A. O. Gross and H. A. Ray. Similar counts can be made by a single observer who records only those birds flushed 50 yards on either side as he traverses fields and woodlands.

Vegetation	Acres traversed	Density of birds per 10 acres
Orchards	118	61.7
Yards and gardens	557	53.4
Swamps	84	30.8
Woodlands	112	28.8
Pastures	5196	16.7
Shrubbery	93	16.5
Meadows	2763	14.2
Wheat, rye, and barley	822	12.9
Waste and fallow	654	12.3
Plowed ground	300	10.5
Stubble	1069	10.5
Corn	6434	9.3
Oats	2486	8.0

An acre equals 4840 square yards. This is the same as a strip 50 yards wide and 96.8 yards long. Ten acres may be visualized as the area 50 yards on either side of a road slightly more than a quarter of a mile long.

Adapted from *Bull. Ill. Nat. Hist. Surv.* 1922.

young men set themselves 50 yards apart and began walking across the state in a given direction. One wrote down all the birds seen *between* the two observers, the other recorded distances and kinds of country traversed and was relied upon to notice birds flushed while his colleague was recording the data.

Since birds seen outside the 50-yard strip are not counted, a partnership cruise of this kind is like the progress of a sweep-net

150 feet wide across the country. Practice in pacing and the help of a tested pedometer enable the observers to compute the acreage surveyed.

Up to the present only one observer, A. A. Saunders, has succeeded in improving on this method. Mr. Saunders is a Connecticut high-school teacher who has done much for bird watching in America. He has recorded the birds observed for 50 yards on either side as he cruised fields and woodlands, and once used data obtained in this manner to estimate the bird population on 16,967 acres in the Alleghany State Park, New York. His inexpensive report (see appendix) is a fine contribution to bird-census work on our continent.

Counting Birds on Study Areas

Some of the best bird counting in the United States has been done by observers who selected study areas with some characteristic kind of bird life. In this way we have come to learn the density of birds on certain kinds of fields, in different types of woods, in swamps and deserts. Only a fraction of the available habitats, however, have so far been investigated.

Some years ago, Ernst Mayr persuaded me to undertake this form of bird watching in the lower Hudson River valley. We picked out a rich deciduous woods adjacent to a reservoir. In April I paced off the tract into subsections 50 yards by 50 yards, and drew my map with the appropriate landmarks. I was then prepared to census the breeding birds—so I felt. They were common birds to be sure, ones I had known for years. They promptly put me through the most searching cross-examination—and I was in for one of the big surprises of my lifetime.

How far does a redstart range about its nest, I soon wanted to know? How far does the flicker range? How far does a *robin* range? These were questions that the fattest bird books could not answer. Pages were devoted, as one annoyed student used to quote, to 'this cheery little songster' or 'that happy little sparrow.' They told very little about the habits of our most common species. I spent the rest of that nesting season learning elementary things about common birds—and I had the time of my life. Partly by accident, I was on an area with a relatively high population of bird life. I was so busy taking notes that—to my surprise—there was no need for human companionship. In the past, my birding had been more or less a competition for rarities. Now, for the first time, I felt what I think Thoreau once called 'the sweet comradeship of nature.'

Perhaps the most satisfying aspect of study areas lies in the opportunities they afford for an intimate acquaintanceship with bird life. A robin is no longer just another robin, but 'the robin from the southwest corner.' Each bird takes on an individual identity and its seemingly casual presence on a new part of the census tract yields a new insight into its daily life and habits.

The usefulness of the final census information is quite apparent. Habitats can be compared from one region to the next, and one habitat contrasted with another in the same region. Populations can be ascertained for each year and all kinds of curious fluctuations noted. I know of only five relatively longtime censuses of breeding birds—a 14-year count by Norman Criddle in Manitoba; two 10-year censuses undertaken separately in Ohio by Lawrence E. Hicks and Arthur B. Williams; another 10-year census completed in Virginia by Wells W. and May Thacher Cooke; and a fourth 10-year count, hitherto unpublished, which is given in Table 14.

A study area need not be large. For a count of breeding birds it might be 30 to 50 acres if it is a field, about 25 acres if it is heavily wooded. I have found fields about three times easier to census than dense woods. A good observer might completely census a field in two or three visits; in a rich woodland he might need four or five counts, depending on his observational efficiency. Sometimes the weather creates complications for this kind of bird watching. In New York I have found that a careful cruise of the study area on the third week end of May (the height of the singing season in that region) often gives the greatest efficiency in recording males.

A very interesting set of breeding-bird censuses from all over the country is annually published in the supplement of *Audubon Magazine*. In the northern states, such censuses are usually begun late in April (to get woodpeckers, nuthatches, and the nests of hawks and crows). In the southern states, they should be started earlier. Census reports should reach the magazine by August 15.

TABLE 14

A 10-YEAR CENSUS OF BREEDING BIRDS ON A MASSACHUSETTS CHESTNUT LOT

This census was taken on 20 acres at Huntington, Massachusetts, by Albert A. Cross. It was based entirely on nests found. The downtrend reflected a parallel decrease in many other places in this region. Winter surveys of empty nests confirmed this trend year after year. The cutting of 873 railroad ties from the blighted trees pointed to diminished numbers in 1922. 'The use of arsenical sprays against the gypsy moth from 1925 to 1928 had a much greater effect. The sprays dripped like rain from the foliage. Insect food for the redstarts simply was not present. In this region, sprays practically wiped out the formerly common black-billed cuckoo and caused the general disappearance of the common garden toad.' The robin concentration was not unusual here, as H. E. Woods had as many as 20 pairs nesting within sight of his house (extracts from letter of Mr. Cross).

	'20	'21	'22	'23	'24	'25	'26	'27	'28	'29
Ruby-throated hummingbird	1									
Flicker						1				
Downy woodpecker			1							
Least flycatcher	2	1		1	1		1		1	1
Phoebe	1	1	2	1	1	1	1	1	1	1
Wood pewee	1						1			
Crow	1				1					
Blue jay								1		
House wren								1	1	1
Catbird								1	1	1
Robin	3	8	2	3	2		2	3	1	3
Wood thrush	1	4	5	3	3	2	2	1		1
Hermit thrush					1	1				
Veery		1	1			1			1	1
Bluebird					1	1				
Cedar waxwing								1		
Blue-headed vireo			3		1			1		1
Red-eyed vireo	4	2	1	4	1	1	1	1	1	
Black-throated green warbler	1									
Chestnut-sided warbler	1					1	1			1
Oven-bird	1	1							1	2
Redstart	1	3	3	3	6		1	2		
Scarlet tanager		1								
Rose-breasted grosbeak					1					
Song sparrow						1				1
Chipping sparrow	1	1			1			1		
Species	13	10	8	8	9	11	8	10	9	11
Pairs	19	23	18	17	20	12	10	13	9	14
Pairs per 100 acres	95	115	90	85	100	60	50	65	45	70

Many students seem to feel that a census can only be interesting if it contains rare and unusual species. Nothing could be further from the truth. What is needed today are bird counts from tracts that are representative of large areas, so that the characteristic bird life of each region may be recorded, compared, and contrasted.

TABLE 15

STUDY AREAS CONTAIN MANY SURPRISES

Regularly traversed tracts, on which breeding birds have been mapped, often disclose marked inefficiencies in bird-census methods. Here are the numbers of birds recorded on morning cruises of a rich warbler woodland totaling 40 acres in the Hudson River valley. Variations in the totals recorded here presumably reflect changes in weather, the breeding cycle, and the time of each field trip. The hours given below are Eastern Standard Time.

	May 22 6:50–10:20	*May 29* 6:50–11:30	*June 5* 8:10–12	*June 19* 4:10–6	*Pairs actually in residence*
Black and white warbler	1	0	1	2	3
Worm-eating warbler	5	1	4	8	8
Blue-winged warbler	2	3	3	1	3
Chestnut-sided warbler	1	3	4	3	3
Oven-bird	12	12	13	19	19
Hooded warbler	2	3	2	4	3
Redstart	16	15	16	17	22
Total	39	37	43	54	61

In the eastern states, bird students are often heard to rue the effects of huge numbers of starlings on native bird life. Who can discuss this with authority? No bird censuses were taken before the starlings arrived—and to what extent they have driven out other birds can only be conjectured. Students in the Middlewest, however, where the starling is only now encroaching, can still obtain an exact picture of local bird life before this bird increases farther. With this in mind, I made a Main Street census of La Crosse, Wisconsin, during the spring of 1942. The density, excluding swifts and nighthawks, was 80 birds per 10 acres—exactly 20 times that of a large abandoned field on the edge of the city. As a sample of urban bird life on the Mississippi River, this may stand comparison with Main Street in your home town. Fifty years hence some other ornithologist will—I hope—find it a good foundation on which to determine the changes in local bird life that half a century is sure to bring.

During the winter accurate censuses of bird life can be made on larger areas of, say, 150 acres. This kind of counting has scarcely been started in our country and practically nothing is known about winter densities. Perhaps this is because acreages represent land

TABLE 16

AN ORNITHOLOGICAL TRANSECT OF LA CROSSE, WISCONSIN

The nesting birds observed for 50 yards on either side of Main Street from the Mississippi River to Losey Blvd. (1.52 miles); based on repeated cruises along this city street from May 28 to June 26, 1942.

Rock dove	4 pr.	Robin	33 pr.
Mourning dove	1 pr.	Starling	2 pr.
Nighthawk	4 pr.	Warbling vireo	5 pr.
Chimney swift	230 pr.	Yellow warbler	9 pr.
Flicker	2 pr.	Redstart	3 pr.
Wood pewee	1 pr.	English sparrow	144 pr.
Purple martin	4 pr.	Baltimore oriole	1 pr.
House wren	1 pr.	Cowbird	1 pr.
Catbird	3 pr.	Cardinal	3 pr.
Brown thrasher	1 pr.	Chipping sparrow	4 pr.

Total for 55.2 acres: 20 species, 456 pairs. Density: 165 individual birds per 10 acres. Also noted: black-billed cuckoo, downy woodpecker, cedar waxwings, yellow-throated vireo, red-eyed vireo, and bronzed grackle. Nighthawks were estimated; the chimney swift figure was arbitrarily taken from 460 birds that entered their roost in back of St. Joseph's Cathedral on June 26. Of the English sparrow nests, 24 were in masonry, 24 lay atop cornices, 12 were in gutters and ventilators, 12 in awnings, and 1 was seen in a tree.

statistics that overpower the minds of many laymen. In many regions government topographic maps can be used to determine these figures. Areas that are one mile by one mile are 640 acres, those one-quarter by one-quarter are 40 acres. In agricultural areas, the county AAA office has splendid aerial photographs, which can be quickly scaled to one-tenth of an acre.

A very special kind of study area is the colonial nesting site. Here scores, hundreds, or even thousands of nests may be counted. I can remember with great clarity my first visit to the great sea-bird colonies of Cobb Island, Virginia, with their barking skimmers, their clouds of laughing gulls, and their scolding terns. I do not like to spend too much time counting birds in colonies like these, for the hot sun unmercifully beats down on the nestlings. On the coast of Texas, a wildlife photographer once told his audience, a young reddish egret could succumb to the sun in about half an hour. Landing on most sea-bird islands is at best an early-morning procedure and one not to be undertaken in cold, rainy weather.

Colonial birds can still be found in many regions, and a number of species, like the great blue heron and the black-crowned night heron, nest in trees where they often permit quick counts of extensive bird populations. Up to the present, however, very few such counts have been compiled in our country over a continuous period. Carried out over a large area, they would inevitably throw much new light on the ebb and flow of bird populations.

TABLE 17

SOME COLONIAL BIRD POPULATIONS IN MAINE
(checked by Allan D. Cruickshank, Audubon Nature Camp)

Nests of double-crested cormorants in Muscongus Bay

As this species continues to extend its breeding range down the coast, its numbers on the coast of Maine continue to build up.

Colony site	1936	1937	1938	1939	1940	1941
Old Hump Ledge	135	188	264	331	337	367
Western Egg Rock	40	91	107	149	138	249
Shark Rock	142	142	367	548	524	540
Little Egg Rock	300+	300+	374	464	455	448
	617+	721+	1112	1492	1454	1604

Estimates on Little Green Island, outside Penobscot Bay

Here ravens, black-backed and herring gulls, preying on both eggs and young of the terns, discourage periodic attempts of these species to renest on the island. In 1941, when sheep were introduced, the loss of grass cover made the laughing gulls also vulnerable to this predation, and many pairs of these birds thereupon deserted. Leach's petrels also nested but could not be estimated with any accuracy.

Species	1936	1937	1938	1939	1940	1941
Herring gull	100	100	100	100	100	100
Laughing gull	150	250	250	250	300	50
Black guillemot	15	15	15	15	15	15
Arctic tern	100	15			150	3
Common tern	50	5			10	
Black-backed gull					2	4
	415	385	365	365	577	172

Counting birds, it can be seen, is a form of bird watching that carries with it many rewards. At large communal roosts and at great concentration places of birds, it offers a high degree of excitement. On study areas it yields the quiet satisfaction that comes with the steady penetration of nature's secrets. I know of no form of bird watching that, carried out over a period of years, is more simple and yet more constructive. Up to the present, at least, its applications have only been touched bv bird watchers, and its successes have been lightly accepted.

CHAPTER FOUR

Explorations in Bird Distribution

THE DISTRIBUTION of birds has received more attention than any other branch of ornithology. During the past century, scores of books have been written on the subject and hundreds of regional lists published in scientific periodicals. As a field of exploration, bird distribution north of the Rio Grande ought to be as dead as the passenger pigeon. *It isn't.*

The subject is admittedly vast and greatly complicated by the movements of migratory birds between breeding grounds and wintering quarters. Yet of all classes of animals, birds have the best-known ranges. Impressive books have now been written on the birds of California, Canada, Florida, Massachusetts, Minnesota, New Mexico, and Oregon. Other bird books concern the Cambridge region, the Connecticut valley in Massachusetts, the New York City region, Cape May, western Pennsylvania, and so on. Birds have been listed by counties and even by townships. For the past hundred years, the primary emphasis has been on *geographic* distribution. During the coming century, *ecological* distribution is bound to occupy the spotlight. Having learned for the most part *where* birds are to be found, we now want to know the *how* and *why* of their presence.

Answers to these new questions will not come from elaborate scientific expeditions, for most museums are no longer interested in cutover forests or in farm lands. Nor will they come from the expensive researches of government agencies, for game commissions are not concerned with songbirds. They will come from the bird watching of laymen, from week-end observations, and from the combined notes of keen-eyed observers seeking to penetrate the mysteries of habitat selection.

The nature of a bird's habitat has often received the notice of naturalists, but outside of the game birds, it has rarely been the subject of intensive investigation on our continent. Perhaps this is in part owing to the failure of many bird watchers to realize that here is one of the most challenging mysteries of nature. Perhaps they do not recognize the unevenness of our present information. We know much about birds' food, but not nearly enough about their needs for water. We have many records on the height of birds' nests, but few specific details on the actual heights at which many species feed by day and roost by night. We know a great deal about birds' song, but almost nothing about their singing perches. For years ornithologists have been generalizing about habitats without ever supplying the many details that combine to make a bird's home. Some of these are easy to observe, and every bird watcher should be alive to the special opportunities each nesting season offers to record them.

Food

Food has been called the burning question in any animal society. Among birds, the truth of this statement probably varies with different seasons and with different climates. In the tropics, for instance, enormous insect populations are available, but in temperate regions these can be relied upon only in summer. In the United States, a vast amount of excellent work has already been completed on the food of birds. This has centered on stomach examinations and is no longer the immediate concern of the bird watcher. Very little is yet known, however, on the density of insect life in various types of woodland. Entomologists have been slow to supply this information, but it may eventually explain the innumerable variations in the diet of many species and why some habitats are so much more barren of birds than others.

Food does have an important and recognizable role in winter bird life in many regions. The many feeding stations are testimony to this statement. Feeding trays have sustained a redstart lingering on Manhattan Island until the end of December; they have kept Baltimore orioles successfully through severe New England winters and undoubtedly caused many half-hardy species to linger in the North far past their usual date of departure. The effect of food concentrations is always interesting and sometimes the results are quite spectacular. Once, in Maine, for instance, Professor A. O. Gross was called upon to verify the presence of over 50 bald eagles which were congregating at a pit containing the offal of over 1000 drought-stricken steers. Local infestations of spring cankerworms sometimes attract great numbers of cuckoos, and they may perhaps be responsible for changes in the density of breeding-bird populations. I know of only one attempt (by C. A. Dambach in Ohio) that has been made to measure this. Here, of course, careful counting is needed to show both the normal and abnormal bird populations.

Every naturalist would do well to record annually in his journal a few pertinent notes on the numbers of grasshoppers, acorns, beech mast, field mice, and pine cones in his region. These are standard foods of various birds and undoubtedly fluctuate from year to year. Some are thought to affect the nesting success of different species. Others are believed to influence the spectacular dispersal movements mentioned in Chapter 3. The actual details of these relationships are still unknown.

Scarcities of acorns and beech nuts may result in local emigrations of blue jays. Piñon crops may affect piñon jays. Peaks of grasshoppers might possibly affect the nesting success of sparrow hawks and migrant shrikes. In Great Britain, mice peaks are

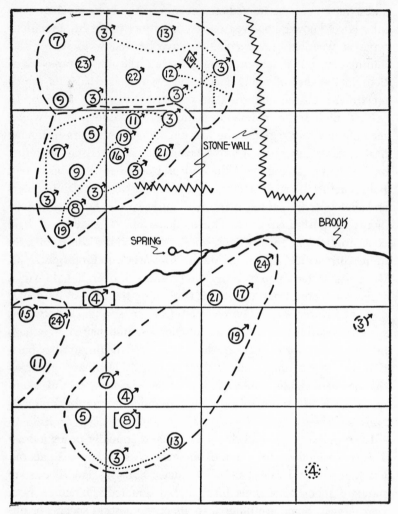

HOW TO PLOT THE PRESENCE OF BIRDS ON A FIELD MAP

It is often relatively easy to determine how far individual birds range during the breeding season. A study area can be paced off into squares, 50 yards by 50 yards. Separate maps can be used for individual species. On each visit the birds' presence can be noted by a separate number for each field trip, and both territory and foraging area gradually determined. Squares, circles, and other figures around the numbers can indicate whether the bird was in song, feeding, seen at a certain hour, and so on. The main elements of three redstart territories can be seen on the map above.

Table 18

FLUCTUATIONS IN BIRD FOOD MAY BE WORLD-WIDE IN CHARACTER

Studies in the cyclic changes of bird food are among the many unexplored by-paths of bird watching. In this table, *autumnal* invasions of Massachusetts by eastern red crossbills are strikingly seen to parallel major *winter* invasions of Europe by Siberian nutcrackers. The crossbills feed on pine-cone seeds, the nutcrackers on cedar nuts.

Crossbills	Nutcrackers
1882	1882
1886	1885
....	1888
....	1892
1895	1895
1899	1899
1903	1903

Condensed from papers by Griscom and Formosof.

thought to affect species like the owls, causing them to lay more eggs, raise more broods, and fledge more young.

These are a few of the many interesting questions underlying bird numbers. For the most part they have been largely ignored by naturalists in our country. In the Canadian Arctic, dramatic cycles of fur animals are everywhere in evidence and have been known to countless trappers for generations. The task of assimilating this vast lode of information has been finally undertaken, not by Canadian or American ecologists but by British scientists interested in the problem of numbers. Some of the finest writing in scientific literature can now be found in Charles Elton's *Mice, Voles and Lemmings,* a recent book of monumental stature which summarizes in its later chapters the fascinating story now known of animal numbers in the Arctic.

How can bird students explore these problems? No one has to go to Ungava or Labrador to study them. They are present in every region. No one, for instance, has to run a trap line just to check on the mice cycle. In Wisconsin, Robert A. McCabe tells me, farmers can readily furnish this information. (In taking up shocks of corn, they consistently count the number of mice that drop out.) Nesting studies of shrikes, sparrow hawks, and the different owls could be carried out over a number of years. Organized co-operative inquiries over long periods are needed to obtain rough estimates on the numbers of grasshoppers and the abundance of acorns and beech mast. If one observer declares that grasshoppers are more plentiful this year than last, his report may not be significant. If 75 out of 100 observers report the same thing in the same state, we would be rather certain that this insect's cycle was on the upward swing. Co-operative studies like these are now being directed in the Canadian Arctic by the British. They might well be organized in the United States by national institutions (like the American Ornithologists' Union and the United States Fish and Wildlife Service) or by ambitious bird clubs.

One of the most surprising blanks in bird study concerns the size of the area in which birds forage for food. For a given species this undoubtedly varies from one pair to another, but within certain limits it is fairly specific. Although many people undoubtedly know the extent to which common birds forage about their nests, they seldom report these details, and the subject is accordingly omitted from every bird book. Does a downy woodpecker range much farther than a brown thrasher? How much? What is the size of a chipping sparrow's territory? I do not know—nor do many of the greatest ornithologists. Yet these are common birds and the information has practical value, especially to census takers.

Foraging areas might be roughly described as the areal equivalent of food requirements divided by available food supplies. The extent of a robin's foraging may vary considerably, depending on weather, variations in individual habitats, and such other factors as the number of its young. These facts are still largely unknown— even for the common birds, like the robins. Data on foraging can best be accumulated by use of the color-banding techniques described in the next chapter. In the breeding season, however, many pairs of songbirds are fairly well separated on their own territories. During this period their movements can often be readily charted in a study area and the foraging distances plotted on a field map.

The word 'territory' has come to have a special significance in bird watching. It is used to describe some area that a bird defends against other members of its own species. Most songbirds are thought to be territorial in the nesting season, but actual observa-

tions in this connection have been reported on relatively few species.
(Among the suspected exceptions are the cedar waxwing, scarlet
tanager, and perhaps the veery.) When a bird has a low density,
its territory tends to be large; when a dense population is present,
territories tend to be more compressed. In my experience, a dense
population of territorial birds is very easy to map in the breeding

TABLE 19

SOME FORAGING AREAS OF BIRDS IN THE NESTING SEASON

Very little has yet been reported on the distances birds forage about their
nests. The following records are largely based on week-end visits in May and
June to a many-aged hardwood forest at Yonkers, New York. Although a
number of birds actively defended the areas here reported, more frequent observations are probably needed to show the complete size of their territories.

No. of pairs checked	Species	Acres foraged Minimum	Average	Maximum
4	Downy woodpecker	3	3.9	5.5
3	Crested flycatcher	3.5	4.1	5.0
5	Yellow-throated vireo	5	8.3	11.0
16	Red-eyed vireo	.5	1.2	2.0
5	Black and white warbler	2.5	3.5	4.0
10	Blue-winged warbler	.6	.8	1.3
9	Chestnut-sided warbler	.6	1.0	1.8
25	Oven-bird	.5	.7	1.0
1	Kentucky warbler	...	4.5	...
43	Redstart	.5	.9	1.5
8	Hooded warbler	1.0	1.5	1.8
6	Red-eyed towhee	1.2	1.5	1.9
4	Northern yellow-throat	1.3	2.0	2.6
1	Indigo bunting	...	5.0	...

season. The males are singing warning songs with commendable
frequency—and their presence is easily recorded.

This outline of territorialism in birds should be kept in mind
whenever foraging studies are made of songbirds. Careful observations abroad have shown that, in some species at least, the foraging
area may be only a part of a pair's actual territory. In colonial birds,
of course, this situation is reversed. These birds have a common
foraging area, and their territories are reduced to small circles
about their nests. Robins seem to possess an especially complex
system, according to my observations in New York. Each pair has
its own territory, which the male rigorously defends against other
males; but many robins in the neighborhood enjoy a common

foraging area. In New Jersey, Charles A. Urner once reported to a Linnaean Society meeting, a pair of robins 'owned' the tree in which they nested, but another pair held foraging and territorial rights to the ground below.

These complications do not, to my mind, make bird watching a hopeless proposition. On the contrary, they add to its attractions. When one considers that actual foraging areas are unreported for at least 80 per cent of our native birds, the opportunities for genuine exploration in local ornithology are nearly without limit.

Cover

Cover plays an important role in the lives of most birds throughout the entire year. It is usually thought of as being some element in the environment that permits birds to escape their enemies. Swifts and swallows, however, require no cover in daylight hours. Being superb fliers, they depend on their wings for escape from enemies. Perhaps their tendencies to nest in colonies and remain in loose flocks at other times help them as a group to detect approaching hawks and falcons. Even the sturdy peregrine falcon requires cover. On wild and remote islands it may nest on a small mound; but on the populated continent it seeks the shelter of high cliffs as protection from its enemies.

Sometimes a single element in the landscape represents quite opposite things to different species. The open water of a bay readily offers refuge to a scaup diving to escape a great black-backed gull, but it may be a falcon's trap for a red-wing.

Some recognition of cover apparently is inherited in birds, but the extent of this varies, I believe, from one species to another. Learning is often extremely important. Dr. Paul Errington, of Iowa State College, who has long carried out predation studies of quail, relates how, for several days following the visit of a Cooper's hawk, bob-whites will take especial care to remain near protective hedgerows. Nor are all quail capable of selecting perfect cover, Dr. Errington has found. In Wisconsin, certain winter territories, which he studied near Prairie du Sac, are lethal year after year. However inviting they look to a covey in the autumn, they offer no real protection in the depths of winter and in them the bob-whites are invariably killed off.

To explore the influence of cover requires both ingenuity and concentration. So little has been done on this subject that the clues are still small, and many may only be observed as special opportunities arise. In making habitat studies it is often important to remember that gales, excessive snows, sleet storms, predation, agricultural operations, hunting, and pole-trapping all affect the numbers of birds, and so leave habitats vacant in various degrees. As a result, most species fluctuate in numbers.

A vacant orchard is no indication that bluebirds refuse to use it. In 1895, for instance, there were severe winter storms in the southeastern states. As a consequence, New England's nesting bluebird population was about wiped out, and for two or three years this species was very scarce in that region. According to E. H. Forbush, it took ten years before the bluebird could recover its normal numbers.

An orchard devoid of nesting kingbirds in late June can signify two things: the orchard does not meet all of the kingbird's nesting requirements; or the kingbird population is somewhere below the optimum. In the case of the bluebird, it might also mean that starlings have taken over the bluebirds' place. Statements on vacated habitats must therefore depend on time, and occasionally upon experimentation.

For the present, I think, bird watchers would do well to record the measurable *minimum* habitat requirements as they are actually seen in use. Take, for example, the yellow-throated vireo. All books report it as a tree-dwelling species. Its cover, then, may correctly be said to consist of trees. Tall trees? Of course. Just how tall? The books do not say. Nests have been found, according to Forbush, from 3 to 50 feet above the ground. Here is a hint of the yellow-throated vireo's preferences—but it is only a hint. No experienced naturalist would expect these birds to spend the greater part of even one day at an elevation of only 3 feet. Other questions come to mind. Must the trees be part of a large forest? In this case, no; for these fine songsters prefer open woodlands, forest edges, and even shade trees. Shade trees offer special opportunities to the bird watcher. How small a row of shade trees will the vireos accept? This question might refer to the number of trees available and in use, or to the average height of the trees under observation. No one has yet given either answer.

Young shade trees are planted, often in new residential areas. As small saplings, they can scarcely attract a single nesting species. But in time, robins, chipping sparrows, and other birds gradually come to nest in them. Thus, the changing age of the trees, their increasing width and height would throw valuable light on the manner of habitat selection.

Farm windbreaks and isolated stands of roadside trees also offer special opportunities to explore bird habitats. In winter, nests of orioles and vireos can here be quickly spotted. If the grove is completely isolated, the number of trees can be actually counted. It would be interesting, I think, if we could say that 12 sugar-maple trees, all 75 years old, were sufficient to meet the entire requirements of one pair of Baltimore orioles in the breeding season.

Landscape measurements are not a final product of bird watching but rather a means to an end. That end is a comprehension of the role of vegetation in bird distribution. There are some persons, of course, who regard bird study as the mere accumulation of statistics. Nests are measured, eggs are measured, young birds are measured, and so on. Facts like these have their place, but unless they are averaged and interpreted they are so many products of the Linear School of Ornithology—uncertain, unwieldly, and underdone.

Mention of the Linear School reminds me of a winter's meeting of the Delaware Valley Ornithological Club that I once attended in Philadelphia. When the program reached the period for discussion of field notes, President Emlen requested that only important notes be related, since the evening was already advanced and the speaker had to catch a train for New York. Something of a silence followed this announcement, and it was evident that each person was weighing the worth of his recent observations. Finally a young undergraduate in the rear of the room slowly rose to his feet.

'I don't know if this is important,' he began. 'I'm sure that if it isn't, Mr. Street will soon tell me.' Up front, J. Fletcher Street, a well-known architect, grinned imperceptibly.

At State College, the young man related, a pair of red-headed woodpeckers had been seen attacking a red squirrel. Every time the squirrel would attempt to ascend the tree, both birds would dive at it, like duck hawks. 'They made a great deal of noise,' the youngster went on, 'and they would dive to within 6 inches of the squirrel's head.'

'How about that, Mr. Street?' he added, sitting down.

'Pretty good,' said Mr. Street, looking soberly at the ceiling. 'Our best previous record was 6½ inches!'

Water

As the basis of plant and animal life, the importance of water is readily obvious. For many birds it furnishes food (fish, insects, and crustaceans), shelter (as when diving ducks seek to escape a hawk), and a place of rest at night (for ducks and sea birds). In a few exceptional cases, it can almost be said to furnish them nests, as when black terns and eared grebes lay their eggs on floating masses of vegetation. Its influence on many species is so apparent that a number of families are popularly grouped together under the all-inclusive term of water birds.

The distribution of all land birds is directly or indirectly affected by water. For some, like the tree swallow and perhaps the pro-thonotary warbler, it attracts large supplies of insect food. For others it offers an abundance of vegetative cover. The importance of this sometimes cannot be appreciated until times of drought. During European droughts, winds have blown down masses of reeds containing the nests of warblers. (In normal times the reeds were firmly anchored in water.) In one part of Montana, during the great drought of the 1930's, the United States Forest Service reported that Smith's wheatgrass was 13 inches high in 1933, 1 inch high in 1934, and 15 inches high the following year. The effect on nesting birds can be readily imagined.

Water is also a very important mechanism that isolates predators. It is for this reason that many ground-nesting species, like the gulls and terns, nest on islands. In this connection an interesting story was once told by Roy Latham, a well-known Long Island naturalist. For many years, Mr. Latham related, a colony of about

5000 common terns successfully nested on the mainland at Orient, New York. The site of the colony had long been a common shooting ground for local hunters, but the birds suffered little interference. Finally the area was made into a public park and all wildlife given 'complete protection.' The tern colony at once deteriorated. Foxes, which for a hundred years had been kept in check, now increased rapidly. Deprived of the artificial predator control and lacking the customary isolation of an island, the colony at once dropped to 500 birds. In another season its numbers were down to 10.

The effect of water on bird distribution is not always obvious— until one begins to think about it. Early in the nesting season of 1942, Harold C. Hanson advised me to watch for the close relation of song sparrows and northern yellow-throats to water. This undoubtedly is well known to many observers, but I had never thought much about it in the East. I drove 5000 miles over the unglaciated hills of Wisconsin before I found a single song sparrow more than 50 yards from a stream or a single northern yellow-throat more than 150 yards from water. Finally I encountered one song sparrow nesting in a village. The lawns and gardens there were so well watered by the residents that I believe the rule still held. Then, late in July, I recorded 3 yellow-throats singing along the dry right-of-way of a railroad crossing on the high prairie of Military Ridge. Their presence on that dry weedy stretch is a mystery that I now find hard to explain.

Water influences the distribution of many land birds by its control of the vegetation. Grasshopper sparrows have preference for dry, rather sparse grass; savannah sparrows prefer thick rank grasses. The kind of vegetation may reflect the drainage of the soil, its amount of humus, and a number of other factors.

How much water each species requires for bathing and drinking has seldom been determined. Many can do quite well without brooks, ponds, and pools. Some birds have been seen to drink drops of dew, others have been seen to bathe by shaking vigorously a rain-soaked twig. Suburban dwellers might add to our knowledge of this subject by reporting the distances that birds in their neighborhood travel to a bird bath. All records of unusual birds nesting in dry sandy regions are especially interesting in this connection. Hermit thrushes are known to nest in the hot pine barrens of Long Island. Yellow-throats are found breeding in the dry barrens of New Jersey. No one knows why. There is something eminently satisfying in exploring the bird life of barren and desert areas. The birds are few in number and there is little in the way of variety. Some avid migration watchers would not 'waste' 10-minutes' time on the landscape. Yet nowhere else are the laws of life and environment expressed with such extreme simplicity, and the pattern of bird distribution set forth with such striking clarity.

Singing Perches

The importance of singing perches has long been disregarded in American bird studies, although Henry Mousley pointed out their importance in 1919. To understand this feature of bird life, it is well to recall first why many birds sing. In the breeding season, most of the males are striving to advertise their presence, and to warn other males of the same species that a territory is occupied and will be defended against trespass. To do this in a heavy forest, woodland species have to sing loudly, like the oven-bird. In fields, the carrying power of the songster need not be so great, and the song may be weak, like that of the savannah sparrow.

In order to advertise themselves, many singing birds therefore take a very conspicuous position, such as the top of a bush or the upper branch of a tree. Here the meadowlark may display his yellow breast or the robin his well-known 'red.' (These colors may serve to advertise the presence of the male and to warn other males of an occupied territory, but the use of color in most species still awaits experimental study.)

The height at which birds sing undoubtedly varies, but within certain limits it is surprisingly specific. This is particularly true in open places, like fields and prairies. Those three small sparrows, the Henslow's, the grasshopper, and the savannah, are quite satisfied with singing perches only a few inches higher than the general height of the surrounding grassland. In the case of the vesper sparrow, I have found it difficult to make observations where fence-posts are absent. An occasional male may sing from a stump, and

I have once even heard one sing from the ground early in the season. In my experience, all other male vespers have used fences or very low telephone poles.

TABLE 20

THE INFLUENCE OF AVAILABLE SINGING PERCHES ON BIRD DISTRIBUTION HAS SCARCELY BEEN STUDIED

Here is a summary of preliminary observations on the *lowest* singing perches that birds will accept. Notes of this kind are best taken in the field by reserving one page in the notebook for each species. These were taken in Wisconsin. Birds preferring wet situations are marked with an asterisk.

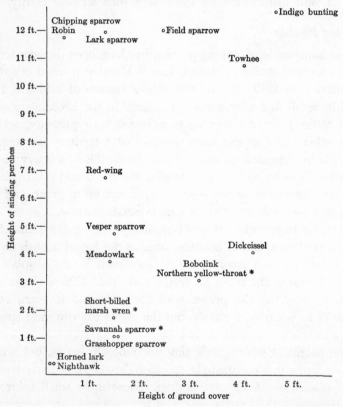

Both the lark and the field sparrows are species that feed and nest in low situations but require much higher singing perches. Indigo buntings are also in this category. As a result, this latter species regularly nests in woodland clearings or along forest edges.

Since these birds also frequently sing from telephone poles and wires, I once asked myself if the telephone pole ever completely became a substitute for a tree. It took time to settle that question, but eventually, on a Wisconsin prairie, I found a pair of indigo buntings that had no trees for hundreds of yards around them. Just

TABLE 21

HOW THE SINGING OF RED-EYED VIREOS VARIES

Red-eyed vireos sing little in the early hours of the morning. At other times the amount of song seems to vary with wind conditions, temperature, and cloudiness. Here are the number of males found singing as the author traversed their territories on a study area at Yonkers, New York. Counts for two years are included; in one (1937) 16 males were present; in the other (1938, dates marked with an asterisk) 18. The hours are Eastern Standard Time.

Date	Start of cruise	Elapsed time	Males in song
May 9	7 a.m.	1 hr., 50 min.	62%
May 16	6 a.m.	2 hrs.	50%
May 23	5:45 a.m.	2 hrs., 42 min.	69%
May 24*	7:30 a.m.	2 hrs.	83%
June 1*	4:35 a.m.	1 hr., 55 min.	39%
June 1*	6:30 a.m.	2 hrs., 20 min.	72%
June 2	5:05 a.m.	3 hrs., 35 min.	32%
June 2*	3:45 a.m.	5 hrs., 15 min.	67%
June 4	6:26 a.m.	1 hr., 52 min.	38%
June 7*	5:40 a.m.	2 hrs., 30 min.	78%
June 19*	5:30 p.m.	2 hrs., 30 min.	28%
June 20	5:45 a.m.	2 hrs., 45 min.	75%
June 26	6:15 a.m.	3 hrs.	50%
June 27	8:00 a.m.	3 hrs., 30 min.	62%
June 28*	3:15 p.m.	4 hrs., 30 min.	72%
		average for all trips	58%

as a bird box is often needed to attract house wrens to a garden, so these telephone poles made it possible for the buntings to nest in this situation. Whether or not the fencepost serves the vesper sparrow in the same manner has not yet been verified.

Among woodland birds, the importance of singing perches is probably less significant. It is known that forest birds often have favorite song perches from which they do most of their singing. How the average height of these varies from pair to pair or from species to species has never been determined. On some occasions birds have been found to occupy three-dimensional territories—one pair keeping to the upper canopy of the forest and another pair of the same species living directly below. I once suspected that this tenement kind of existence was applicable to two pairs of red-eyed vireos on my study area, but I never could be absolutely sure.

Sometimes a naturalist can have a good deal of fun pointing out the perches that birds will mount to sing. This is fairly easy in fields and meadows, although extremely difficult in woodlands. When the moving-picture industry first developed sound films, one company decided that recordings of bird song would be the most dramatic demonstration of its newly found abilities. It was the right season of the year for this undertaking, and two top-ranking cameramen were sent to scour the countryside. Near the end of their field work (some two weeks, as I remember) the two experts had to admit their failure. They had cruised hundreds of miles of rural roads, but not a single bird's song had been recorded. In desperation the two men drove to Ithaca, New York, and appealed to Dr. Arthur A. Allen, Cornell University's professor of ornithology. If they only could get one species on their sound tract, the cameramen confided, at least some of their reputation would be salvaged. To Dr. Allen this did not seem like a difficult problem. Directing the sound truck to some brush along a roadside, he told the two explorers to set up their equipment. There were no birds singing at the moment, but this did not seem to matter to Dr. Allen.

'If you will focus your apparatus on the top of this bush,' he predicted, 'you ought to get a fine recording of the song sparrow.'

Completely baffled by this time, the harassed cameramen followed directions. They had not long to wait. As soon as their activity subsided, a male song sparrow rose to his favorite singing perch. For the motion-picture men, the quest had ended. For Dr. Allen a new career was just beginning. The appendix of this book describes the superb recordings of bird songs that he has since completed.

Other Factors in Habitat Selection

Several elements in habitat selection, already well emphasized by other authors, remain to be mentioned. Among these is the kind of anchorage that birds demand for their nests. Robins, for instance, require a firm foundation, like the crotch of a tree or the ledge of a porch. Quite in contrast, Baltimore orioles want a hanging structure of twigs. In an interesting little book on this subject, William J. Beecher (see appendix) declares that the vegetation substrate is of primary importance in determining the local distribution of breeding birds. Substrate, to Mr. Beecher, embraces various physical characteristics of vegetation. Some of these are used by nesting birds to anchor their nests, others for weaving the nest itself, still others for cover. In habitat analyses, each of these elements deserves separate consideration by the bird watcher.

It seems not unlikely, for instance, that nest anchorage is an important factor in the selection of habitats by some species, but it must only limit others to certain broad classes of vegetation. A red-eyed vireo requires a small horizontally forked twig of a deciduous tree. Mr. Forbush reports that this species may nest as high up in a tree as 50 feet. I once found a nest only 2 feet off the ground. Nest substratum, therefore, may be quite important to each pair but distinctly unimportant in the eyes of a naturalist.

Last year, my wife and I were surprised to find six red-wing nests in a timothy field in the Mississippi valley. We had seen hundreds of seemingly similar fields in the past but those had been devoid of red-wings. Intermixed in the timothy were occasional plants of dock. Their strong stems made a sufficiently sturdy foundation for the red-wings' nests. A neighboring pasture was extremely swampy and excellent for foraging. How necessary the adjacent high-tension wires were as singing perches I could not determine, but apparently some combination of factors like these accounted for the presence of the red-wings.

If habitat studies are to be completely successful, they will have to include, I think, a large series of nests and give equal consideration to each of the various elements in habitat selection. Many interesting variations in nesting behavior can then be brought to light. In the New Jersey oak barrens, brown thrashers have been reported as ground nesters. In the timothy field, mentioned above, one female red-wing did attach her nest to the fragile stalks of timothy. In this latter case, every other nesting requirement was presumably satisfied. However surprising these exceptional birds are, they may help us in the end to evaluate the use of substrate in the nesting activities of each species.

How much emphasis birds place on roosting is another unsettled question in habitat selection. During the winter it may be quite important. I am inclined to think that birds pay much more attention to the selection of their roost than most writers have led us to suspect. On the porch of my office, an ancient electric-light fixture offers an excellent roosting place in the ceiling for English sparrows. In November it was frequently visited during daylight hours by one or more sparrows that were settling into their winter routine. This roost was selected, I feel sure, at mid-day, and not by any last-minute activity. A great deal about the individual habits of roosting birds is still unexplored. How often they visit the roosting site each day, how far they travel in winter to their roosts, how often they shift the site during the winter, the spring, and the summer, how birds select a night roost on migration—these are some of the interesting aspects of this subject that merit the attention of the bird watcher.

As this chapter has already shown, birds have many environmental requirements during the breeding season. Sometimes these can be satisfied by a homogeneous block of vegetation, such as a pine plantation or a grassy meadow. More frequently they are met by several plant types. A pair of mourning doves, for instance, may nest in an apple orchard where hay is also being grown. For food the birds can repair to other cultivated fields. For dust baths they might visit a near-by road. Being creatures of great mobility, mourning doves can utilize these scattered places with facility. To other birds, access to a variety of environmental types may be a much greater problem.

Partly as a result of this, or perhaps because border vegetation is generally rich in character, many birds tend to nest near the edge of certain habitats. Some nest on the edge of fields, or in hedgerows, or along roadsides. Others nest on the edge of forests, along woodland paths, or in small woodland clearings. In his book on *Game Management* (described in the appendix), Aldo Leopold has called this tendency the 'edge effect.'

Edge in this special sense has sometimes been confused with the boundaries of study areas. Actually it is used to represent those lines in a landscape where an animal can obtain simultaneous access to more than one type of environment. The edge effect is so impressive in many game-bird studies that Professor Leopold was once led to postulate its existence as a law of dispersion. In a given area, he declares, the *potential* density of game of low mobility will, when two or more types of environment are needed, be roughly proportional to the sum of the type peripheries. In other words, where two or more types converge, the length of their mutual boundaries should suggest the maximum number of territories available for nesting birds. Up to the present, statistical proof of this statement has not yet been accumulated. On an extensive marsh, which Mr. Beecher studied in northern Illinois, the *actual* nesting density is said to increase in each plant society directly with the number of feet of edge per unit area. As this is written, only an incomplete report on this extensive nesting study is available.

Although its effects are noticeable, Professor Leopold points out, edge does not lend itself too well to significant measurements. What looks like edge to us may not be edge to birds. Many species have special requirements, and—as Table 20 implies—different species probably require different combinations of environment during the breeding season. During 1937 and 1941 in Westchester County, New York, I was able to study the effect of edge on two wooded census strips, each 100 yards wide and 750 yards long. Although one strip was dry and situated on top of a ridge, it contained 15 per cent more nesting birds than the one near by which bordered a reservoir. Actually the dry strip contained more clearings and hence more edge (see Table 22).

It can be seen that there are many elements making up a bird's habitat. Which factor is most important? At this stage of our knowledge, it is best not to generalize. Peregrine falcons (duck hawks) give great emphasis to cover; but on at least one occasion they have nested in a barrel on a marsh in California. Here, I think, food was the deciding factor. In arid country, peregrines are replaced by prairie falcons. Cover is still plentiful, but food, water, or perhaps climate then limits their distribution. It would seem likely that, for a given species, the critical factor in habitat selection varies from one region to another, and that even in a single locality it might change over a period of years.

In many species there is a strong attachment to locality, once the adult birds have nested for the first time. I have known redwings to nest persistently in an area for several years after their swamp had been drained and the cattails obliterated. Breeding-bird censuses by Wendell P. Smith have likewise shown that wood warblers returned to their old nesting grounds in New England

TABLE 22

THE 'EDGE EFFECT' CAN INCREASE THE DENSITY OF BIRD LIFE

A two-year study of the nesting birds on two strips of woodland in southern New York is summarized here to show how a mixture of habitats can increase the density of bird life. Actual measurements of the boundaries (edges) of the clearings in these 15-acre samples gave, however, only a slight suggestion of the different densities encountered.

	Average number of pairs	Length of edge	
Dry strip near top of ridge	45 (54%)	850 yards	(68%)
Somewhat rocky strip along reservoir	38 (46%)	400 yards	(32%)
	83 100%	1250 yards	100%

after their forest habitats had been partially destroyed by the great hurricane of September 1938. In a few years these adult birds disappear, usually, I think, through death. Since no young birds take up territory in the altered environment, changes in the numbers and kinds of birds may not be marked. The response of some species to habitat destruction is often delayed in this manner. It might be likened to the reluctance of farmers to abandon lands that have become obviously unfit for agriculture.

Under natural conditions, a great many habitats change over a period of years and, as a result, shifts and changes in bird life are constantly taking place. These bring us to the concept of succession, one of the most fascinating aspects of nature.

Succession in Bird Life

No naturalist can fully appreciate the changes taking place in the bird life of his region until he possesses a working knowledge of the local sequence of habitat changes. All too often these are completely overlooked by ornithologists, although their importance is fundamental to an understanding of both zoölogy and conservation.

Several habitat successions lend themselves well to study by bird watchers. In some regions, these successions are relatively simple, as when a plowed field reverts to prairie. In other regions, successions may be fairly complex.

SIMPLE PLANT SUCCESSIONS

Whenever a field or cutover area gradually reverts to forest, an orderly sequence of plant communities takes place. Many of these communities attract different species of birds. In the beginning, the field-loving species give place to the brush dwellers. The brush dwellers in turn are succeeded by certain woodland birds. As the forest matures, it attracts additional species like the woodpeckers, and so the succession continues until the mature forest is reached.

Temporary stands of oak or aspen may precede the growth of pine; or pine may first occupy a field and later be followed by a deciduous forest. A great many plant successions are known to botanists, but up to the present only a few have been studied for their effect on bird life.

It should be said in passing that studies of the succession of bird life in a sequence of plant communities are (at least for the present) best confined to events during the breeding season. It is then that the habitat preferences of birds reach their highest degree of rigidity. During their migrations, birds greatly relax their habitat requirements, and in the winter they may dwell in environments that have little resemblance to their summer homes. Myrtle warblers, which nest in the northern coniferous forests, may be found in many types of deciduous trees and shrubbery while they are migrating. In winter, along the coast of the middle Atlantic states, they almost exclusively resort to bayberry bushes—a far cry from their summer homes in Canada.

As a simple example of succession, mention might be made of the open aspen and birch woods community that Charles C. Adams once described for northern Michigan. Here dwell slate-colored juncos, oven-birds, white-throated and chipping sparrows, red-eyed vireos, flickers, and Wilson's thrushes. As these woodlands increase in age, the deciduous trees are gradually replaced by conifers. New birds come in and in the final stage of succession (often called the climax), black-capped chickadees, golden-crowned kinglets, red-breasted nuthatches, Canada jays, white-winged crossbills, and four kinds of woodpeckers (downy, hairy, pileated, and Arctic three-toed) are residents of the mature balsam-spruce forest.

A relatively simple succession in Maine, following the complete cutting over of the mature spruce forest, has recently been described by Roger T. Peterson in *Audubon Magazine*. The rough outlines of this sequence of bird communities may be summarized as follows:

1. Fields:
   Savannah sparrow
   Bobolink
   a. Where wet and brushy:
      Northern yellow-throat
      Song sparrow
2. Low brush:
   Towhee
   Field sparrow
   Nashville warbler
   Chestnut-sided warbler
3. Birch and aspen:
   Oven-bird
   Redstart
   Red-eyed vireo
   Ruffed grouse
   a. With mixture of small evergreens and deciduous trees:
      White-throated sparrow
      Hermit thrush
      Solitary vireo
4. Evergreens dominant:
   Magnolia warbler
   Myrtle warbler
   Olive-backed thrush
5. Later stage:
   Blackburnian warbler
   Black-throated green warbler
6. Climax spruce:
   Golden-crowned kinglet

Cape May warbler
Bay-breasted warbler
Several woodpeckers

Of even more interest is the bird succession in a maple-beech forest which Lawrence E. Hicks has reported from northeastern Ohio. This surpasses other analyses in its details, and it may well serve as a model, until a better one is found, for similar studies in other regions.

1. When sprouts and seedlings are from 1 to 10 feet high, and there are large open spaces between the crowns, 5 species of birds predominate:

Indigo bunting   Blue-winged warbler
Field sparrow   Chestnut-sided warbler
               Red-eyed towhee

In moist areas at this stage, the northern yellow-throat is also found.

2. From about 10 to 18 or 20 feet, when the forest crown converges and slowly closes over, and humus begins to accumulate, the species above begin to disappear and are replaced by the following:

Robin   Rose-breasted grosbeak
Red-eyed vireo   Goldfinch
Oven-bird   Least flycatcher

3. At 20 to 30 to 40 feet, when herbaceous plants have developed on the forest floor (and in certain localities, young hemlocks have sprung up), the second group of species continue, while several new birds come in:

Ruffed grouse   Blue jay
Scarlet tanager   Slate-colored junco
               Black-capped chickadee

4. When the forest is 30 to 50 feet high, smaller trees are shaded out and die. The black-throated green warbler now appears and, in some areas, the blue-headed vireo.

5. At 50 to 60 feet, many large dead trees are present in the forest. The rose-breasted grosbeak now drops out and a large number of new species of birds are now found for the first time. These include the following:

Wood thrush	Downy woodpecker
Hairy woodpecker	Crow
Magnolia warbler	Veery

and in certain areas:

Black-throated blue warbler	Blackburnian warbler

6. When a mature forest finally develops, from 65 to 90 feet in height, with numerous old stumps and logs, the herbaceous plants are shaded out by a considerable amount of undergrowth. The habitat becomes modified here and there by storms, windfalls, and upturned roots. Three species disappear:

Robin	Ruffed grouse
Chickadee	

Three others appear for the first time:

Wood pewee	White-breasted nuthatch
Hooded warbler	

A few years after Dr. Hicks reported this sequence of bird life, A. A. Saunders described a similar succession in the same kind of forest at Alleghany State Park, some 80 miles to the east. Although Mr. Saunders' statements are more cautious and represent tentative conclusions to a certain extent, his succession follows Hicks' almost bird for bird.

Does this mean that each type of woodland has its characteristic bird life? Perhaps yes, but there are other factors influencing the distribution of bird life. Both Hicks and Saunders worked in maple-beech forests containing a mixture of hemlocks. Both reported certain species that are northern in their distribution, like the slate-colored junco, the magnolia warbler, and the blackburnian. Sixty miles to the southwest of Ashtabula County, where Hicks made his observations, Mr. and Mrs. R. E. Clisby have more recently been conducting a breeding-bird census in a climax beech and sugar maple forest. Here the northern influence is missing; there are no hemlocks, and the northern birds are absent. Red-bellied woodpeckers, Acadian flycatchers, and tufted titmice all give testimony to a southern fauna. Although the woodland type is essentially the same, 60 miles is enough to bring out a new emphasis in the resident bird life.

In setting out to discover the succession of bird life in a given region, the student need not wait, of course, until a field has actually grown up into a mature forest. At Star Island, Minnesota, it was once estimated that the forest required 500 years to reach its climax. Under ordinary circumstances, this period is much less, but it is still beyond the lifetime of the average naturalist. In many regions different-aged woodlands can be readily spotted, their bird life noted, and a synthetic picture of succession put together.

No consideration of succession is complete without some word about the changes in the density of bird life that must take place. Mr. Saunders believes that, as the forest crown rises in height, there is a parallel increase in the density of breeding birds. Thus, the greatest density is found in the climax woodland, which in effect has the greatest volume of habitats available for birds. He suggests that the original forest in Alleghany State Park, New York, perhaps contained about 15 per cent more birds than are now present there in the second-growth forest. On the other hand, from 15 to 20 species present in the park today would have been absent in the virgin forest, or found there in greatly reduced numbers.

TOPOGRAPHIC AND PLANT SUCCESSIONS

A slightly more complex sequence of habitats involves changes in topography as well as in plant life. In many coastal regions, tides and storms are constantly destroying sandy islands, or changing their shapes, or building them up. Wind and wave action have been known to shift barrier beaches as much as 18 feet every year. Beaches may be extended for miles, or islands created where shoals once existed.

These landscape changes are accompanied by equally interesting changes in bird life. On Long Island, the initial stages are fairly evident, once the new land is free from high tides and from human interference. A new sandy area along the ocean shore is usually first occupied by piping plovers. These pioneers are frequently accompanied by least terns, less frequently by common terns, and only occasionally by black skimmers (which invaded that part of the coast in the 1930's). With the early growth of beach grass, common terns tend to increase in abundance; piping plovers and least terns tend to decrease. Roseate terns or herring gulls may come in at this time. As grass begins to dominate the landscape, it attracts savannah sparrows, and the pioneers dwindle in numbers or shift to the edge of the vegetation. Roseate terns and herring gulls may temporarily increase, although the gulls (when present) usually manage to drive off the smaller terns. The beach grass is eventually followed by shrubs like the bayberry. The colonial nesters are now entirely eliminated and a new community of birds takes over. The northern yellow-throat now predominates; catbirds and song sparrows appear for the first time. In many localities this is as far as the succession ever gets. The accumulation of humus is extremely slow, and the sea may at any time take back what it once created. Later stages involving the development of a pitch pine forest should not be very difficult to observe and study at points on the Atlantic coast.

Topographic successions also occur in many inland communities where lakes and ponds are filling up with organic and inorganic debris. These often encompass long periods of time (many hundreds of years in some cases) but they enable us to predict with a fair degree of accuracy the future changes in the bird life of certain localities.

A very interesting analysis along these lines was once offered by Charles C. Adams as the result of a study of the wildlife communities at Isle Royale, Michigan. There, in Lake Superior, the aquatic plant communities are first inhabited by herring gulls, common loons, American and hooded mergansers, and by pied-billed grebes. As marsh lands are slowly built up, American bitterns, lesser yellow-legs, marsh hawks, and swamp sparrows become the residents. With the growth of alders, cedar waxwings, white-throated sparrows, and redstarts come in. Later, as the bog-forest becomes continuous, these birds diminish in numbers and finally disappear, their places being taken by chickadees, Canada jays, golden-crowned kinglets, yellow-bellied flycatchers, and white-winged crossbills.

The plant and topographic successions just discussed are so intimately connected with our local birds today that they deserve a prominent place in every regional bird book. The theory of succession in bird life is not new. It was known to Adams as early as

TABLE 23

THE PROBABLE SUCCESSION OF MARSH BIRDS IN THE FOX LAKE REGION, ILLINOIS

Given time enough, successive plant communities can fill up a small lake and change it to a field or forest. Each plant community tends to attract certain kinds of nesting birds. Here is the most detailed bird succession ever worked out in America. It was recorded by a young commercial artist, William J. Beecher, whose observations were limited to week ends. This table, adapted from Beecher's interesting book, lists the birds in the plant societies in which they nested, with the densities calculated for 10 acres of each community.

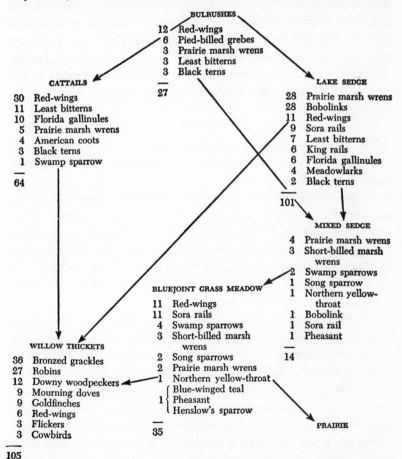

BULRUSHES

12	Red-wings
6	Pied-billed grebes
3	Prairie marsh wrens
3	Least bitterns
3	Black terns
—	
27	

CATTAILS

30	Red-wings
11	Least bitterns
10	Florida gallinules
5	Prairie marsh wrens
4	American coots
3	Black terns
1	Swamp sparrow
—	
64	

LAKE SEDGE

28	Prairie marsh wrens
28	Bobolinks
11	Red-wings
9	Sora rails
7	Least bitterns
6	King rails
6	Florida gallinules
4	Meadowlarks
2	Black terns
—	
101	

MIXED SEDGE

4	Prairie marsh wrens
3	Short-billed marsh wrens
2	Swamp sparrows
1	Song sparrow
1	Northern yellow-throat
1	Bobolink
1	Sora rail
1	Pheasant
—	
14	

BLUEJOINT GRASS MEADOW

11	Red-wings
11	Sora rails
4	Swamp sparrows
3	Short-billed marsh wrens
2	Song sparrows
2	Prairie marsh wrens
1	Northern yellow-throat
1	{ Blue-winged teal / Pheasant / Henslow's sparrow
—	
35	

WILLOW THICKETS

36	Bronzed grackles
27	Robins
12	Downy woodpeckers
9	Mourning doves
9	Goldfinches
6	Red-wings
3	Flickers
3	Cowbirds
—	
105	

PRAIRIE

Condensed and adapted from Nesting Birds and the Vegetation Substrate. 1942.

1908, but his brilliant work at that time was virtually disregarded by bird watchers for a quarter of a century. The exploration of bird life along these lines is still in a pioneer stage. It requires thinking by the naturalist, and notes taken in the field on the many plant communities that attract characteristic communities of birds.

In some regions very elaborate plant successions have already been worked out by botanists. Sometimes these are made up of plant societies too small in extent to have a significant effect on bird distribution. Others may be characterized by differences that are of no importance to birds. Yet many provide suggestions and theories that can be tested in bird watching. Plant successions are now listed in modern American books on plant ecology, and newly recorded ones can be found from time to time in the pages of two periodicals, *Ecology* and *Ecological Monographs*.

CLIMATIC AND GEOLOGICAL SUCCESSIONS

The greatest changes in bird habitats have undoubtedly occurred in geological time. For the most part these are only of historical interest today.

As the last glacier retreated northward, there ensued in its wake an orderly sequence of progressively warmer climates in the northern portions of the United States. The first of these permitted the existence of a great expanse of tundra in the wake of the ice-cap. In time, the tundra was replaced by fir trees. These were followed by a forest of spruce, and by pines, and finally by the deciduous forests that are present today.

The succession of bird life that accompanied these changes in habitats can now only be conjectured. In all likelihood, the northern states were once inhabited by nesting redpolls, numerous shore birds, gyrfalcons, and snowy owls. As firs and spruce took over the landscape, pine grosbeaks probably came in to breed along with birds like the northern shrike and the great gray owl. Eventually these were replaced by a new community composed (presumably) of spruce grouse, three-toed woodpeckers, hawk owls, and many small species like the kinglets. As the climate gradually grew warmer, the conifers gave way to deciduous trees and an entirely different avifauna, much like the present one, occupied the forest.

Farther south, still other birds, like the Carolina wren, the mockingbird, and the summer tanager, marked an additional stage in the succession.

Geologically speaking, this succession is relatively recent, but to most bird watchers interest in it is confined to those regions where a few relicts of these former habitats are still present. In the Middlewest these are represented by hundreds of scattered tamarack swamps, which are rapidly being lumbered and drained. (At the present rate of destruction, they will soon disappear forever.) Other relicts are stands of hemlocks and sphagnum bogs far south of their normal range. For the most part the former bird life of these habitats has already disappeared, although occasionally they attract nesting birds like black-throated green warblers, blue-headed vireos, and brown creepers beyond their regular limits of distribution. Many relicts are now too small in extent to have any appreciable attraction for birds. In the winter, however, they are often the best places to look for rare stragglers from the North.

LAND-USE SUCCESSIONS

Other studies in local distribution can be correlated with the use of land by man. In western Wisconsin, once the home of the prairie chicken, the silt loams of the tableland lent themselves well to agriculture. Inevitably the prairie chickens gave way before the plow and the gun. Today they breed on the sandy soils in the center of that state. Similarly, in the southeastern states, repeated fires have left a covering of conifers in complete possession of the landscape. It is said that if fire is ever eliminated, a deciduous forest will reoccupy much of that country. The ensuing changes in bird life are not hard to imagine.

In the Middlewest, I have seen bank swallows breeding at one place because of accelerated soil erosion. Topsoil had been washed off the neighboring hills and had raised the floor of the valley by about three feet. Ensuing rains had cut a channel through the fill, leaving a bank for the swallows.

The cattle country, in which I have had no field experience, must offer many interesting examples of the effect of overgrazing on bird distribution. Farther east, in Wisconsin, the changes caused by grazing in a woodland are particularly noticeable. When cattle first begin to graze a forest, the underbrush starts to disappear. Continued grazing finally eliminates all undergrowth and seedlings. The culmination of this stage marks the disappearance of ground-dwelling birds, like the ruffed grouse, the northern yellow-throat, the oven-bird, the indigo bunting, and song sparrows nesting along the edge of the forest.

In the second stage of forest degeneration, the soil becomes impacked, grasses are replacing the former litter on the forest floor, trees begin to die here and there, and the forest canopy is opened. The ensuing changes in bird life are complex. Woodpeckers appear to increase temporarily, while other birds, like the red-eyed vireo and redstart, begin to decrease with diminution of the forest canopy. The robin replaces the wood thrush. Crested flycatchers seem to diminish in numbers. Yellow-throated vireos and Baltimore orioles increase. Bewick's wren invades the area during this period.

The next stage of grazing witnesses an almost complete destruction of the woodland community. Trees still survive in a few clumps. Robins are still left; bluebirds, starlings, killdeers, meadowlarks, and lark sparrows have now come in. Typical woodland birds, like the red-eyed vireo and the redstart, are gone. Here and there flickers and warbling vireos persist. Continued heavy grazing finally eliminates even the tree-nesting species, and in the end only killdeers, prairie horned larks, and nighthawks can occupy the landscape.

Land-use successions may include changes brought about by irrigation, by drainage, by dredging, and by the damming of rivers. Usually these involve relatively rapid changes in bird life, which can be compared and contrasted from one year to another. Census methods may be used as the occasion requires, but the greatest value to the records thus accumulated will come from the careful use of the same census technique over a period of years. In some localities a study area can be easily selected. In others a cruising technique may be more advisable. Each can give a clear picture of the changing character of the bird life, the cruise-type emphasizing the variety of species and the census area yielding the most accurate densities.

Life Zones and Forest Types

Most regional bird books discuss the distribution of breeding birds in terms of faunal zones. In the western states and in the mountainous regions of the Americas, these are especially noticeable. As one climbs to a high altitude, the vegetation is seen to change and with it are corresponding changes in bird life. These zones are given names, like the Carolinian zone, the Canadian zone, and the Hudsonian zone.

In recent years a good deal of criticism has been leveled at the concept of faunal zones. It has been said that the original zones were based on erroneous calculations of temperature, and that birds primarily respond to types of vegetation. Thus, it is claimed, bird life is distributed according to the deciduous forest, the coniferous forest, the tundra, and so on.

It seems likely that much can be said for both these schools of thought, and that both have their weaknesses. Some ornithologists like to believe that the faunal zone still identifies a definite group of birds regardless of how the zone is relabeled. But sometimes even the same zones are used to refer to different species in different regions. In Wisconsin I might report that Carolinian birds are breeding in La Crosse County; and in New York I might say the same thing about the breeding birds of Westchester County. The same statement would refer to some entirely different species. To call all of them birds of the deciduous forest and let it go at that is scarcely any improvement on the old conceptions of distribution.

TABLE 24

CAROLINIAN ZONE BIRDS DIFFER FROM ONE REGION TO ANOTHER

Generalizations about the zonal distribution of birds are subject to many exceptions. All of the following species breed in the deciduous forest and are said to belong to the Carolinian zone. Yet the birds listed for La Crosse County do not breed in Westchester, nor are those listed for Westchester County known to breed in La Crosse.

La Crosse County, Wisconsin	Westchester County, New York
Bewick's wren	Carolina wren
Bell's vireo	White-eyed vireo
Prothonotary warbler	Worm-eating warbler
Blue-gray gnatcatcher	Kentucky warbler
Red-bellied woodpecker	Hooded warbler

The theory that each major type of forest has its own character-istic community of birds would meet its most critical test if blocks of coniferous woodland could experimentally be taken out of their natural range and set down in some more southern environment. The cost of such a transplantation would be enormous, and—as a matter of fact—completely unwarranted. Nature has already per-formed the task for us. In many parts of the so-called transition zone, relict tracts of hemlocks, pines, or tamaracks still exist. I have frequented one of these for nearly 20 years—a mature stand of hemlocks covering several hundred acres in the New York Botanical Gardens at Bronx, New York. During this entire period, this coniferous forest has never once attracted a single pair of so-called coniferous-nesting birds.

To the bird watcher, all these theories might well be left to authorities who have the time to map carefully the distribution of many species. Ornithologists will agree, I think, that within certain rather wide limits, birds are not interested in the species of trees. During the nesting season they have many requirements. Each species has its own degree of flexibility. This may be very wide, as in the case of the robin, or narrow, as in the case of a crossbill.

The possibilities for explorations in bird distribution are seen to include many approaches. In every case careful note-taking is neces-sary. A day's hike might cover a score of different communities for birds. As a result, a score of different bird lists are possible. It is on such occasions that the old-type field card exhibits its strength and weakness. It does permit the quick recording of birds in a single habitat, but not all observers can afford to use 20 cards on a single trip. It is in this respect that a pocket notebook shows to advantage. Field notes can be taken on different communities, on different factors, or on a single species. At home the pages can be torn out and transcribed or pasted onto more permanent sheets in loose-leaf notebooks.

As his studies in bird distribution progress, every bird watcher will find stimulating ideas in the literature that has been published by workers in other fields. Local soil maps take on a new signifi-cance when one is interested in bird distribution. Geology textbooks offer basic ideas. Periodicals on plant ecology contain unsuspected suggestions. The distribution of birds is seen to be an expression of climate, landscape, and land use, interrelated in complex ways with the psychological requirements of a species and often reflecting a condition in its population. In the last century of American ornithology, only the main outlines have been sketched in. The field is now wide open for exploration.

CHAPTER FIVE

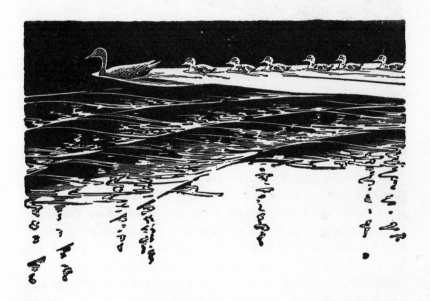

The Romance of Bird Banding

BIRD STUDY in America has witnessed two revolutions within the past half century. The first of these, the substitution of field glasses for the collector's gun, around 1900, has already been described. Of even greater importance has been the inauguration of systematic bird banding about 1920. It has now become possible to study the individual wild bird under natural conditions, to trace it on long migrations, to identify it after long absences, to compute its age, and even to study its heredity. No other class of animals can now be watched under such superb conditions in the wild.

The Beginnings of Bird Banding

Like the development of field identification, appreciation of the value of banding has not been developed overnight. Early in the nineteenth century, Audubon placed silver wires around the legs of two fledgling phoebes. After the passage of a year, he had the satisfaction of seeing them again in the same locality. Many decades later a lightship captain fastened a small box (with a message inside) around the neck of a tired duck hawk that had sought rest on his vessel off the capes of Hatteras. Within a few weeks, this unfortunate bird expired in an emaciated condition on the coast of Florida.

Marking birds is no longer so haphazard. The basis of our present technique was worked out by a Danish schoolmaster, who placed aluminum rings on the legs of starlings, white storks, European teal, and several birds of prey. Measured by present-day standards, Hans Mortensen's work would scarcely startle a museum curator, but in 1899 his report echoed throughout the ornithological world.

In 1903 the ringing of birds was begun at the famous migration station of Rossitten in Germany. When one of its banded gulls was subsequently found in France, there was much debate by the natives about what the band could possibly mean. By some it was thought that the ring had been attached by a shipwrecked sailor from a vessel named *Rossitten;* by others it was regarded as a token sent by a sentimental maiden to her lover who kept a bird shop. Not long after, when a Bulgarian shot a spotted eagle, banded with the number 1285, the local press carried a report of a bird over 600 years old.

In our own country, scientific bird banding was inaugurated by Paul Bartsch, a well-known conchologist whose hobby was bird study. During 1902 and 1903, Dr. Bartsch ringed over 100 black-crowned night herons in the District of Columbia. For two decades, the new method of bird study led an uncertain life. Bands were somewhat expensive and no one knew quite what to band. Organizations like the Smithsonian Institution, the American Ornithologists' Union, the New Haven Bird Club, the Linnaean Society of New York, and the American Bird-Banding Association strove to keep up with the mountain of clerical details that were inevitable as the program grew.

By 1919 the success of this new type of bird study was well established and the United States Bureau of Biological Survey (now the Fish and Wildlife Service) assumed entire responsibility for supplying all bands and keeping records. This was followed by an agreement between Canada and the United States to use a common set of numbers. Banding had now come of age. Its future, in North America at least, was permanently assured.

Most of the growing pains of bird banding are now forgotten, but one of them, related by Frederick C. Lincoln, deserves recounting. This concerned the early efforts of the Government to obtain a source of bands. When the Service first took over the program, practically every manufacturer of aluminum smallware in the United States was approached for bird bands without success. Finally, as its supply was nearly exhausted, the Government placed an order in England. When the rings reached America, a typographical error had resulted in a startling legend. Instead of 'Biol.Surv.,Wash.,D.C.' the finder was advised, in effect, to Wash, Boil, and Surv.

The methods of banding are very simple. A small aluminum band is carefully fastened to the leg of a bird that usually has been found in a nest or caught in a trap. This ring may bear some number such as 43-273829 and some description such as 'Notify Fish and Wildlife Service, Wash., D.C.' When a banded bird is found somewhere and its number forwarded to Washington, the finder receives a thank-you card stating when and where the bird was banded, and the bander is notified of the place and date of recovery.

The homely origins of American bird banding have done much to retain this branch of bird study for enthusiastic laymen. I know of no museums that operate trapping stations. Among the universities, banding generally varies according to the particular problems on which graduate students are working from time to time. Governmental agencies remain dedicated to game birds. Banders now count among their numbers lawyers, civil engineers, physicians, farmers, men from nearly every walk of life. They are exploring the birds' world with a sureness and a thoroughness undreamed of by Audubon and the early ornithologists. Throughout North America, they have helped to band over 4,000,000 birds in the last 20 years, and to accumulate some 260,000 records of returns and recoveries scattered over 4 continents.

Since its inauguration, bird banding has been marked by periodic improvements. These have tended to divide the movement into three stages. The first was the ringing of fledgling birds; the second was the trapping of adults; the third was color marking. Their relative advantages and disadvantages, which will now be discussed, should be clearly understood by every bird watcher.

The Ringing of Fledglings—the First Phase of Banding

Early in the history of banding, thousands of fledgling birds were ringed throughout the country in the innocent hope that whenever and wherever the birds died, people could be relied upon to report the band number to the Government. This worked out fairly well for birds like the hawks, owls, and herons, which are often shot. It was rather successful, too, with gulls and terns, the dead bodies of which so often wash up on a beach. Very few of the smaller birds, however, died on sidewalks and lawns where they could be conveniently noticed. Recovery percentages for the banded fledglings of songbirds were close to zero.

As the first phase of banding, however, the ringing of fledglings has had its own successes. It has, for instance, given some insight into the little-known movements of birds that cross the Atlantic. Apparently kittiwakes cross from England fairly frequently, and Arctic terns are now believed to fly due east from America before they turn south and go down the western side of the Atlantic to their wintering area. The migration of many other individual birds has likewise been traced to Central and South America.

Undaunted by the relatively small percentages of recoveries, many banders have concentrated on ringing fledglings in the great sea-bird colonies. These are often banded in large numbers, although the work involved is laborious and exacting. Each band must be fitted perfectly so that it will not catch in grasses or rub the bird's leg. When frightened, young herons and gulls have the unpleasant habit of regurgitating their food.* Colonial birds are best banded by a team of banders who are able to work rapidly

* In order to avoid having this happen, I have found it convenient to throw an old hat over the head of a fledgling gull about to be banded. The ensuing darkness quiets the youngster. It then docilely permits its legs to be pulled out toward the tail, and the band can be affixed quickly and securely without further commotion. This method works very well for banders with strong backs and weak stomachs.

TABLE 25

HOW MANY BANDED BIRDS HAVE CROSSED THE ATLANTIC?

In spite of the vast numbers ringed in North America, only 4 or 5 banded birds are now known to have crossed the Atlantic Ocean from east to west. Among more than 30 banded birds recorded as having crossed in the opposite direction was a racing pigeon. This bird was lost on a flight from Land's End, England, to North Ireland in June 1927. It was shot later the same month at Belle Isle, Newfoundland.

Species	Where banded	Date banded	Place of recovery	Date of recovery
		EASTWARD CROSSINGS		
Arctic tern	Maine	July 3, 1913	West Africa	Aug. 1917
Arctic tern	Labrador	July 22, 1927	France	Oct. 1, 1927
Arctic tern	Labrador	July 23, 1928	South Africa	Nov. 14, 1928
Caspian tern	Michigan	July 14, 1927	England	Aug. 1939
		WESTWARD CROSSINGS		
European widgeon	Iceland	July 17, 1927	Newfoundland	Oct. 5, 1927
European widgeon	Iceland	Aug. 4, 1936	Prince Edward Island	Sept. 26, 1936
European widgeon	Iceland	July 2, 1926	Nova Scotia	Dec. 10, 1926
European widgeon	Iceland	July 2, 1927	Massachusetts	Nov. 14, 1927
European widgeon	Iceland		Maryland	Nov. 29, 1929
European widgeon	Iceland	July 12, 1930	North Carolina	Dec. 1930
European widgeon	Iceland	July 1927	British West Indies	Oct. 28, 1937
European pintail	Iceland	June 30, 1930	Quebec	May (1), 1932
Lapwing	England	May 1926	Newfoundland	Dec. 27, 1927
Northern skua	Scotland	July 3, 1939	Massachusetts	Feb. 4, 1940
Black-headed gull	Germany	July 18, 1911	Barbados	Nov. 1911
Black-headed gull	Germany	July 1911	Mexico	Feb. 1912
Black-headed gull	Holland	June 21, 1932	Labrador	Sept. 1933
Kittiwake	Russia	June 19, 1937	Newfoundland	Sept. 20, 1937
Kittiwake	Russia	July 25, 1938	Newfoundland	Fall 1939
Kittiwake	Russia	Aug. 9, 1939	Newfoundland	Nov. 14, 1939
Kittiwake	England	June 21, 1936	Greenland	Oct. 1, 1936
Kittiwake	England	July 2, 1929	Davis Strait	July (15), 1931
Kittiwake	England	June 30, 1924	Labrador	Oct. 28, 1925
Kittiwake	England	June 28, 1923	Newfoundland	Aug. 12, 1924
Kittiwake	England	June 23, 1928	Newfoundland	Dec. 10, 1930
Kittiwake	England	July 1, 1929	Newfoundland	Dec. 24, 1930
Gull-billed tern	Denmark	June 17, 1937	Windward Islands	Sept. 5, 1937
Puffin	Scotland	Aug. 4, 1939	Newfoundland	Dec. 21, 1939
Puffin	Scotland	Aug. 10, 1939	Newfoundland	Dec. 20, 1939
Purple sandpiper	Iceland	May 20, 1942	Baffin Island	Apr. 1943

Compiled from various sources and with the assistance of May T. Cooke.

through the colony and, at least in point of time, reduce to a minimum the disturbance among the birds.

In recent years members of the Florida Audubon Society have made annual excursions to the Dry Tortugas, where they band as many as 6400 sooty terns on a single visit. In the Cape Cod region, vast numbers of common and roseate terns have been banded each year by Dr. O. L. Austin and his assistants. Between 10,000 and 18,000 fledgling herring gulls are annually banded in the Great Lakes region and along the Atlantic seaboard, but here again the percentage of recoveries for these species has not been very large. Recent reports indicate that it is at least 1.4 per cent for Caspian terns and at least 3.3 per cent for herring gulls. Ordinarily, these small percentages would not justify random banding. In the case of colonial sea birds, an enormous number of fledglings have to be ringed in order to obtain an appreciable number of returns and recoveries. On a single island off the coast of New Brunswick, Canada, large-scale banding by Bowdoin College students has already yielded a rich harvest of some 800 herring gull recoveries. To achieve this record, over 23,000 gulls were banded in a 5-year period.

TABLE 26

YOUNG HERRING GULLS DISPERSE WIDELY AT THE CLOSE OF THE NESTING SEASON

Before they migrate to the south for their first winter, young herring gulls do a good deal of wandering. Banding at Bowdoin College's scientific station on Kent Island, New Brunswick, now discloses that, until November, more of these young birds are reported north than south of their natal colony.

Distances recorded from nest site	July	August	September	October
501– 800 miles north	..	..	9	2
101– 500 miles north	..	1	13	21
0– 100 miles north	2	4	12	11
0– 100 miles south	..	..	6	2
101– 500 miles south	1	2	1	14
501–1000 miles south	..	..	1	10
1000–2000 miles south	..	..	1	1

Condensed from *Bird-Banding*. 1940.

The wholesale banding of fledglings has yielded many interesting records on the longevity of birds. In 1939 a black-headed gull was caught in central Europe 25 years (less 2 months) after it had been banded as a nestling. The band was by this time as thin as paper, but it was still legible. A starling is also reported to have lived 15 years and 10 months—an extraordinary age for such a small bird in the wild. Predation and extremities of weather help shorten the lives of the smaller birds to but 2 or 3 years. Larger birds live longer. Dr. Austin, the New York surgeon who has done

so much banding on Cape Cod, has found that 10 years are necessary for a given age class of terns to be wiped out by mortality. In
discussing the recoveries of herring gulls, Professor Gross has noticed a sharp drop in the number of recoveries at the end of the
eighth year. He believes, however, that with another ten years of
accumulated records we shall be able to obtain a more precise
concept of the life expectancy of this species.

One of the current problems of both ornithology and conservation
concerns the relation of breeding grounds to wintering areas. Do
the crows nesting in British Columbia winter in the same region
as crows that have bred in Oregon or California? No one knows—
yet. It is not impossible that a given species may be composed of
a number of different populations that breed in distinctly different
regions and perhaps winter in equally separate areas. Banding has
actually proved this situation to exist in certain waterfowl, like the
Canada goose. It has also been demonstrated by taxonomists working on subspecies of birds like the fox sparrow. It is even known
that the most northerly nesting birds of a given species may winter
the farthest south.

The accumulation of migrational banding data at this time seems
to be a hopeless task on birds like the warblers and the flycatchers,
which may winter in Central or South America and are rarely recovered away from the original point of banding. After all, the
wintering range of the chimney swift is still unknown. There remain, however, a number of species on which the banding of
fledglings is certain to yield some recoveries. In general these include all birds that are still shot or trapped in numbers. All large
hawks and owls and many of the herons are included in this category. Crows likewise offer possibilities for the bander. Finally there
are the water birds, such as the gulls, terns, pelicans, and cormorants, all nesting in colonies and offering splendid opportunities
for wholesale banding. Although restrictions on metal prohibit the
promiscuous banding of fledglings in wartime, every bird club
might well possess a standing committee on bird banding to concentrate and co-ordinate the work of its members on the wholesale
banding of some local species whenever bands become available.
Vigorously carried on for a period of years, such a program would

do much to build up a picture of local bird life, its habits of migration, and its specific (if any) wintering range in southern regions.

Trapping Stations—the Second Phase of Banding

Although the banding of fledglings is still carried out today on a somewhat limited scale, it has been replaced to a considerable extent by the trapping station. The appearance of this institution marked the second phase of bird banding, which in America was largely brought on by the initiative and example of S. Prentiss Baldwin, a Cleveland lawyer and real-estate operator. By systematically operating a series of traps, Mr. Baldwin was the first to capture large numbers of adult birds. He was the first, too, to prove that birds winter in the same locality year after year, returning to the same gardens and shrubbery. Largely owing to his influence, the operation of garden traps is now the standard practice of many banders. That great numbers of birds are now being marked in this way may be seen from some of the totals reported by the Fish and Wildlife Service. During the fiscal year 1940, the following birds were among those banded, the vast majority of these undoubtedly trapped as adults:

Junco	21,399	Robin	8,312
White-throated sparrow	21,147	Purple finch	8,028
Grackle	11,844	White-crowned sparrow	6,569
Cowbird	9,985	Catbird	3,922
Song sparrow	8,939	Chipping sparrow	3,490

Bird traps sometimes create surprises for their operators. There is, for example, the story of the ambitious Chicagoan who, having secured from Washington the necessary permits and bird bands, enthusiastically set his traps for migrants. During the first two days he caught a rat, a red squirrel, and a skunk—all very much alive and presumably somewhat excited.

Trapping stations have this merit, however: they often can be conveniently located near one's residence and even watched by members of the family. Among my friends is a busy physician whose small son sets the traps each evening a half hour before his father rushes home from the clinic. Another is a housewife who found she could iron and watch her traps at the same time. The success of a station does depend, though, on the kinds of birds that frequent the vicinity. If these are mostly small migrants, the percentage of recoveries is apt to be very small. Thus, on Long Island, Mrs. Marie V. Beals trapped over 30,000 birds in her garden over an 11-year period; only 152 of these were eventually retrapped in her locality and only 210 were recovered away from the trapping station. Here the combination of abundant bird food and all the skill of one of the ablest bird trappers in the country could not produce a record of recoveries better than 1.1 per cent.

To obtain any considerable number of recoveries away from their trapping station, many banders of nongame species have therefore been forced to ring large numbers of birds. As one bander has put it, the smaller and less conspicuous the bird, the fewer the recoveries. Commenting on this fact, M. J. Magee some time ago reported that, in a total of over 18,000 birds banded, his recoveries of evening grosbeaks averaged 1 out of 86 banded, and for purple finches 1 out of 940.

Where birds have settled down for the winter, banding traps will often catch the same birds year after year. In South Carolina, W. P. Wharton has reported, out of 11,886 birds banded, 1895 (15.9 per cent) were recaptured again in some subsequent winter. These returns ran as high as 19.6 per cent for chipping sparrows, 18.4 per cent for white-throated sparrows, and 18.4 per cent for red-eyed towhees. As in Mrs. Beals' experience, the recovery of small songbirds away from the trapping station was disappointingly small: only 4 out of 3753 chipping sparrows, and only 5 out of 3112 white-throats.

Much of the incentive back of bird banding has doubtless come from a desire to learn more about the migration of individual birds. Banding has confirmed, for instance, the presence of two distinct migration routes used by ospreys and duck hawks in the East. One of these obviously follows the coast, the other follows the Appalachians.

In England, more than half of the recoveries of kittiwakes banded come from our side of the Atlantic. New and specialized migration routes have also been found for many species of waterfowl. These have been well described in Frederick C. Lincoln's

The Migration of American Birds, a book which contains the best
available summaries of the many spectacular discoveries made by
North American banders of migrating birds (see also appendix).

Special routes for most of the other birds remain largely undis-
covered. Among certain species such routes undoubtedly are not
present, since these birds disperse over wide areas as they migrate.
The use of highways by other species may vary considerably. Professor Gross has shown that his herring gulls, banded off the coast
of New Brunswick, closely follow the eastern seaboard, while those
banded by Lyon and Wilson in the Great Lakes region have been
recorded in practically every state from North Dakota and Texas
east to the Atlantic.

Because the trapping of small songbirds yields so few recoveries
of migrants, many banders have found new and no less important
uses for their bird traps. Before releasing their birds, they carefully examine each of them for external parasites. These may include mites, flies, ticks, or lice which have made their way to different parts of the bird's body. They can be removed with small
tweezers, and sent in small vials of 70 per cent alcohol to the Department of Agriculture's Bureau of Entomology in Washington.
The great potentialities of this work have not, I think, been fully
appreciated by banders. The parasites are often small, and an
examination of a bird's entire body is necessary to discover all of
them. Many species of parasites have not yet been described. For
others, the complete life cycle is not yet known; for some, their
significance as disease carriers still remains to be determined. Do
infected birds tend to shorten their migration? Do they sing less,
have a shorter life, duller plumage, and a generally smaller size?
Here the bander can penetrate to one of the important frontiers of
science. He is blessed with material that is the envy of other
workers. He can make exact observations on the effect of parasites
on their hosts, help work out their geographic range, and interest
himself in their life-history cycles. This is a little-worked field, but
one which is more and more being associated with the bird-bander's
traps.

Another bypath of bird banding concerns the weighing of live
birds. Scales have always been difficult to operate in the field, since

the slightest breeze affects their balance. Partly on this account, the weight of many wild birds is still unknown. Wherever trapping stations are located in a garden, a captured bird can be placed in an old sock and readily weighed indoors. One bander, Mrs. K. B. Wetherbee, weighed over 2700 birds in a 2-year period. At another station, Baldwin and Kendeigh made 13,546 weight determinations for 5812 individuals over a 9-year period. Another bander, Mrs. M. M. Nice, secured 746 weights of 455 song sparrows. It is evident that a bird's weight increases during the day (depending on air temperatures, the amount of food taken, and other activities). During the night, when no feeding takes place, there is a loss of weight. Birds have also been found to change in weight according to the season. They may grow heavier in winter and lighter in summer. They also tend to lose weight while they are feeding their young. Before this subject is fully explored, it is obvious that a vast number of weight determinations must be made. Bird banders can best supply these records.

The trapping of birds has also placed many bird banders in the enviable position of being able to enlarge our knowledge of bird molts. Among the first to do this were Mr. and Mrs. T. T. McCabe, who studied the wing molts of pine siskins in British Columbia. Subsequently, Mr. and Mrs. Harold Michener published a report based on a study of some 8000 to 10,000 house finches that they had banded in California over a 4-year period. At Saulte Ste. Marie, Michigan's famous bander, M. J. Magee, has made plumage notes on more than 10,000 purple finches. Not only do some banders handle large numbers of birds but they often constantly retrap the same individuals for successive weeks, months, or even years. Under such unrivaled conditions, the opportunities for weight and plumage studies are limited only by the note-taking ability of the bander.

Bird traps for banding purposes are described by Frederick C. Lincoln and S. Prentiss Baldwin in a government manual (U.S.D.A. Miscellaneous Publication 58). Improvements on these are reported from time to time in the magazine *Bird-Banding* and in mimeographed publications of the regional banding associations. I shall never forget one ingenious device that made local history in New York City a few years ago. One of my friends, a diamond broker

TABLE 27

DO BIRDS HAVE MANY DEFORMITIES?

There is no telling what the bird banders will next discover. Here are the more conspicuous abnormalities of 10,000 starlings observed by Dr. Lawrence E. Hicks of Ohio State University, when he and two students handled more than 25,000 birds that roosted at night in the towers and superstructures of buildings in Columbus, Ohio. All birds that are trapped in large numbers can be studied in the same way.

One toenail absent	314	Both legs crooked	6
Two toenails absent	210	Red legs	3
Three toenails absent	163	Pink legs	1
Four toenails absent	49	Giant size	7
Five toenails absent	12	Pigmy size	6
Six toenails absent	8	Tail missing	1
Seven toenails absent	3	Swallow tail	1
Eight toenails absent	1	Giant crossed bill	14
One toe absent	182	Split bill	5
Two toes absent	104	Stub bill	2
Three toes absent	68	Sparrow bill	2
Four toes absent	28	Grosbeak bill	1
Five toes absent	3	Hooked bill	6
Six toes absent	1	Curled bill	3
One foot absent	21	Transparent bill	3
One leg absent	12	Chalk bill	2
Club foot	18	One eye blinded	46
One broken or crooked leg	83	Broken or crooked wing	6

White feathers present   11

Total birds with abnormalities, 535, or 5.35 per cent of the 10,000 captured

Slightly condensed from *Bird-Banding*. 1934.

named Irving Kassoy, had for some time been studying barn owls. One evening, at a meeting of the Linnaean Society of New York, Irv informed us that he had located a new nest of these birds only a few miles from the site of his old banding operations. Some weeks later, he again reported. Much to his surprise the female owl was wearing a bird band. No one had ever before found a barn owl in such circumstances. To a veteran owl bander, the responsibility of getting that band number was quite apparent.

In a matter of this kind, Irv left nothing to chance. Local experts were canvassed for the very latest ideas. The safety of the eggs was considered, as well as the state of the female's mind. In the end, it was decided to pull a net over the old bird when she entered the abandoned building. Some time later, some friends and I accompanied Irv to the abandoned coal yard to witness the historic capture. The trapping device bore witness to the fact that improvements had been borrowed from more than mere ornithologists. As the female crossed the threshold, she had to pass over a treadle. With this, a light would flash in the next room. Here Irv, tightly clenching a rope, stood like the Statue of Liberty with one arm raised high in the darkness. On some occasions, we found, he had to hold this pose for an hour—but in every case the female escaped. Some thought that Irv pulled too quickly. Others averred that his pull was too slow. The whole contraption was even said to be at fault. In the end, the female became extremely nervous and after several nights Irv had to abandon his efforts.

A sage from Westchester, Michael Oboiko, was called in for consultation. To a veteran squirrel trapper like Mr. Oboiko, the situation was undoubtedly an enjoyable one. The city experts had failed and even their government manual offered no consolation. The remedy, said he, was simple. The New York barn owl trap was to be scrapped entirely. Its place was to be taken by the Oboiko Squirrel Trap (unpatented). Not all at once, decided Mr. Oboiko, but one piece at a time—one piece each week, so as not to frighten the birds. This arrangement proved to be quite acceptable to the barn owls, albeit hard on Irv's blood pressure. In due time, he succeeded in capturing the female. The band revealed that it was not one of his own birds after all, but one that had been ringed as a nestling the year before in Massachusetts. Such is the history of the first banded barn owl to be trapped in America. Moral: if you can't catch it yourself, call in a squirrel expert.

Studies of a Single Species—the Third Phase of Banding

With the growth of trapping stations, bird banders became increasingly aware of the broader implications of their studies. The return of birds to the same area year after year was a noteworthy fact to discover, but it in turn provoked other questions. If a set of relatively immovable traps could show a 20 per cent wintering return for banded chipping sparrows, how much higher would the returns be if the traps were systematically moved about a much larger neighborhood? Then too, if the birds annually nest in the same locality, do they choose the same mates year after year? Do they ever inbreed with their own offspring or with their brothers and sisters? Many questions like these began to receive attention.

Almost inevitably, thoughtful bird banders realized that they did not want to wait for birds to come to their immovable traps. From this point on, they moved their traps after the birds. A few began to concentrate their work on a single species. Smaller numbers of birds were trapped, but the percentage of returns was higher. As the scope of their investigations gradually became enlarged, banders soon asked themselves if individual birds built the same type of nests year after year, and at the same height; whether skill in nest building is acquired with age; whether birds use exactly the same territory from one year to another, and so on. This marks the modern phase of bird banding: the effort to trace the life of the individual bird throughout its entire life cycle. It involves nest-watching and note-taking. Not only have new methods of trapping made this new step possible, but the whole emphasis of banding studies has matured as well. Banding has become a means to an end, not an end in itself. This change did not, I think, come about merely from a new appreciation of the value of specialized studies. Complete life-history studies have both a diversity of activity that is stimulating to the observer, and a final satisfaction that fragmentary work can never equal. Stated simply, they are much more fun.

Among the first to specialize on a single species was S. Prentiss Baldwin, who, with characteristic foresight and thoroughness, began a long-term study of the house wren. One of his first discoveries disclosed that the marriage relations of this species differed widely from certain concepts held by the clergy. So busy were the female wrens feeding the first fledglings of the season that the males deserted them to pair with new females for their second nesting. (Biologically, this is an economy in point of time, since it permits more young to be raised in a short period.) All over the country banders began to find that adult birds trapped in their nesting territories could often be recaptured in the same place in some subsequent breeding season. This phenomenon is now accepted as a fact. The degree to which young birds return to their birthplace has been, however, something of a stumbling block.

The ease with which certain hole-nesting species can be captured on their nests has encouraged banders to produce some of their finest studies. Among these are reports of bluebirds, tree swallows, plain titmice, black-capped chickadees, and white-breasted nut-hatches. Up to the present, however, there has been no extensive trapping of purple martins, tufted titmice, Carolina wrens, rough-winged swallows, or belted kingfishers. Nor has there been a thorough study of nesting starlings on our continent.

It should not be supposed that banders have been unable to study species other than hole nesters. In the breeding season, many birds still come to traps into which water is dripping from a can or bucket. Although feeding trays may not attract them when other food is plentiful in the spring and summer, running water is hard to resist.

After they have been incubating for some time, ground-nesting birds will allow simple drop traps to be placed over the nest site. In this way large numbers of adult common terns, herring gulls, and piping plovers have already been caught. For other species *that nest in the open,* like the killdeer, black skimmer, Wilson's plover, prairie horned lark, and least tern, this method offers a splendid opportunity to capture the adults.

Another trick is to put all the young birds (when they are fairly well grown) into a small cage or trap. If this is placed fairly near the nest, the old birds will enter it to feed their youngsters. Birds nesting in thickets and deep grasses can be rather easily captured in this manner. I have found that this method works well with fledglings that are not yet able to fly, and with traps so wired that the adults cannot feed their young through the mesh.

Using these techniques, a bird student will often be able to band every bird of a given species in his neighborhood or in a given area. The chances for returns are enormously increased as a result. Even young birds, which year after year tend to settle short distances from their birthplace, can be recaptured in this manner. In studying the song sparrow, Mrs. Nice recaptured only 1.6 per cent of her fledgling birds in her garden, but by moving her small traps about the neighborhood, as new nesting pairs were located, she raised her recoveries of 1-year-old birds to 13 per cent. Here one sees the weakness of the immovable trapping station and the superiority of the specialist. Measured by returns, it would seem that one is about 8 times better than the other.

Concentration of banding on a fairly small population of birds requires some judgment in the selection of the most available species, and this naturally varies from one region to another. Some species, for instance, may breed in such considerable numbers that a single bander had best work in a relatively small area in order to trap all the adults. Time is always a factor in the field studies of laymen. The birds must be fairly accessible. Some years ago I set out to band all the adult Kentucky warblers nesting in south-eastern New York State. It was a nice problem: how does a species maintain itself in small numbers at the periphery of its range? Only 6 pairs, I believed, were involved. Of these, I only succeeded in banding 2, along with their broods. Time was lost not only in find-ing nests, but also in traveling to widely scattered localities. The papers published by banders conclusively demonstrate that the most interesting results are obtained with common species of birds. Banders as a class have no greater leisure than the average man, and very little is gained by rushing madly all over the country in a motor car.

Bird clubs have an especially good opportunity, however, to spread a network of banding over a fairly wide area. Since swallow nests are easily found, these lend themselves well to a carefully planned program of extensive banding. The rough-winged swallow, for instance, is often restricted to river valleys. In 1929, according to John B. May, only 21 colonies were known in New England, all of them in Massachusetts. It would be extremely interesting to band thoroughly all of those in a given region, like the Connecticut valley. Swallow banding is relatively easy, the adults being caught in an angler's net placed over the entrance to their nests when the young birds are being fed. Dayton Stoner used to average about 40 adult bank swallows per day.

Several other species of birds can be marked on a wholesale scale. Barn swallows, which at first might seem to be difficult sub-jects, can be readily caught on their nests at night. The barn doors should be closed on such occasions, and a certain amount of care exercised in returning the birds quietly to their nests. The young, of course, can be readily banded during the daytime.

Extensive banding by a bird club necessarily involves the careful mapping of nesting pairs in a given locality. If the species is a well-known one, country and rural newspapers are always glad to publicize such a project. One of the most interesting nesting species still awaiting large-scale banding is the chimney swift. In recent years, enormous numbers of these birds have been banded by members of the Tennessee Ornithological Society in areas where as many as 7000 migrants spend the night in a single chimney. In the nesting season, however, the opportunities for annual returns are much greater. Chimney swifts lay 4 to 6 eggs, are subject to but little predation, and I strongly suspect that they live much longer than other small birds. In Europe some almost incredible returns of swifts are already reported, some nesting birds being recaptured after a period of 10 years. A peculiarity of chimney swifts is a tendency for three birds to remain together as they forage for insects. This is so striking that it must have some significance, but only careful watching can eventually disclose the reason. Like the tree sparrows that Mrs. Baumgartner studied at Ithaca, swifts should lend themselves to special markings by means of colored feathers. All the birds in one chimney might be given red-colored plumes, those of a near-by chimney white-colored plumes, and so on. Banders who wish to study individual swifts in a small colony might possibly retain the identity of a few individuals in the air by cutting notches in those feathers of their wings called the primaries.

Color Marking—the Climax of Bird Banding

As banders began to concentrate their activities on a single species, their interest in the daily life of a bird grew accordingly. Some wanted to study the role of territory in bird life—how much of the time a breeding male remains in the area of his selection, what are the movements of female birds, and so on. The aluminum ring can give a permanent number to a bird in one's garden, but identity of the individual is usually limited to brief intervals in the trap. The uncertainties of trapping thus hamper all observations that depend for their value on the bird's freedom of movement. To overcome this, a new technique was developed. Various colored bands were arranged on the legs of birds, and their order and sequence used to give a field identity to each bird regardless of trapping.

With this final development, banding has thrown wide open the door to a new exploration of bird life. During the 1920's, contributions by bird banders emphasized new and better techniques of trapping. Today this trap is still necessary, but it is used sparingly and its importance is decreasing. From trapping, the emphasis has changed to watching.

Although celluloid bands were actually placed on penguins in the Antarctic near the beginning of this century, colored bands were not used extensively until the 1930's. Among the pioneers in this field were J. P. Burkitt and W. K. Butts. Working, I believe, as a county surveyor, and cut off in northern Ireland from stimulating contacts with well-read ornithologists, Burkitt produced some of the most remarkable papers on bird watching in the 1920's. Studying English robins, he would capture them in the field, take them home in his pocket, give each bird four bands, and release them at the point of capture. Burkitt found that his birds did not seek area for their territory as much as what we now call 'edge': each pair averaged 180 yards of hedge, or about 1.5 acres. In one year, 2 of his 9 males were unmated; in another year, 4 or 5 out of 13 failed to obtain a mate. These unmated males, he reported, sang steadily far into the summer, while song in the mated males declined with the progress of the first and second nesting.

As a graduate student at Cornell, Butts explored the various ways in which birds could be marked for field identification. He reported that colored celluloid bands are the most conspicuous and most permanent in field studies. These bands are now furnished by the Fish and Wildlife Service, and almost all modern studies of bird behavior rely on them. Black-capped chickadees, white-breasted nuthatches, black-crowned night herons, mockingbirds, and song sparrows have so far been studied in this manner. The limitations of the system depend on the length of a bird's leg (more bands can be carried by a heron than a sparrow) and the proximity with which the colors can be observed (red is conspicuous at fair distances, but in the field dark blue often appears black). Colored bands can be set on a bird's leg in various combinations, such as green over blue on the left leg and black over the metal band on the right. One bander, a young Long Island engineer named Frederick P. Mangels, has computed the number of combinations possible according to the number of bands used and the number of colors chosen. Counting the metal band of the Fish and Wildlife Service as a part of each combination, the possibilities are considerable:

Number of bands	Number of colors						
	1	2	3	4	5	6	7
2	6	12	18	24	30	36	42
3	12	48	108	192	300	432	588
4	10	80	270	640	1,250	2,160	3,430
5	6	90	486	1,536	3,750	7,776	14,406

Color marking is a great help in homing studies, since some birds cannot always be captured upon their return. Paints are useful up until the time a bird molts its feathers. Occasionally, however, too much has been applied too conspicuously . . . and the marked bird is driven away by its fellows! A very neat invention was once used on tree sparrows by Marguerite Heydweiller Baumgartner. In order to study her birds at a distance, this Cornell student glued colored feathers to her tree sparrows' tails. They could then be followed with considerable convenience. More recently, Richard Weaver, a Dartmouth ornithologist, added tail plumes to 350 purple finches when this species invaded Hanover, New Hampshire, by the thousands. All over New England, bird watchers were soon reporting these unusual migrants at their feeding stations.

Parallel development in bird study has centered around the marking of thousands of gulls with celluloid bands. On the Pacific coast, glaucous-winged, western, and California gulls have been ringed in colonies stretching from British Columbia to Mexico. On the Atlantic seaboard, over 20,000 herring gulls have been color-banded from Long Island Sound to the Gulf of St. Lawrence. In wholesale marking of this kind, each colony is given its own combination of colors and this is changed every year. As a result, the age and

TABLE 28

A BIRD CENSUS OF THE FUTURE

On December 23, 1939, 11 members of the Linnaean Society of New York made a new kind of bird census. Concentrating their observations on herring gulls in the general vicinity of New York City, they reported the exact birthplace of 59 birds and the exact year in which they had been born. The gulls wore combinations of colored bands which gave this information.

| Region of birth | Years hatched | | | Total | Actual colony |
	1937	1938	1939		
Quebec	1	1	..	2	St. Mary Islands
Quebec	2	3	4	9	Razades Islands
New Brunswick	6	9	6	21	Kent Island
Maine	..	2	..	2	Duck Islands
Maine	2	10	3	15	Muscongus Bay
Maine	2	..	..	2	Heron Islands
New Hampshire	..	..	3	3	Isles of Shoals
Massachusetts	1	1	1	3	Penikese Island
New York	1	1	..	2	Wicopesset Island
Total	15	27	17	59	

Condensed from *Proceedings of the Linnaean Society of New York.* 1940.

origin of every marked bird can be readily determined in the field. Fishermen, lightship keepers, and all kinds of bird students have recognized these interesting birds as they migrated. Fish docks have been the source of many such records. All that is necessary is to note carefully the color of the celluloid bands on the gulls' legs and write down at once the particular order in which they are placed, as for instance, blue over red, or black on one leg and yellow on the other, and so on. Should you ever see one of these birds in the West, record of the observation should be sent to Pacific Gull Project, Scripps Institute of Oceanography, La Jolla, California. Eastern records, which now number over 2000, are kept by Gull Survey, American Museum of Natural History, New York City, New York.

Colored bands can be used for all sorts of studies—territorial habits, the relation of song to weather and the nesting cycle, the social dominance of certain individuals in a winter flock, the share of the two sexes in incubating the eggs or feeding the young, and so on. Some banders have found it advisable not to place colored bands on young birds until they have returned and settled down as adults. Other banders think that a single red band helps them to locate young in another year. They have obviously found a new frontier to explore in bird life.

A Florida Odyssey

Of all the stories that have circulated about banders, I think I like best the one that Richard H. Pough tells about a Winnipeg banker, C. L. Broley. Mr. Broley is a modest man and only a few American ornithologists know his story. Some years ago this gentleman stopped in at the New York office of the National Audubon Society. Having retired at the age of 60, he was now on his way to spend the winter in Florida. To Mr. Broley, Pough (pronounced Poe) described a hawk-banding campaign that he was promoting throughout the country. Recoveries of banded hawks told many things to a conservationist: which species was most persecuted, where such birds were being shot, and so on. In Florida there were many bald eagles nesting. If Mr. Broley could find some local youth to climb to the nests, Pough would be glad to send some bands for the young eaglets.

Early in January, the gentleman from Manitoba made his first report. Ten bald eagles had been located near Tampa. If Mr. Pough would send some bands, he would see what he could do.

A few weeks later, Mr. Broley made his second report. Seven eagles had been banded; nine others were in sight, and more bands were suggested.

In a subsequent letter, the transplanted Canadian explained that he was putting the bands on himself. A weighted rope was first thrown over the lowest limb of a tree, and the actual ascent made by rope ladder. It was in climbing up and over the sides of the eagles' great nests that the greatest difficulties were encountered.

In some cases, great horned owls had driven off the nesting adults, eaten the young, and taken over the nest. To Mr. Pough, visions of a retired banker climbing those great pine trees were bad enough; the thought of horned owls in the vicinity was even worse. The ferocity of these birds is extremely variable. Mr. Pough warned his correspondent that the owls were 'bad actors.'

Undaunted, Mr. Broley continued his campaign. 'Today,' he eventually reported, 'a great horned owl nearly knocked me out of a tree. It struck me from behind and tore the right shoulder of my shirt off, leaving the mark of all 8 claws on my back and arm.' When the season ended, he had lost 15 pounds in weight, but he had ringed a total of 44 young eagles.

Within a few months, the recoveries of these banded birds began to raise the eyebrows of scientists. On May 8, one eagle was shot in the Hudson River valley, 1110 miles north. On May 30, another was killed on Chesapeake Bay, 760 miles from the point of banding. Only 58 eagles had been previously banded, but scarcely any movement like this had been suspected.

As time went on, Mr. Broley continued to concentrate on eagles. In 1940 he banded 73; in 1941, 79; and in 1942 the amazing total of 106. Between seasons he kept in good condition by chinning the bar frequently. Even a second encounter with an enraged owl, which struck him on the face, failed to daunt him. In his second year of banding, he began to utilize a 5½-foot iron hook to get over the overhanging edge of many nests. 'Climbing is now just commonplace,' he finally advised Mr. Pough. 'The more difficult the tree the more I enjoy it.'

His visits to scores of bald eagle nests have convinced Mr. Broley that these birds feed mostly on fish and that they richly deserve protection. One nest that he reached contained 20 large fish at the time of his visit. Others have held such interesting items as opossums, raccoons, eels, an odd duck, and a cormorant. Only once has he found poultry present. At another nest he was surprised to find the remains of two pelicans and two Ward's herons. One of his more exciting discoveries in one high nest seems to have been a nest of hornets. 'Had to descend in a hurry,' he reported laconically.

Watching eagles from a distance has helped Mr. Broley carry out his banding program with maximum efficiency. In 1942, he had 85 nests under observation, many of them in dead trees that were becoming more dangerous every year.

'It is not a comfortable feeling,' he now admits, 'to climb a rotten tree and have limbs breaking off under you right along. As long as the tree stands, I climb it. I have been relieved to find four or five of them blown down since last year and the birds established in a sound tree in the vicinity. Eagles become very attached to a certain locality. If they lose their tree, through lumbering or other reasons, they will foolishly risk an unsecure crotch for their nest rather than leave the spot. I have had two or three nests blown right out of such trees.'

With so many nests on his list, Mr. Broley keeps full records of their location and the date on which the birds begin incubation. Female eagles with eggs or very small young, he finds, sit low in their nests so that only their heads are visible to a bird watcher studying them from a distance with binoculars. Minor points like these help him decide when to return, climb to the nest, and band the young.

On one occasion, Mr. Broley writes in a letter, he was surprised to notice one of his eagles sitting low in her nest long after the normal period of incubation. It was Saturday afternoon, and he was taking a young friend in to Tampa.

'Jimmie,' said Mr. Broley, 'that bird has been sitting for five weeks. Her eggs must be bad. In a few days I will take them from her, or she will incubate them for perhaps two months.'

Just then, to his great astonishment, a young bird about six weeks old stood up in the nest. Although Jimmie, dressed in his only good suit of clothes, was impatient to get to the city, Mr. Broley felt that the tree should be climbed at once. In the nest he found two fine young eaglets, six or seven weeks old, and a bad egg half buried in the spanish moss.

'First time I have found what would be three eggs to a nest in Florida,' he reported down to Jimmie. Banding the young, he paused to pick up the egg—and found that it was only a white rubber ball. The long incubation period was now explained.

Looking over the nest, Mr. Broley saw Jimmie still intently watching the proceedings. 'Catch this rotten egg,' he called, and hurled the ball right at him. Jimmie's horrified back flip set an all-time Florida record.

Besides rubber balls, the eagles of Tampa adorn their nests with many other curiosities. Mr. Broley has found a powerful electric-light bulb, large 'conk' shells, a fish plug (probably arrived with a fish), a cob of hard corn, and large turtle shells. One nest contained a Clorox bottle and a clothes pin.

The recovery of these banded eagles has continued to be remarkable. A few were reported locally. Others were shot 350, 540, and 640 miles north. Once, in April, a bird turned up in Connecticut. Still others were reported in Quebec on May 11 and in New Brunswick on May 23. One was even shot on Prince Edward Island on June 1, some 1675 miles north and 3 months and 20 days after having been ringed as a fledgling.

The final story of this remarkable exploit in banding may not be available for years to come. As this is written, no birds have been recovered with a banding age of over six months. The new bald eagle Act of Congress will undoubtedly cut down on shootings, and some of these magnificent birds may live for years. Mr. Broley is not worried about that. For the 1942 season, war-bound Canada permitted him to leave its boundaries only because his work was scientific. As this is being written at the start of the banding period for 1943, Mr. Broley is more concerned about getting gasoline to cover his eyries. 'I feel that if I drop this work now,' he recently wrote to Mr. Pough, 'I may not resume it again. I am 63.'

How to Become a Bird Bander

The willingness of the Federal Government to underwrite the cost of bird bands has done much to make bird banding the hobby of the average citizen. Until fairly recently, British banders had to buy their own rings. I imagine that they were much more prudent in ringing fledglings as a result. Here in America the government budget for banding work has never been a large one, but officials have never turned down a bona fide request to trap birds for scientific purposes. It would require little effort to double the number of banders in the United States and Canada, but lack of funds has never encouraged authorities to work for such an expansion. Hence, in recent years, the number of bird banders here has usually fluctuated around 2000 persons. Most of these are laymen, and the amount of time they have for bird study varies widely. Some of the most famous banders have been women: Mrs. Margaret M. Nice in Ohio, Mrs. Mabel Gillespie in Pennsylvania, Mrs. F. C. Laskey in Tennessee, Mrs. Kenneth B. Wetherbee in New England, Mrs. Harold Michener in California, Mrs. Marie V. Beals in New York, and Mrs. F. M. Baumgartner now of Oklahoma. Their combined scientific papers would do credit to the staff of any museum or experimental station.

In order to trap wild birds for scientific purposes, the prospective bander usually must secure two permits. The first of these must be obtained from the Chief, Fish and Wildlife Service, Department of the Interior, Washington, D. C. The second is ordinarily obtained from the conservation department of the state where the banding is to be carried out. The chief prerequisite of banding has long been a knowledge of the identification of birds. Banders who do not know the difference between a cowbird and a grackle not only are unable to add to our knowledge of bird life, but they might actually contribute records of the most invalid nature. Such errors would impair the whole structure of facts that other banders have gradually compiled on bird life. To avoid this, the Government usually requires an applicant to present a letter of recommendation from at least one reputable ornithologist who knows the applicant and can vouch for him.

Another prerequisite, now increasing in importance, is the nature of the problem that the would-be bander intends to explore. If he is simply interested in banding fledgling robins or trapping birds at random, his net contributions to banding will be close to zero—and the filing of his all but worthless records an added expense to the Government.

To prospective banders who have no experienced ornithologists to help and guide them, my advice would be this: Learn first to identify all the common birds of your vicinity. They afford the best opportunities for bird watching. Start a nesting study of your own. A good deal of information about the habits of birds can be picked up by simple observation and note-taking on a single species. These things might include a complete account of the population's arrival in spring, a census of the breeding pairs, a map showing local nests, and a table showing the nesting success for both eggs and fledglings. A preliminary report containing observations of this kind sent to the Chief, Fish and Wildlife Service (Washington, D. C.), will do more to convince officials that you are a real student of bird life than the most commendatory letter from some naturalist (who, after all, might have been an old classmate of your father).

It has always been a surprise to me how many of our present banders restrict their thinking to traps and baiting techniques. Some seem to feel that if they can band more birds than they did last year they have done a good job. However commendable this ideal may be, it has its pitfalls. Birds may be banded with little hope of recovery, just to swell some annual total. Fifty birds accurately weighed and thoroughly examined for molt, deformities, and parasites, and *then* banded are worth 500 others ringed in promiscuous fashion and promptly forgotten.

No new bander should, I think, engage in this revolutionary type of bird watching without subscribing to *Bird-Banding,* an inexpensive but stimulating periodical, which was founded in 1930. For a number of years, this little magazine has consistently carried excellent abstracts of the literature of field ornithology. These have become a fountain head of ideas for bird watchers in North America, and the present volume owes much to their inspiration. The fact that only a fraction of our present bird banders now subscribe to this periodical is proof that the banding program in this country is still haphazard and carried on with little attention to the work of others.

In this chapter, I have tried to show that bird banding is one of the most important tools of the bird watcher. It offers a delightful opportunity to handle wild birds, and at the same time to check their ages, weights, ectoparasites, and plumages. More or less in a hit-or-miss fashion, it has added new pages to our books on bird migration, but its most impressive results are now coming from long-term studies of small populations of a single species. On a large continent like North America, nearly every species of bird has now been banded (as many as 443 kinds were ringed in 1939), but relatively few have been watched intensively. The spotlight of exploration can still be focused on common species, and a new insight into bird life awaits those who are enterprising and observ. ing.

CHAPTER SIX

The Art of Bird Watching

THE ART of bird watching has different meanings among different people. To some it is the art of identifying birds in the field, or of recognizing their songs year after year. This is the Field Card School of Ornithology, which measures success in terms of the rarity, the first migrant, and the big list. At its best it is a sport, testing the eye, the ear, and one's legs. At its worst, it is a mad rush to the next oasis, with birds ticked off on the run, and a great reliance placed on both gasoline and brakes. Birds are *scanned,* but it scarcely can be said that they are *watched*—especially when one has an eye incessantly searching for a rarity in the next tree.

Bird watching is much more than this. It is the art of discovering how birds live. Through it the naturalist can cross the frontier of knowledge and explore an unknown world. His reward is more than a mere check on a field card; although personal and intimate, it can still be a contribution to science.

Bird Study in the Past

Glancing back toward the past, one is impressed with the difficulties under which earlier bird students labored. Until fifty years ago naturalists scarcely dared to trust their own eyes, and the only safe method of recording a strange bird was to shoot it. No competent bird student was without his gun, and his cabinet of bird skins invariably dwarfed the size of his library. Until 1808 there was no American bird book that students could consult, and until 1850 no professional ornithologist to whom they could turn for advice. The center of the continent was still called the Great American Desert, and naturalists wishing to explore the West had to contend with the vicissitudes of Indian warfare.

Yet in spite of these difficulties, the foundations of bird study were laid firmly, piece by piece, and by many men. By 1781, 190 species of American birds had been described by the great Swedish botanist, Carl Linné (Linnaeus). In Philadelphia, at the beginning of the next century, a Scotch emigrant named Alexander Wilson began to gather all that was then known about American birds. A brilliant nephew of Napoleon began to place the birds of the country into a systematic and scientific order. By 1825, nearly all the eastern species had been discovered, and Audubon was exploring the swamps of Florida and the wild coasts of Labrador. Less than a decade later, the last great collecting expedition crossed to the Pacific. (On it, 15 new species were discovered.) Wilson and Audubon did more than describe new species. They set a tradition for bird study in America, a living tradition that inspires students to this day.

As the tide of civilization edged slowly across the Great Plains, there developed at least one safe way of traveling in the West— with the United States Army—and naturalists made the most of it. Many entered the Medical Corps, and at least 36 of them were sufficiently noteworthy to occasion a recent book of biographical sketches by Colonel Hume.* Of these, Elliott Coues was generally recognized by contemporaries as one of the most brilliant ornithologists of all time. The long introduction to his encyclopedic *Key to North American Birds,* described in the appendix, can still be read with profit.

As the nineteenth century progressed, American naturalists occupied themselves with a primary question: *what* and *where* are the birds of America? To answer this, they climbed mountains, crossed deserts, waded through swamps. New species were harder to find, but closer study revealed many new subspecies. The

---

* E. E. Hume. 1942. *Ornithologists of the United States Army Medical Corps.* Johns Hopkins Press, Baltimore. 583 pp.

handling of so many dead birds created special opportunities for other kinds of studies. Some naturalists took copious notes on the molts of birds. Others, in skinning their specimens, availed themselves of the chance to study anatomy. Still others worked on distribution and the compilation of county lists. Gradually, and with due regard to priority, each subspecies was baptized with its own scientific name. More museums began to spring up to house the growing collections. The dignified study of birds' eggs became a fad, was overdone, and largely dropped. In the 1890's bird photography attracted attention, although the first subjects literally and figuratively were lifeless and stuffed. The year 1910 saw the first of the enormous, superbly illustrated books on the birds of a given state, with local distribution now given in great detail and thousands of migration dates cited (generally of first arrivals). So much information had accumulated in a hundred years that state bird books sometimes spanned as many as four volumes.

Bird Study Today

Today the amateur naturalist is apt to look upon American ornithology with something of a bewildered eye. In universities he hears of students being trained in parasitology, in physiology, in ecology, and all the other 'ologies.' In the government agencies he sees experts devoting their full time to wildlife research. In the museums he sees attention turned to far-off places where scores of new subspecies can still be discovered. He hears vaguely of scientific expeditions, but he knows of none that have been made to his locality for generations.

Is it any wonder, then, that the student is led to regard bird study as a closed subject, and to believe that his own occupation with it must be confined to a simple compilation—for his own satisfaction only—of the birds he has noticed in his own locality?

Let no layman suppose for a moment that to him have been left the crumbs of ornithological exploration, and that in his region the last pages of his favorite science have been written. To the naturalist of today has been delegated a vast field that challenges every movement of his eye in the field. Bird study has always demanded a fresh point of view, but in every generation there are timid souls who forlornly decide that its possibilities have been exhausted.

'It is amusing,' writes E. M. Nicholson in *The Study of Birds,* to find an author of Yarrell's period (1784-1856) in what we should call the Dark Ages of Ornithology, apologizing for his work and merely venturing to hope that, everything of importance being already known, he had presented the subject in rather better arrangement than his forerunners. Ornithology, as a matter of fact, has hardly begun . . . What was venerated yesterday as the Alpha and Omega of the study of birds will be regarded tomorrow as a mere collector's handbook, giving without remarkable accuracy, the descriptions of species with their nests and eggs, the crudest account of their distribution and practically nothing else besides.'

It is not the scarcity of problems, but stringent financial restrictions that prevent government and private institutions from multiplying their professional staffs a hundredfold. The great mysteries of bird life still crowd our very doorsteps. We are still living in an age of wonder. We are still wondering about the exact relation of birds to their environment, about the mechanics of bird populations, about 'the migratory instinct,' about 'the homing instinct,' about 'the nesting instinct,' and about the whole pattern of behavior which makes birds so immensely fascinating to sophisticated *Homo sapiens.* These are the aspects of bird study still awaiting the laymen's enterprise. Perhaps an increasing number of professionals will enter these fields, but unquestionably the amateur's opportunities are almost unchallenged and virtually unlimited.

'I know, of late,' Robert T. Moore wrote some years ago in a publication of the Delaware Valley Ornithological Club, called *Cassinia,* 'there has been a tendency to belittle the chances of adding to the knowledge of birds of this region; to believe, because so much has been accomplished . . . that little is left for the younger generation. It is true that the searcher for new species will shoot in vain, that the blower of shells will note his consuming fad deprecated more and more, that the maker of mere lists will find his wares unsalable; but this merely means that the age of the indefatigable observer has arrived. The work of the past has been hardly more than fundamental. The structure of life histories has just begun . . . We have exhaustive studies of bird feathers; we have learned little of how they fly; we know much of throat mechanism, we know practically nothing of bird songs. The past, splendid as it has been, has not made effort useless; it has merely swamped out the main road in the wilderness, whose pleasant bypaths it shall be our duty to cut, and so reveal secrets unsuspected.'

Beginners in bird study seldom realize the rigidity that dominates the research of professional ornithologists. In the government agencies (many of which are entirely supported by the sale of hunting licenses) every effort is now directed toward the conservation and management of game species. In the museums, great world-wide collections of birds may wait for years before they can be classified and studied. Even to glance over a collection is no easy matter. Merely to inspect for only one minute each bird skin now at the American Museum of Natural History in New York City would require over five years. This would involve a 48-hour week, no vacations, and presumably the services of an endless belt transporting the specimens to one's desk.

The limited budgets of both public and private institutions virtually insure to the ordinary bird student a kind of public domain in the bird world that will be his to explore for years to come. He should not be awed by the weight of his state bird book. Part of it summarizes the accomplishments of previous generations, which had their own interests and their own problems. Books are seldom printed with blank pages to show the great gaps in our knowledge, and bird books are no exception.

Take a truly monumental work, *The Birds of Massachusetts*, and see just what is known about a common species. Here is an oriole, the Baltimore. Its feathers are described in detail, its measurements are added, and summaries are given of its molt, range, distribution, habitat, nest, eggs, incubation, voice, haunts, and habits. Has anything been left for the layman to discover? These call notes and alarm notes—just when are they given? How do the birds react to blue jays, to cowbirds, to red squirrels, and to cats? Does singing decline when the male secures a mate, or does it continue unabated until eggs are laid? Does the male have a territory that he defends against other male Baltimore orioles? Does he exclude orchard orioles from his territory? How large is the actual territory? Does the male patrol its boundaries or does he have irregular singing perches? Does he forage for food in all of the territory or just in part of it?

These are simple questions that can be answered by simple observations. Other questions, more complex, require more elaborate studies. In courtship the male is said to display his 'gorgeous' colors before the 'admiring' eyes of the female. Can we honestly say 'admiring'? What would happen if we dyed the male's colors a dirty gray? Would she still 'admire' him?

These embrace but a few aspects of one species' life. They invite backyard bird study. They require no motor cars. They do demand careful note-taking, the keenest sort of observation, and the clearest kind of thinking. They are so many *minutae* in themselves. Yet the underlying questions involve elementary concepts in zoölogy. What is the function and use of bright colors and fine songs in bird life? Have these evolved as a means of sexual selection? Does their primary function serve to advertise territorial possession by the male and to warn intruding birds against trespass? Or are they used as recognition marks between the sexes of each species?

The Student and His Bird Club

The average bird student may be overwhelmed by a barrage of such questions. His handicaps are clearly apparent. He is out of doors, for instance, only on week ends. He enters the field with little or no technical training. He has but the scantiest knowledge of the fascinating literature of his subject. He has no ready access to current periodicals except by personal subscription. No wonder he sees little of significance in the behavior and exact distribution of the most common species. No wonder he holds firmly to his one bit of knowledge, identification, and keeps on compiling his county or regional list.

The task of orientation in the complexity of modern bird watching can be simplified by a well-organized program in a local bird club. Bird clubs have responsibilities that individuals do not. It is a bird club's task to serve as a medium for the dissemination of our present knowledge of bird watching. It is a bird club's duty to promote the scientific study of the ornithological features of its own local region, the behavior and interrelationships of both its common and its rare species, and especially the intensive classification of its own local habitats.

It is a common mistake to assume that the layman has no ambition in his hobby. Beneath his early pursuit of the 'life' bird and the rarity there already lies a sense of dignity for his efforts. How else can one explain the journals that nearly all bird students seem to have? It is this sense of the dignity of bird study that forms the basis for contributions to ornithology by the amateur. He may dislike having to rush and arrive at his office by 9 A.M., but he enthusiastically arises an hour before dawn to wade with wet feet in a mosquito-ridden marsh. He often produces notebooks dating back 20 years.

It is an oft-repeated complaint that the great problems of field ornithology must be given back to the professionals because business commitments permit only week-end birding. Government men are often months afield, it is true. Yet this great group largely confines itself to game birds, and many of its members have no opportunity to settle down in one region. How many museum men have you met who, like Thoreau, had an office in the woods? How many university instructors can you name who do not have classes? By and large, we can safely say that protracted field work comes to one only as vacation time. Amateurs and professionals are all in the same boat. It is just that some have longer vacations than others.

The problems of bird study and the course of its progress are chronicled in English in about ten periodicals of national and international circulation. Every student would relish looking through one of these each week. But how many can? Here and there reference libraries are open to the public, but many are closed on evenings, holidays, and week ends, when businessmen would like to visit them. The layman, faced with the task of earning a living, must absorb ideas for his hobby more or less on the run. The prized state volumes on his own shelf of bird books emphasize accomplishments of the past, while on problems of the present and the near future they are all too often noncommittal. They are dedicated to the variety of species, and when and where you may find them.

But beyond this all-important introduction to bird study, they yield to the periodicals the inspiration for new ideas in bird watching.

Happily enough, bird magazines are fairly inexpensive in price. To buy all of them, however, is not always practical; but by donations and annual subscriptions it is extremely easy for bird clubs to build up circulating libraries of immense inspirational value. Where budgetary considerations are of the utmost importance, a club's expenses can be reduced to a minimum by having different members subscribe to different publications and then, after they have read them, donate each issue to the club library. Another useful plan is to have frequent meetings given over to reviews by members of interesting articles on bird watching.

The layman can still indulge in any aspect of bird study that suits his fancy. He can watch a bird roost, or a migration highway, a pair of birds building a nest, or young birds learning to fly. Limited as he is in his week-end field work, he is limited in his reading time as well. He should skim through many papers and concentrate on mastering only a few. Much of the fun in bird study and the solution of its problems jointly depend upon eyes that know what to see, upon a knowledge of what has already been done, upon common species of birds, upon intensive studies of small tracts of land, and upon a corps of observers working together in a common purpose. He should realize also the tremendous significance of two great and relatively recent milestones in field ornithology. One of these, the development of bird banding, at last permits the comprehensive study of the individual bird (in one's own backyard if necessary); the other, the recognition of the function and use of territory in bird life, forces the rewriting of the life histories of nearly all our most familiar species. The student can write a footnote to the science of bird study; his bird club can write even a chapter.

Opportunities to Explore Bird Life

The field exploration of bird life today might be said to fall into three main channels: life-history studies, regional studies, and special problems. This is by no means a perfect classification but it does outline three important ways by which bird watchers can approach the subject. In the first category the emphasis is laid on a single species, its breeding cycle, its migration, its winter life, its behavior. In the second, observations are broadened out to include all birds, but the center of focus is a single region. In the third, field work is concentrated on some one problem, like the molts of gulls, or the diseases of songbirds, or the food of owls.

LIFE-HISTORY STUDIES

A life-history study is an attempt to work out the complete story of a bird's life. In the past many writers have felt that this could be summed up in a page or two. Today many naturalists regard the subject as large enough to require an entire book for a single species. There are many reasons for this change in attitude. Birds are now known to possess great individuality. To draw adequate conclusions about the life of a given species, it is best to observe a large population (if that is possible) instead of but a pair or two. This permits better averages to be calculated for the number of eggs laid, the percentage of infertility, the number of eggs that hatch, and the number of young that fledge. It also lends greater significance to conclusions drawn on bird behavior, homing, longevity, and similar matters.

Outside of the government agencies and universities, most life-history studies have been started more or less fortuitously. Bird banders have often found themselves ringing more of one species than of others. Records of returns arouse their curiosity and banders enlarge the scope of their observations. They watch the fighting of the males, the displays in courtship, the share of the sexes in incubation, and other details of bird life. In the end, they have a concentrated mass of information that may cover one species' entire life story.

Partly because so many of our birds are only summer residents, complete life-history studies are fairly rare. Nesting studies, on the other hand, are becoming increasingly popular. This is owing, I think, to three fairly recent developments in bird watching. The first of these, the rise of bird banding, has already been discussed in Chapter 5. The second is the recognition of the use of territory in bird life. The third is a new desire to obtain exact statistics on population-turnover in birds.

The present significance of territory is rooted in an important oversight that Charles Darwin, the famous English naturalist, made nearly a century ago. In studying the effect of evolution on bird life, Darwin found it easy to explain the somber colors of birds like the sparrows. In the struggle for existence, these had benefited by protective coloration. But the beautiful song of the nightingale and the startling colors of the male peacock were quite another matter. Darwin finally decided that these had evolved through sexual selection year after year: the female birds had selected the finest males. This seemed like a logical explanation, but only one or two naturalists were subsequently able to support it with actual observation in the field. Other naturalists more or less accepted Darwin's theories.

About 1920 Eliot Howard, an English businessman, convinced the scientific world that—among other things—song is used by the male bird to warn other males of the same species against invasion of its territory. A whole new field of bird watching opened up as a result. It is now suspected that some colors in birds may be warning colors, since they advertise the presence of a male to his rivals. It is not impossible, of course, that these colors may serve dual functions. Hence, in each species, the closest attention to displays should be given. Variations in the size of territories have already been discussed in connection with food and foraging distances (Chapter 4). This relatively recent acceptance of the territory theory by ornithologists now permits new and original observations on the behavior of hundreds of species in North America.

Nesting studies also furnish an important insight into the mechanics of bird populations, and form a basis essential to the understanding of many conservation problems. Valuable contrasts in population characteristics can be made between common and rare or vanishing species. Carefully planned banding can eventually determine the average life expectancy of adult birds for most species, but many nests will have to be checked before one can determine how many eggs must be laid to produce a single adult. In the song sparrow, often quoted as the most thoroughly studied

bird in America, little is yet known of the relative importance
of each brood of the season in the composition of next year's population of adults. Other questions that can be attacked in a nesting
study are listed in the appendix.

Life-history studies by the amateur are obviously a matter of
convenience. They are best conducted on a common species, especially one that can be conveniently trapped, color banded, observed every week end and, if possible, at odd moments throughout
the week. The time necessary for such field work varies greatly,
according to the species involved and the detail with which it is
investigated. During 1938, Mrs. A. R. Laskey carried on a nesting
study of 36 pairs of bluebirds scattered in boxes along 12 miles
of roadside in a suburban park of Nashville, Tennessee. Complete
notes on three nestings required, she reports, 45 visits between
late February and mid-August (about twice a week). After brooding started three- or four-hour trips in the field resulted in the
successful capture on their nests of all the adult females, as well as
the ultimate banding of all the young. Dr. Lawrence H. Walkinshaw, a Michigan dentist, has mentioned in one of his excellent
nesting studies of the prothonotary warbler that his field work was
carried out on Thursdays.

Housewives will doubtless minimize their opportunities to make
nesting studies of backyard birds, but the greatest life history of
a songbird ever completed stands to the credit of a Columbus,
Ohio, woman who was raising five children. Her report, a monograph on the song sparrow, should be read by every life-history
student. It is described in the appendix.

Nesting studies are usually carried out over a two- or three-year
period. During the first year, skills in such matters as nest finding
often have to be developed. Occasionally it is found that the study
was begun too late in the season and that important elements of
the bird's courtship had been missed. Not infrequently, the student
simply lacks the ability to see and record quickly the many things
a bird is doing. It is always best to *note down at once all details,
regardless of their seeming unimportance.* A half hour later they
may otherwise be forgotten. At the end of the season, minor details
often assume considerable importance.

Amateur naturalists who consider their week-end opportunities too limited for nesting studies often overlook an interesting fact about professional wildlife research in this country. Already concentrated on game species, many of these studies are further restricted under Pittman-Robertson funds to definite three-year periods. Only rarely are such projects renewed and the same biologists permitted to continue for another three years. In the university field, graduate students are also compelled to complete their studies in as short a time as possible. As a result, the amateur occupies a singular position of advantage: despite his inability to be daily afield, he can conduct long-term studies to an extent that is impossible under professional conditions. He is under no pressure to publish work that is incomplete. He can pick any bird to work on that he chooses. He can, if he wishes, produce a monograph, and bring his name into permanent association with that of a given species.

REGIONAL BIRD STUDIES

One of the commonest forms of bird study centers around the bird life of a given region. In most bird clubs this is the principal form of bird watching, and many clubs have an officer charged with the responsibility of collecting the random notes of members on this subject. Sometimes these are recorded only because they are easy to record; only occasionally is emphasis given to the actual gaps in our knowledge of regional bird life. In many bird clubs, members are still reporting only the first spring migrants, after the manner of the last generation. The theme has become overworked and, bored by the repetition, the older members drop out. Club officers wonder why their membership exhibits such a turnover.

Regional bird life may be considered according to the spring migrants, the breeding birds, the fall migrants, and the winter bird population. In most localities these exhibit tremendous differences both in the kinds of species and in total numbers, but in very few regions have all four received equal attention. In many parts of the West, the adjustment of birds to wet and dry seasons offers a parallel problem that still requires study.

Many migration watchers have their favorite study areas but they often tend to drop their intensive watching soon after they have witnessed the peak of the migration. A good migration study would endeavor to show the migration classes in each species: the vagrant birds, the resident birds that immediately take up territory, the transients that rather silently pass through, the percentages of males and females, the status of stragglers, and in the fall the numbers of young. These groupings undoubtedly vary among different species and in different regions, but the degree of variation has yet to be established.

A number of interesting migration studies are linked to species that are known to possess geographic races. The order in which these subspecies migrate through a given locality is often unknown, and it sometimes can only be established by collecting representative samples of the birds encountered. In a recent letter, Dr. Jean M. Linsdale reminds me that this is especially important on the Pacific coast. To a lesser extent this is true for a few subspecies in the East. Every region should have a collector to work out such problems as collecting can still settle, and every effort made to see that the specimens go to a museum of repute. The glass has undoubtedly replaced the gun in the esteem of the last generation, but it can never completely substitute for it in all problems of identification.

Breeding populations offer an especially fine opportunity for field work. Shall we call our local birds common or uncommon, and let it go at that? Or shall we work out their distribution and numbers in detail? How much detail?

'What would the present-day New England naturalist give,' wrote Dr. Glover M. Allen a few years ago, 'if he might have an accurate picture of the conditions here 300 years ago. Forbush's wonderful volumes on the habits and history of New England birds show only too clearly how little record we have of birds in Massachusetts, even so recently as three generations since. It is evident that a clear record of current conditions must now be kept for the benefit of those who will in future find it useful.'

Many other ornithologists have advocated this policy. Periodically at Linnaean Society meetings in New York, I have heard the late Charles A. Urner maintain that we should leave to our successors the most exact picture possible of our local bird life.

There are many ways to do this. The breeding records of all uncommon species can be mapped and their habitats described in detail. Counts of colonial birds can be made from year to year. Maps can also be worked out showing the predominant plant types that influence the distribution of local birds today. In each of these types, censuses can be taken to determine the density of breeding birds and wintering species. I know of only one region—around Cleveland, Ohio—where quantitative work on local habitats is being systematically pursued. There, the Kirtland Bird Club and the Cleveland Museum of Natural History have been conducting breeding-bird censuses on climax forests, fields, second-growth timber, suburban areas, and many other types of local environment. This is not a short-term program, but neither is bird watching an ephemeral hobby.

In late summer and fall, the dates and movements of migrating birds are much less known than those for transients in spring. Not only can separate arrival and departure records be kept for both male and female birds, but important data on immature birds can also be recorded. What, for instance, is the ratio of old birds to young? The value of the latter information is well recognized today by game managers, but the possibilities for other species have scarcely been touched.

From late summer on, communal bird roosts can also be mapped, their flyways determined, and the numbers of birds counted from time to time. Many roosts are so located that the foraging area about each of them can also be ascertained. In this way an overall density of the birds can be worked out, and comparisons made with other regions. The same density would give a picture of local bird life that would be of great value to future observers in the same region.

Winter birds offer equally good opportunities for exploration. For over 40 years *Audubon Magazine* (née *Bird-Lore*) has been publishing Christmas bird counts. These have furnished an admirable insight into the *variety* of bird life in many regions, but almost nothing is yet known about actual winter *densities*. Since in winter birds forage fairly extensively, study areas of 100 or 200 acres are advisable.

Some winter birds lend themselves readily to weekly or biweekly counting. Such regular counts make it possible to study population decreases over this very critical period in the lives of birds. 'Winter kill' in some upland game birds has been found to reach 50 or 60 per cent. In the song sparrows studied by Mrs. Nice in Ohio, the winter loss of breeding males ran as high as 26 per cent between October and April. The subject of winter losses has received much attention from research workers on game species but has scarcely been touched in connection with songbirds in North America.

In itself, any one aspect of life-history work or regional bird watching might be called a special study. A great many of the scholarly papers now published about birds fall into one or the other of these two broad fields. Sometimes, however, the exploration of bird life crosses the boundaries of many regions or touches the lives of many species. The investigation of hawk migration in the Appalachians now stretches across many states and concerns many species. Monographs have been written on the molts of birds, their incubation, and their food. Banders can work on the weights of birds, their plumages, parasites, and deformities. A very worthwhile study could be built around the ratio of males to females—beginning, say, with one species and eventually carrying it out through many species. Sex ratios can be worked out for different seasons and for different years. They can be studied for adult birds and even for fledglings. The ubiquitous English sparrow is potentially the guinea pig of the bird world, since hundreds can be collected for large-scale biological investigations. One bander I know kills over 1500 every year, but makes no effort to record their sex, their weights, their ages, or their external parasites. Few of us like the sparrow, but no one should waste a scientific opportunity like that to record a mass of data.

Special studies have this advantage: by extending his observations over a large number of species and by concentrating on one aspect of their lives, the bird watcher can obtain a broad picture of bird biology that is extremely revealing. There is almost no limit to the number of topics. Song, territory, courtship, nest building, care of the young, persistence of the family flock, and use of roosts are a few that come to mind. Other questions can be found in the outline for a life-history study given in the appendix.

Co-operative Bird Watching

Although bird watching is often the most individualistic of occupations, it also embraces a wealth of opportunity for co-operative exploration. This approach to the study of natural history involves something more than two anxious and intent naturalists stalking a nervous bird from opposite sides of a bush. It is the welding together of diverse talents in a field study of bird life. Very roughly, it might be said to comprise research partnerships and organized inquiries.

RESEARCH PARTNERSHIPS

A simple but well-established partnership now exists between field men and laboratory workers. The opportunity for bird banders to secure the assistance of parasitologists has already been mentioned. In the past, bird watchers have been slow to appreciate the dramatic stories back of studies in bird parasitology, and to realize their great opportunities for furthering our knowledge of this very important field.

The life histories of bird parasites demonstrate some of the most complex and fascinating interrelations found in nature. Their exploration involves detective work far beyond anything Sherlock Holmes ever attempted. Many birds pick up external parasites in their food. In one species, liver parasites of prairie dogs develop into intestinal tapeworms when their hosts are eventually eaten by hawks. Reproduction in this simple cycle takes place in the hawk; segments of the worm containing eggs are passed out in the feces to reinfect more prairie dogs—and, of course, more hawks.

Snails are often an intermediate host for another type of parasite called the fluke. Adult worms of this type are known to inhabit the mouths of great blue herons. The unworried heron swallows the eggs of the parasite and these pass out with the feces. From the eggs, swimming forms hatch and infect snails. In the snails, burrowing forms of the parasite develop and then leave their intermediate host. They are next found on the skin of fishes as small yellow grubs. Their last step, to the mouths of the herons, is obvious.

It should be clear that bird watchers can share in the complicated task of solving many riddles in parasitology. Bird banders with trapping stations are in an extraordinarily fine position to detect (external) ectoparasites on adult birds. Every nestful of young offers an equally interesting opportunity. The lining of the nest can be examined, the ears and soft parts of the fledglings carefully noted, and a thorough search made of the young birds' skin and feathers. Fleas, ticks, mites, and lice are a few of the curious animals birds may carry externally. These can be readily preserved in small vials of 70 per cent alcohol obtainable at one's local drugstore. Although tens of thousands of young herring gulls have been banded, I am told by Dr. B. B. Morgan that relatively little is yet known about their parasites.

Another great group in which new species can still be named and life cycles worked out in detail comprises the (internal) endoparasites. Research on many of these creatures has long been impeded by the lack of wild birds available for autopsy and dissection. Bird watchers are often in a position to make specimens available. 'Vermin' campaigns—however inexcusable—occasionally result in wholesale killings of crows, magpies, hawks, herons, and kingfishers. Such birds can be examined for bands and external parasites. Fresh specimens can often be packed in dry ice and shipped to near-by parasitologists. Along the ocean beaches, excellent opportunities are present to collect birds that have recently died of some disease. Many scientific agencies are only too willing to receive such specimens (in the right condition) and to identify the parasites present. The importance of these to public health has been recognized more and more in recent years, but a vast amount of work remains to be done on the subject. Endoparasites can always be sent for identification to the Bureau of Animal Industry, Department of Agriculture, Washington, D. C.

Other research partnerships can be worked out with botanists, entomologists, mammalogists, and others, who are carrying out field work in the bird watcher's own region. Association with specialists like these inevitably broadens the ornithologist's point of view and increases his knowledge and enjoyment of nature. It can occasionally be climaxed by research partnerships of the greatest value. Botanists can often furnish vital information on plant succession and help in the local mapping of various habitat types. Entomologists might be willing to help in the study of the insect food of birds and the relation of insect densities to breeding-bird densities. Mammalogists often find their paths crossing ornithologists' when their study of rodent populations necessitates visits to owl roosts and an examination of owl pellets. One extremely useful type of project is the censusing of all the animals, vertebrate and invertebrate, on study areas. This, of course, can best be conducted near university towns and large cities, where many specialists of diverse types are apt to be present.

Another type of partnership still awaits organization. This involves the field worker who has neither the time nor the patience to publish his observations, and some other naturalist who would assume the responsibility of preparing the field notes for publication. I believe that many excellent papers could be printed on bird watching if more amateur naturalists could receive help in writing up their observations. Professional ornithologists are often only too glad to help the amateurs when they can, but many businessmen seem to feel that the writing up of their notes is an activity that can be taken up after they retire, or when their physician tells them they are no longer physically able to take to the field. This personal utopia is seldom realized and many excellent observations die with the naturalist. The journals and field diaries that are left behind are too cryptic and too illegible to become anything but sentimental symbols of contributions to natural history that are lost forever.

Many young bird watchers would also profit from a partnership that would insure the publication of their observations in a professional manner. Competent partnerships in publication would, I think, tend to emphasize the most important aspects of the field work completed, and capitalize both on the technical background and the extensive reading of the senior author. With both writer and field worker appearing as joint authors, responsibility and credit would not be exaggerated.

ORGANIZED INQUIRIES

Bird watching can often be divided into intensive and extensive studies. The former include field work carried out in relatively small areas, such as those emphasized in this book. The latter involve the compilation of data from a large or extensive area, and usually require field notes or reports from a number of observers. Situations of this kind usually can be met by organized inquiries.

Inquiries are not new in North America, although we are now rapidly falling behind British bird watchers in such activities. During 1884 and 1885, 170 observers pooled their migration records in the Mississippi valley to give a picture of bird migration that is still quoted today. Wells W. Cooke, who organized this co-operative study, later inaugurated (in 1914) a remarkable series of breeding-bird censuses, chiefly on farm lands through the United States. Some of these counts covered a five- to ten-year period, but the project died a premature death in the 1920's. Another series of breeding-bird censuses was initiated in 1937 by William Vogt in *Bird-Lore* (now *Audubon Magazine*). About 30 to 40 bird watchers contribute to this every year from all over America.

Most organized inquiries are on a much smaller scale. Usually a questionnaire is sent out and some kind of follow-up instituted. In this way, Robert P. Allen has mapped the black-crowned night heronries of Long Island, and J. T. Emlen, Jr., the winter crow roosts of California and New York. A particularly interesting questionnaire was one sent out in 1926 by the Royal Ontario Museum of Zoölogy. This inquiry aimed to gather up fragmentary data on passenger pigeons in the province. It ultimately resulted in an excellent study of this extinct species by Margaret H. Mitchell.

Questionnaires among English bird watchers are now an accepted way of gathering scattered information about birds. Inquiries have been used to bring out new facts about the great crested grebe, swallow nestings, the populations of a heron, the food of an owl, and the habitats of a plover. Begun by *British Birds,* an excellent monthly magazine devoted to bird watching, these inquiries have been continued by the British Trust for Ornithology, a private organization set up to co-ordinate bird-watching activities in the United Kingdom.

Organized inquiries have also been successfully used by the Bureau of Animal Population (at Oxford University) as a means of gathering information about cycles in the Canadian Arctic. They can readily be adapted to canvass the members of a single bird club, a series of bird clubs, an entire state, or many states. Many of these co-operative studies in Britain have been based on the reports of 50 to 100 or more observers. In my experience, Canadians are definitely more co-operative than Americans in such affairs, so that the method of questionnaires in the United States must be used with caution. The number of questions should be few, perhaps four or five is enough. A good idea, passed on to me by Robert A. McCabe, is to give the correspondent several squares or boxes in which he can merely check off his answer.

Double postcards are one inexpensive way of instituting a widespread inquiry. (These can usually be multigraphed for not more than a dollar per hundred.) They might be used to locate communal roosts of birds and colonial nesting sites, and to check the bird populations there from year to year. They would be useful in roughly determining the numbers of winter birds like the rough-legged hawk, the horned owl perhaps, the northern shrike, and so on. Each bird club could probably support some venture of this kind from year to year—and in the course of a decade make a sizable contribution to our knowledge of bird life.

Bird Watching by the Layman

Amateur naturalists consider successful bird watching to be simply the effective use of their spare time. Birds have been studied under all kinds of conditions. Railroad travelers have made cross-country counts of birds, and motorists have furnished most of the facts now known about the speed of bird flight. There is one story of a soldier who was always volunteering for lookout duty in the crow's nest of a troop transport crossing the Atlantic. More sea birds than submarines were seen by Lester L. Walsh on that trip, but somehow the vessel got through. Less known is the story of the biologist who noticed flickers courting and nesting outside his window. In the end a very interesting paper on the behavior of these birds was published in *The Auk*. Although the observations here were daily in character, each lasted but a brief period. They were made, for the most part, while Dr. G. K. Noble was shaving —apparently with a safety razor.

The art of bird watching is based on some knowledge of what should be recorded about bird life. Only occasionally may it involve the spectacular. 'The invariable mark of wisdom,' Emerson once said, 'is to see the miraculous in the common.' I have found that the pleasure of being in the field has increased with my reading of bird books and periodicals. Flushed with new ideas about what others have seen, I constantly see possibilities of making parallel discoveries about other species. There are some naturalists who believe that reading does not enhance their powers of observation. 'I have heard a man say,' wrote President Van Hise of the University of Wisconsin many years ago, ' "I observe the facts as I find them, unprejudiced by any theory." I regard this statement as not only condemning the work of the man, but the position as an impossible one.'

'Speculation and theory are not always mischievous or futile,' E. P. Bicknell once pointed out. 'At the threshold of an unstudied subject they often have the effect of stimulating investigation and giving direction to research.'

Without having some idea of what other naturalists have found, the student is certain to miss many of the subtle things that are constantly happening in bird life. Suppose, in watching a pair of robins feeding their young, he notes in his journal:

> 10:23 male came to nest with food, paused, fed nestlings,
> and left at 10:24
> 10:29 female fed the young
> 10:35 male back with more food.

Is this all that took place? Some adults are said to approach their nests by routes that are invariably the same. Did these robins have different routes, or the same routes? How many young were fed at each feeding? Did the adult bird feed the nearest mouth or the

TABLE 29

HANDBOOK INFORMATION STILL WANTED ON NORTH AMERICAN BIRDS

No *complete* handbook has ever been compiled for North American birds. One reason is this: some of the most elementary facts about our native bird life have yet to be recorded by bird watchers. The approximate status of this information today is shown in the table below. The perfect handbook will some day give all these data for every species of bird in North America—only if bird watchers record their observations in nationally accessible publications.

C = complete   FC = fairly complete   I = incomplete

Plumage descriptions

color of soft parts	FC
weights	I
other measurements	C
molts	FC
field marks	C
feathers	C

Voice

significance of calls and songs	I
factors affecting song	I
song period	I

Nesting habits

relation of substrate to nests	I
role of sexes in nest building	I
size and color of eggs	C
manner and dates of laying	FC
period of incubation	I
role of sexes in incubation	I
rhythm (if any) in incubation	I
length of fledgling period	I
duration of family flock	I

Habitats

use of singing perches (if any)	I
food relationships	I
use of cover	I
relation to water	I
effect of edge	I
relation to soils and forest types	I
place in successions	I
relation to land use	I

roosting sites	I
size of foraging area according to season	I
type and size of territories	I

Population characteristics

average number of eggs in clutch	FC
number of clutches and broods	I
percentage of infertility	I
average number of eggs that hatch	I
average number of young that fly	I
percentage that die at each age	I
life expectancy	I
local densities recorded	I
sex ratios	I

Migratory habits

diurnal or nocturnal migrant	C
principal local migration routes	I
average arrival dates for local males, females, and immatures	FC
average arrival dates for transients of same species	I
effect of winds and temperature on migration	FC

Parasites

internal	I
external	I
diseases carried	I

highest mouth? Some young birds are said to extend their mouths straight upward for a certain number of days and thereafter direct their open mouths toward their parent. Which were these baby robins doing? Will all the young birds develop the second kind of response on the same day, and at much the same time? In these *minutae,* the naturalist can ascertain the habits of birds and the maturation of instinctive behavior.

In 1937 the Linnaean Society of New York informed its members that over 20 species of birds, which bred in that region, had unknown or uncertain incubation periods. It was rather surprising to see what birds made up this list. Some of them were relatively common in that region; others were common only in other regions.

King rail	Black-throated blue warbler
Piping plover	Black-throated green warbler
Willet	Pine warbler
Black skimmer	Kentucky warbler
Rough-winged swallow	Hooded warbler
Tufted titmouse	Canada warbler
White-breasted nuthatch	Savannah sparrow
Brown creeper	Grasshopper sparrow
Winter wren	Henslow's sparrow
Blue-gray gnatcatcher	Sharp-tailed sparrow
Parula warbler	Seaside sparrow

Within two months of publication of this list, one member of the Society determined the incubation period of the parula warbler and the black-throated green; another approximated that of the Florida gallinule. In a few more months, I suppose, the list was largely forgotten. Yet this little reminder had helped close two small gaps that had existed in the biology of birds for years.

Bird watching is obviously a matter of seizing available opportunities. All too often the naturalist spends hours traveling back and forth from some 'ideal' study area which he can only reach with considerable difficulty on week ends. A much more convenient area near by may sometimes be less aesthetically satisfying in its vegetative cover, but, if it contains birds that can be watched for a half hour each day, in the long run it will probably yield more concrete and new facts about bird life.

On Publishing Observations

Bird students have long been noted for their confused notions on how and where their observations should be published. Perhaps this is inevitable in a field containing so many scattered devotees of varying shades of experience. The problem is well worth the attention of every bird watcher.

One of the commonest ideas among beginners is that every observation is important and should be brought to the attention of others. This exaggerated idea makes for two hardships: on the one hand, the older and more experienced naturalists are forced to listen to interminable tales of unimportant migrants; on the other, editors are flooded with accounts of allegedly exciting rarities. For the most part, the older ornithologists accept these burdens philosophically, remembering their own excitement and their own youthful questions. Yet they also know of the many bird books that have already been written. To be unaware of local migration data that have already been compiled is an increasingly inexcusable ignorance in this day of public libraries. When a rare bird is to be reported, its status should be checked against all available sources of information. Records that change the status of a bird as given in the *A.O.U. Check-List* might well be published in *The Auk*. Lesser rarities should be reserved for more local publications, or sent in to one of *Audubon Magazine*'s regional editors of 'The Season.' These reports should always be concise and to the point.

A number of bird clubs now keep the lists of their regions up to date by putting out mimeographed magazines or even more pretentious publications. These serve a very commendable function by preserving purely local observations in one place, and by leaving to the national organizations the task of publishing articles of national interest. This would be a happy situation in bird study if the officers of each bird club could retain their sense of perspective. Not infrequently, however, important papers are printed in periodicals of very limited distribution. This not only makes for bibliographical difficulties among professional ornithologists, but it also strangles the development of amateur naturalists in other regions. I have known many bird watchers whose life-long interest in their hobby dates from reading a single article or a single book. My own absorption stems from a book by an Englishman and a paper on a Greenland bird in a Dutch periodical.

The future of bird watching obviously depends on the accessibility of its results. Many bird clubs can contribute to the common good by helping to support the national periodicals and by keeping their own local publications reduced to a minimum. Sometimes papers are written that are of interest both regionally and nationally. When these are published in organs like *The Auk, The Condor, The Canadian Field-Naturalist, Bird-Banding,* and *The Wilson Bulletin,* reprints can readily be purchased by a bird club and redistributed to the membership. Decorative line drawings with the club's name can even be added by a local printer at a small cost. An increasing number of organizations are now finding reprints a useful way of simplifying their budgets and of making better known the work of their members. The cost differentials can be seen in this example. In one eastern city, a local bird club has been printing an annual publication (circulation about 250) at a cost of $3 a page. An equal number of reprints from some national periodical like *The Auk* (circulation 1500) would cost the club $1 a page for a paper of average length. Should this club restrict the more important researches of its membership to its own essentially local publication? Does it owe anything to bird watching throughout America? If it has an ample budget for publications, should it use the reprint method and make an added financial contribution to the national periodical that publishes the work of its members? The officers of every bird club should face these questions. In times of economic depression, they become especially important.

In writing his observations for a scientific periodical, the bird student has the satisfaction of making a contribution to knowledge. Having profited by the birdlore of past generations, he pays a debt by passing on to future generations his own experiences. To write a scientific note or a scientific paper is not easy. Neither can be dashed off like a letter; for each superfluous word ultimately is costly to print and time-wasting to read. A short note in a scientific journal can be a work of art, condensed and polished, with not a single wasted word. The aim of the writer should be a communication giving all the pertinent facts in the shortest possible space. I believe that some writers are prouder of their general notes than of some of their much longer papers. Wordiness has never been a sign of wisdom; in scientific writing it is an imposition.

In writing a paper, the student might well observe the following rules. Some of these have already been pointed out by Dr. Linsdale in *The Condor*.

1. *Learn what others have published on the subject.* If a life-history paper is to be written, Chapman's handbook will list the important papers published on eastern species up to 1931. The 10-year indices to *The Auk* and *The Condor* are other useful sources of titles. Bent's *Life Histories* summarize many scattered fragments up to the dates when they were written. The subsequent annual indices of *The Auk, The Condor,* and *The Wilson Bulletin* can be used in a search of this kind. Reviews in the files of *Bird-Banding* are also important. Inaccessible papers can often be obtained from authors, many of whom have available reprints of their articles. (Not infrequently these have been paid for by employers.) The address of an author is usually given at the end of an article; it can often be found in the A.O.U. membership list published from time to time in *The Auk.* The free distribution and exchange of reprints is now an accepted courtesy among contemporary scientists.

2. *Prepare a logical outline.* This can be modeled after some paper that is especially well written. Even one on some other species will do. Sections of the outline that are found to contain insufficient data can be readily dropped or incorporated with some other part of the outline. Be sure to include acknowledgments, if necessary, and a summary.

3. *Select a periodical and follow its style.* This should be the publication to which the paper will ultimately be submitted. Notice how references are handled (as footnotes or in a bibliography at the end of the paper). See if minor material can be summarized and placed in small type. Follow, wherever possible, the names of birds as given in the *A.O.U. Check-List.* Use names of plants and other animals only with care, avoiding colloquialisms and specifying some authoritative source from which the names have been taken. In scientific periodicals it is also best to give all measurements in both English and metric systems. One or the other can be left in brackets. Most periodicals contain, inside the front or rear cover, additional instructions regarding typewritten material and the manner of including illustrations.

4. *Let the first draft be comprehensive.* Writing is a tremendous stimulus to clear thinking. It enables one to develop perfectly unexpected points of view. It often shows up glaring gaps in one's own observations and emphasizes the need for further field work. Even when additional field work on the same subject is already planned for the following year, a preliminary draft on the past season's observations is well worth making.

5. *Make the second draft concise.* Avoid personal references; stick to the subject. See how much it can be condensed. Try graphs and tables as a means of summarizing material. The title of the note or article should be short (in order to spare bibliographers for years to come). Give full details where required for a clear indication of the significance of your observations. In the summary, avoid a mere listing of the topics presented; make it a true abstract of the paper.

6. *Read the paper for punctuation, logical sequence, and clarity.* Most public libraries have good books on the former. The University of Chicago's *Manual of Style* is widely used in this connection; John Benbow's *Manuscript and Proof* will also be of help. Base general statements on the evidence you present, not upon some generally accepted theory or supposition. Use terms in their generally accepted meaning or else define them. Make up a neat copy of your article before trying the next step.

7. *If possible, have the manuscript read critically by some experienced naturalist.* The critic need not be elderly; if he is, he may already be flooded with such requests. I think he could be asked to look for two things: wordiness and insufficient data. He may also be able to detect errors in logic, but this kind of criticism often involves a special effort or a large amount of time. To read a paper very critically is an arduous task requiring immense powers of concentration, and relatively few ornithologists have time for extracurricular activities of this nature.

8. *In making the final copy, check each reference against the original source.* By some quirk of the human mind, the papers most familiar to the author are often mentioned in the bibliography with incorrect titles. Above all, do not pad the bibliography. Include only references that you have examined yourself and read thor-

oughly. Isolation from good libraries is no sign of intellectual weakness; if an abstract or review of a paper is the only source of a quotation, quote the actual source you used. Check carefully the spelling of all scientific names used in the text. Verify the spelling of names of persons.

To some, the routine of publishing articles may seem to exceed the time that the amateur naturalist has for his hobby. Yet amateurs have made some of the greatest contributions to ornithology. Charles Darwin, for instance, was an amateur, but his is now a household name. Eliot Howard, who focused the attention of scientists on the importance of territory, was an English businessman. A. C. Bent, who has been compiling the monumental *Life Histories of North American Birds,* is a New England textile manufacturer. The author of the great monograph on the song sparrow is the wife of a midwestern college professor.

'There are two ways of constructing our picture of the bird,' wrote T. T. McCabe a few years ago, 'one is a mosaic, an effort to patch together a large number of fragments of observation, of many shades of significance and reliability, the other a direct and continuous drawing in which the whole picture is at least laid in, with the necessary sense of composition and subordination.' With experience and resolution, more and more bird students may contribute to our knowledge of birds.

Bird Watching and America

Bird watchers are often the first to detect serious downward fluctuations in the numbers of wild birds, and in this respect they represent the eyes of the conservation movement. It seems to me logical, therefore, that this chapter should close with a plea for clear thinking and a broad point of view on this aspect of our rather dizzy and discouraging world. To millions of our citizens, nature still means some outdoor picnic table beside an imported Japanese cedar. To others a park is merely a place to spread newspapers on the grass or to feed bears.

With the grim specter of accelerated erosion now stalking many of our national forests, every attempt to restrict grazing privileges on public lands is bitterly contested by cattle- and sheep-men.

Millions of dollars go for irrigation; millions more for drainage. Thousands of miles of mosquito ditches are dug, while in some states malaria has gone up and ducks have gone down.

In the Middlewest, which some like to regard as the enlightened center of America, red-tailed hawks are still shot on sight, considerably less than a quarter of the badly eroding farms are now plowed with a thought to the future, and state conservation officials were dismissed without hearing as late as 1942. Some Americans are still like the old-timer from the Illinois river bottoms a few years ago, when waterfowl were facing a serious crisis. Told that the continued slaughter there might reduce some ducks to the status of the passenger pigeon, this elderly citizen (perhaps thinking of his radio, his telephone, and the WPA) is reported to have said: 'So what? We're doing pretty well right now without the damned pigeons, ain't we?'

Conservation means more than preserving a few species of wildlife. It means the wise use of all the natural wealth of a great continent so that other generations of Americans can benefit by its resources and enjoy the same opportunities that we do today. We could clear the buffalo from the plains and use their bones to fertilize the fields of California. We cannot, however, cut down our vast forests without some penalty in floods and misery. We could pollute our streams, waste our fishes, drain our marshes, and so make barren deserts of our waters. We cannot, unfortunately, farm *all* our lands without the inevitable bankruptcy of soil erosion. Other evidences of an uncertain future appear in our depleted reserves of oil, our diminishing supplies of coal, our burned-over lands that are struggling to raise new forests.

As one who is close to nature, the naturalist is especially sensitive to the impact of our civilization on the natural resources of the continent. In the past he has all too frequently been content with the passage of a few laws and with the inauguration of a few sanctuaries. He is still confused about the function of education, about the efficacy of lobbying, and about the diversity of problems in national and international conservation. He sees bird-protection agencies quarreling among themselves, government bureaus practicing predator control on the one hand and managing national refuges on the other. It looks like a cockeyed world, and it nearly is.

In a world full of prejudice and politics, loose thinking and laziness, it is hard to keep one's feet on the ground and face squarely in the right direction. There are, I think, certain principles that should govern the thinking and conduct of every bird watcher.

1. Every citizen now has inescapable obligations to see that conservation becomes a major force in North American politics and thought. Patriotism is not something that one dons like a uniform every time war is declared. It involves duties that enter into our daily lives in times of peace as well as international strife.

2. More than ever before, the conservation movement now demands the mutual co-operation of many people interested in diverse things. Bird watchers *must* help sportsmen get better hunting, hunters *must* help garden clubs abolish roadside billboards, garden clubs *must* help fishermen get better trout streams, and fishermen *must* encourage farmers to manage their wood lots. Selfishness has been the curse of our race; in conservation it inevitably leads to distrust, embitterment, and defeat.

3. Many of the needs of conservation can be met by community action. Pious resolutions are next-door neighbors to the subservient mass mentality that is the menace of our generation.

4. Last-minute laws and eleventh-hour sanctuaries are sorry efforts to correct long-continued land abuse and a lack of long-range planning. All the wealth of Massachusetts could not prevent the doom of the last heath hen. Our present inability to save the few ivory-billed woodpeckers that are now left in the South is not due simply to the lumbering industry (as Table 30 might imply). The underlying cause goes back, I think, to failure of an earlier generation more concerned in the spoils system than in a national program of forestry.

5. Misuse of wildlife is but a symptom of universal land abuse. If we are to save our disappearing whooping cranes and trumpeter swans, we must provide for efficient mining, scientific utilization of oil fields, soil-erosion control, correction of stream pollution, and the development of protection forests in a co-ordinated program in each state. Even in high places there still exists the innocent ex-

TABLE 30

HOW BIRD LIFE IN AMERICA HAS BEEN AFFECTED BY MAN

Many changes in American bird life can be traced directly to human agencies. Sometimes a number of agencies act together upon a single species, and it is extremely difficult to single out the one factor that is most important. Changes in bird life are not necessarily as simple as this table would imply.

Agency	Method	Species affected	Some results
Farmers	Clearing of forests	Prairie horned lark	Extended range from plains to seaboard
Farmers	Clearing of forests	Killdeer and field birds	Occupied former forest lands
Farmers	Clearing of forests	Oven-bird and forest birds	Decreased wherever forests fell
Farmers	Plowing of prairies	Woodland birds	Encroached westward with woodland as prairie fires ceased
Farmers	Marshland drainage	Waterfowl	Only remnant now breeding in central states
Farmers	Marshland drainage	Whooping crane	Now nearing total extinction
Farmers	Marshland drainage	Everglade kite	Now nearing extirpation in the United States
Farmers, orchardmen	'Vermin' control	Louisiana and Carolina paroquets	Both now totally extinct
Farmers, gunners	'Vermin' control	Golden eagle	No longer breeds in eastern states
Ranchers, gunners	('Vermin' control?), random hunting	California condor	Near extinction; remnant left
Market hunters, etc.	Slaughter	Passenger pigeon	Wiped out forever
Hunters	Overshooting	Wild turkey	Gone from nothern part of range
Hunters, farmers	Overshooting, plowing	Prairie chicken	Eastern race (heath hen) now extinct; southern race 99% exterminated; remnants of other races left
Market hunters, etc.	Overshooting	Eskimo curlew	Probably extinct
Hunting clubs, game commissions	Introduction from Europe	Pheasant and Hungarian partridge	Now common in many states
Bird-liberation groups	Introduction from Europe	English sparrow	Now abundant throughout the United States
Bird-liberation groups	Introduction from Europe	Starling	Rapidly spreading westward
English sparrow	Takes over nests	Cliff swallow	Great decrease in southern part of range
Starling	Takes over nests	?Red-headed woodpecker	Decrease in eastern part of range
Millinery trade	Plumage hunters	Gulls, terns, herons	Near extinction about 1910
Audubon societies	Feather laws	Gulls, terns, herons	Great increase in numbers since 1910
Big cities	Garbage dumps	Ducks, rails	Locally extirpated
Big cities	Garbage dumps	Herring gull	Continued increase since 1930; lessened mortality in winter
Herring gull	Predation	Common and Arctic terns	Loss of eggs and young
Mosquito commissions	Drainage	Rails, ducks	Reduced in numbers locally
Lumbermen	Cutting southern hardwoods	Ivory-billed woodpecker	Rapidly nearing total extinction
Lumbermen	Cutting northern conifers	?Red crossbill	Great decrease in numbers since 1906
Commercial fishermen; mattress industry	Killing for food and feathers, respectively	Great auk	Exterminated in North America by 1840
Fish hatcheries	Pole-trapping, etc.	Osprey	About 70% down inland in New England

Compiled from various sources.

pectation that worn-out soils can always find some use as wildlife preserves.

6. The real progress of conservation is rarely measurable by the events of any one year. New laws and new sanctuaries are sometimes symbols of advance, but their seal of success stems from new folkways and cultural concepts that gradually attain an accepted place in the conduct of our people.

It seems obvious that the task of preserving our national wealth will be an endless one. 'Write your congressman' is said to be a tepid technique in conservation. Perhaps it is. Yet the Bald Eagle Act passed by Congress a few years ago is said to be largely the work of one lady, Miss Maud G. Phillips of Springfield, Massachusetts. Almost unknown in wildlife circles, she plagued her representatives for years until, in desperation, they got the measure passed. Conservation is the product of intelligence times persistence. I should like to see bird watchers have plenty of both. I believe it worth while and pleasurable for us to explore the mysteries of wildlife. It would be in a sorry predicament, however, if we all buried ourselves in bird blinds and left nature to work out its own salvation.

Appendix A

AN INTRODUCTION TO BIRD TRACKS

THE IDENTIFICATION OF BIRDS by means of their tracks is about as well known today as field identification with an opera glass was fifty years ago. A few ambitious souls take up the idea from time to time, but most naturalists regard the technique as a blind alley to be shunned and distrusted.

Bird tracks can, however, yield useful information to the naturalist. In recent years, the footprints of quail in the snow have often been counted to ascertain winter losses in different coveys of this species. Naturalists who like to wade through swamps find tracks a good indication that secretive rails are present. The time is now ripe for a collective effort to report the tracks of all the larger species and to work out methods of separating these in the field. Herons, gulls, terns, upland game birds, rails, gallinules, coots, crows, ducks, and geese all leave tracks that can be reported. Many will be virtually impossible to identify. Others will be found to possess unsuspected characteristics that make them absolutely distinctive. As a sport, the endeavor has its possibilities; as a contribution to birdlore, it has its own potentialities.

The most sustained and thorough field work ever carried out in this connection stands to the credit of the late Charles A. Urner,*

---

* Charles Anderson Urner died suddenly at Elizabeth, New Jersey, on June 22, 1938, at the age of 56. A graduate of the University of Wisconsin, he was associated throughout his life with the wholesale butter-and-egg business of New York City and was vice-president of the Urner-Barry Publishing Company there at the time of his death. For many years he was an ardent hunter; later he became the most active field ornithologist in New Jersey and a dominant figure in the Linnaean Society of New York. Extraordinarily expert in the field identification of coastal bird life, he completed nesting studies of the short-eared owl, compiled important and characteristically thorough counts of migratory shore birds and waterfowl, conducted breeding-bird cen-

179

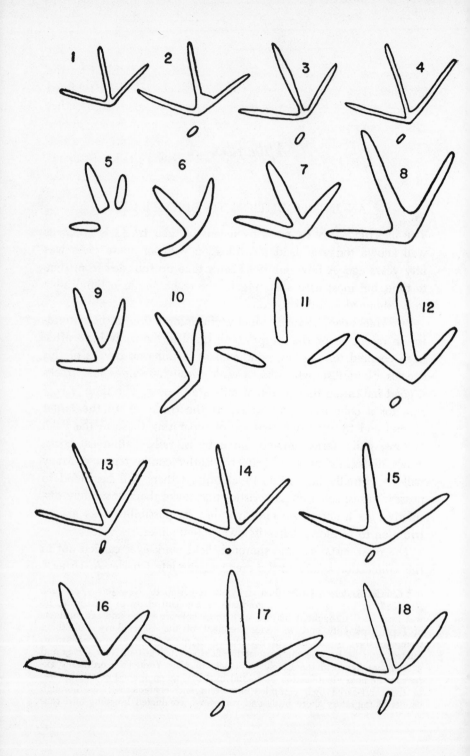

whose notes and records on this subject are here published for the first time. The Urner Collection of Bird Tracks is chiefly confined to shore birds, but its value is great by any standard. Altogether 376 tracks were obtained in the field, by wax impressions, plaster casts, or by careful measurements. For each species, studied attention was given to the way the birds toed in, the distances between running and walking steps, and the various conditions in which the tracks were made (hard sand, soft mud, film of dust, etc.). Prints were carefully redrawn on large cardboards and notations made on many of the 30 species recorded.

Since only a part of this great collection can be reproduced here, two important sources of variation in bird tracks should be clearly emphasized:

1. *Differences in tracking conditions often lead to considerable variation in the tracks of a single bird.* In very hard mud or sand, the heel of the bird fails to show and the mark of a hind toe may

suses, worked on successional studies of marshland bird life, and wrote in 1930 one of the most complete county bird lists ever published. In his last years, his week-end field work was directed toward a detailed mapping of the birds of his state, analyses of habitat selection, counts of curlew roosts, and behavior studies of robins and catbirds. The completion of these projects now rests with his many friends who shared in his field studies and who still remember the richness of his personality and the matchless vigor of his mind. The inspiration that he instilled in so many younger men (among them the writer) may yet constitute one of his most important contributions to bird watching.

PLATE 1

1. Least sandpiper
2. Semipalmated and male western sandpiper
3. Female western sandpiper
4. White-rumped sandpiper
5. Piping plover
6. Piping plover
7. Sanderling
8. Killdeer
9. Semipalmated plover
10. Semipalmated plover
11. Red-backed sandpiper
12. Ruddy turnstone
13. Spotted sandpiper
14. Solitary sandpiper
15. Stilt sandpiper
16. Knot
17. Dowitcher
18. Pectoral sandpiper

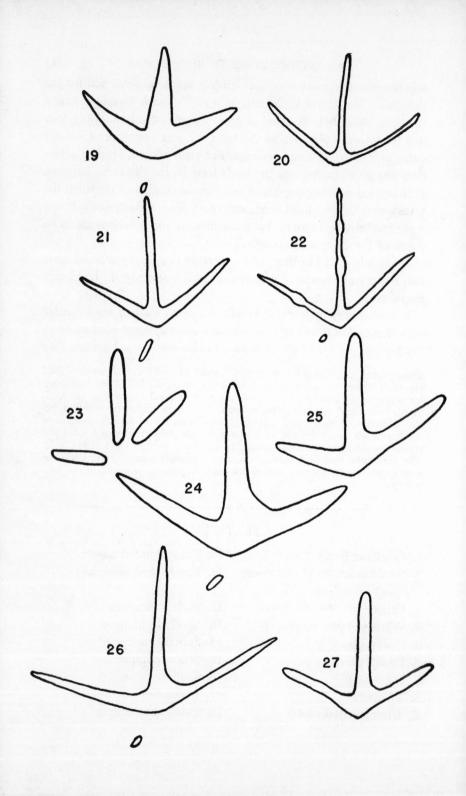

also be absent. These imperfect tracks are illustrated by Mr. Jaques between pages 186 and 187 (the footprints being faithfully based on actual samples in the Urner Collection). As far as possible, perfect tracks are illustrated in Plates 1, 2, and 3.

2. *Differences among individual birds of the same species likewise produce variation in the size of the tracks.* Mr. Urner rightfully regarded certain extremes as due to differences in sex. In most species of shore birds, the female is larger than the male. In dowitcher tracks, this size difference may possibly be due to a difference in subspecies. It was some years after his prints had been made that Mr. Urner established the existence of the long-billed dowitcher flight late each fall down the Atlantic coast. (In doing so, he convinced eastern ornithologists that the call note of these birds was by far their most distinctive character.) Practically all the tracks are undated and no distinction between the tracks of this and the western race of the dowitcher is now possible. A similar uncertainty exists for some of the measurements reported here for the willet. The large footprint reproduced in Plate 2 was recorded by Mr. Urner at Barnegat Inlet, New Jersey, on September 7, 1930; it is the largest willet track in the collection and almost certainly is that of a western willet. While the western is the predominant willet each autumn along those portions of the New Jersey coast that Mr. Urner habitually covered, minimum measurements for this species reported here should not be arbitrarily assigned to this race until further field studies are reported.

The tracks illustrated in the accompanying plates have been grouped somewhat arbitrarily to avoid crowding. Each print represents a right foot and is life size. Care has been exercised to illustrate how each species toes in, and the birds may be regarded as

---

PLATE 2

19-20. Wilson's phalarope	24. Western willet
21. Wilson's snipe	25. Black-bellied plover
22. Woodcock	26. Greater yellow-legs
23. Golden plover	27. Lesser yellow-legs

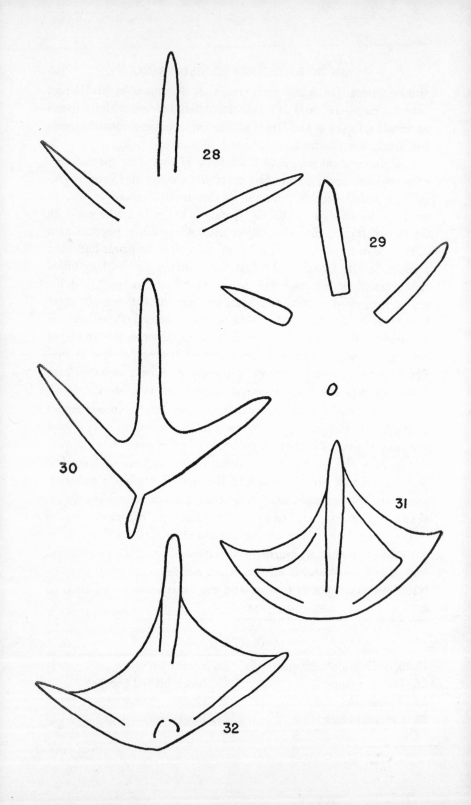

walking from the bottom of the page directly toward the top. Slight differences always exist in the amount of 'toe in' for a given species, and variations from the tracks shown here must therefore be expected in the field.

TABLE A

A SUMMARY OF THE CHARLES A. URNER COLLECTION
OF SHORE-BIRD TRACKS

Species	Middle toe Length in mm. Ex-tremes	Aver-age	Width in mm.	No. of prints secured	Pal-mation[1]	Hind toe[1]	Stride in mm.[2]	Track number on plates
Least sandpiper	17	17	1	4	.....	.....	66–75	1
Piping plover	17–20	19	2–3	17	.....	.....	70–80	5–6
Semipalmated sandpiper	19–22	20	1–1½	21	43%	33%	50–53	2
Sanderling	20–24	22	2–3	16	.....	.....	90	7
White-rumped sandpiper	21–25	23	1–1½	9	22%	100%	55–87	4
Western sandpiper	22–26	24	1½–2	3	67%	100%	71	2–3
Semipalmated plover	22–26	24	2–3	15	.....	.....	70–80	9–10
Spotted sandpiper	23–28	25	1–2	29	10%	66%	75–95	13
Red-backed sandpiper	23–29	28	2–3	18	.....	11%	85–107	11
Killdeer	25–30	28	2–4	17	24%	.....	90–130	8
Turnstone	25–31	29	2–4	15	.....	88%	80	12
Solitary sandpiper	26–28	27	1–2	13	100%	15%	15–60	14
Stilt sandpiper	27–31	28	2–3	17	71%	71%	....	15
Knot	28–32	30.5	3–5	31	21%	14%	115	16
Golden plover	29–35	31	3–4	10	trace	.....	120–150	23
Dowitcher	29–41	34	2½–3½	26	trace	69%	80–119	17
Pectoral sandpiper	30–32	31	2–3	5	.....	100%	43–47	18
Wilson's phalarope	30–36	32	2–5	4	50%	25%	....	19–20
Lesser yellow-legs	33–36.5	34.6	3	18	100%	.....	84–87	27
Black-bellied plover	35–39	36.5	4–5	16	75%	.....	125–170	25
Wilson's snipe	35–41	37	2–3	18	trace	100%	45–110	21
Woodcock	36–37	36.5	2	2[3]	.....	100%	....	22
Greater yellow-legs	37–46	43	2–4	17	40%	33%	150–180	26
Western willet	41–47	43	4–6	17	65%	35%	90–110	24
Hudsonian curlew	41–48	46	5	7	.....	71%	....	29
Avocet	47–58	51.5	4½–5	6	66%	.....	....	28–31–32
Marbled godwit	57–62	58	5	5	60%	100%	....	30

[1] Number of times these characters occur in the collection.
[2] Based on from 2 to 5 samples for each species; more records could easily be made of birds running at full stride.
[3] Dead bird only.

In Table A, shore-bird tracks have been arranged according to the relative length of the middle toe. In compiling these, I measured from the distal end of the toe to the rear edge of the bird's

PLATE 3

28. Avocet   30. Marbled godwit
29. Hudsonian curlew   31-32. Avocet

heel. Measurements of a hind toe were not included. In several species only a few tracks were available. The presence of these gaps demonstrates the need of more records of these birds and the caution that must be exercised in using the following tentative key to shore-bird tracks.

A Preliminary Key to Shore-Bird Tracks

(Known cases of overlapping measurements in the Urner Collection are marked with asterisks; other cases may be encountered in the field.)

A1 Lateral toes equal in size, or nearly so
    B1 Lateral toes curving slightly inward
        C1 Midtoe 17-20 mm. long......................piping plover
        C2 Midtoe 30-36 mm. long..................Wilson's phalarope
        C3 Midtoe 47-58 mm. long.............................avocet
    B2 Lateral toes straight
        D1 Outer toe equal in length to inner toe or nearly so (sandpipers *et al.*)
            E1 Lateral toes forming angle of 90° or more. .ruddy turnstone
            E2 Lateral toes forming angle of more than 90°
                F1 Hind toe quite pronounced under good tracking conditions, 3-10 mm. long
                    G1 Lateral toes widely spread (about 125°), midtoe 29-41 mm. ....dowitcher
                    G2 Lateral toes less widely spread (about 110°)
                        H1 Midtoe 30-32 mm. long, hind toe mark 8-9 mm. ....pectoral sandpiper
                        H2 Midtoe 35-41 mm. long, tapering, hind toe mark 5-10 mm. ....* Wilson's snipe
                F2 Hind toe usually or often present as a dot or small streak
                    J1 Palmation absent under good tracking conditions
                      K1 Toes 2 mm. or more in width
                        L1 Toes tapering, 2-3 mm. wide, midtoe 23-29 mm. long....red-backed sandpiper
                        L2 Toes stubby, 3-5 mm. wide, midtoe 28-32 mm. long.................knot
                        L3 Toes broad, 5 mm. wide, midtoe 41-48 mm. long......Hudsonian curlew
                      K2 Toes 2 mm. or less in width
                        M1 Midtoe 21-25 mm. long, 1-1.5 mm. wide .... * white-rumped sandpiper

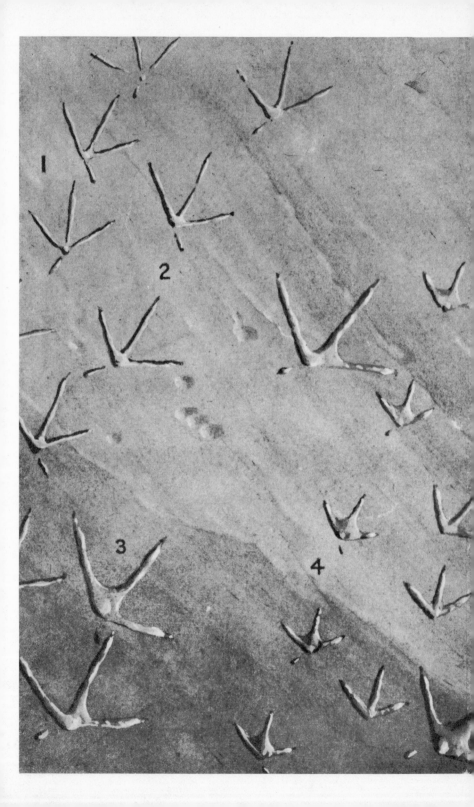

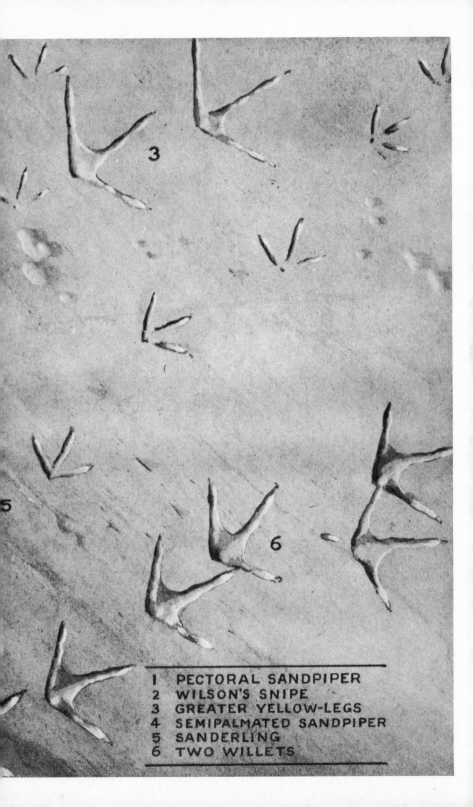

3

5

6

1 PECTORAL SANDPIPER
2 WILSON'S SNIPE
3 GREATER YELLOW-LEGS
4 SEMIPALMATED SANDPIPER
5 SANDERLING
6 TWO WILLETS

    M2 Midtoe 23-28 mm. long, 1-2 mm.
      wide . . . . * spotted sandpiper
   J2 Palmation present, or usually so, between middle and outer toe
    N1 Toes narrow (1-2 mm. wide) but not markedly tapering
     O1 Midtoe 19-22 mm. long, 1-1.5 mm.
      wide . . . . * semipalmated sandpiper
     O2 Midtoe 22-26 mm. long, 1.5-2 mm.
      wide . . . . * western sandpiper
    N2 Toes markedly tapering, 1-2 mm. wide, midtoe 26-28 mm. long. . . .solitary sandpiper
    N3 Toes fairly broad, 2-4 mm. wide
     P1 Tracks toeing slightly inward, midtoe 27-31 mm. long, 2-3 mm. wide
          stilt sandpiper
     P2 Tracks with middle toe not turned in
      Q1 Midtoe 33-36.5 mm. long, 3 mm. wide. . . . . . . .lesser yellow-legs
      Q2 Midtoe 37-46 mm. long, 2-4 mm. wide. . . . . . .greater yellow-legs
   J3 Palmation present between toes
    R1 Midtoe 19-22 mm. . . .semipalmated sandpiper
    R2 Midtoe 30-36 mm. . . . . . . .Wilson's phalarope
    R3 Midtoe 41-47 mm. . . . . .willet
    R4 Midtoe 57-62 mm. . . . . .marbled godwit
  F3 Hind toe absent
   S1 Toes narrow (1-1.5 mm.), midtoe about 17 mm. long. .least sandpiper
   S2 Toes stubby or broad
    T1 Midtoe 20-24 mm. long, 2-3 mm. wide
          sanderling
    T2 Midtoe 47-58 mm. long. . . . . .avocet
   S3 Toes broad, but tapering to some extent
    U1 Midtoe 23-29 mm. long, 2-3 mm. wide
         red-backed sandpiper
    U2 Midtoe 28-32 mm. long, 3-5 mm. wide. .knot
A2 Lateral toes unequal in size; outer toe markedly longer than inner, hind toe marks always absent; tracks with pronounced toe in
  V1 Palmation absent in good tracking conditions; inner toe usually exceeding 90° to direction in which bird is walking
   W1 Midtoe 17-20 mm. long. .piping plover
   W2 Midtoe 22-26 mm. long. . . . . * semipalmated plover
   W3 Midtoe 25-30 mm. long. . . . . * killdeer
  V2 Palmation very reduced but evident in good tracking conditions; inner toe rarely exceeds 90° to direction in which bird is walking
   X1 Midtoe 25-30 mm. long, 2-4 mm. wide, tapering. . . . . * killdeer
   X2 Midtoe 29-35 mm. long, 3-4 mm. wide, stubby. . . .golden plover
   X3 Midtoe 35-39 mm. long, 4-5 mm. wide. . . . . .black-bellied plover

Appendix B

SOME RESULTS OF BREEDING-BIRD CENSUSES

CONSIDERING THE SIZE of our continent and the great variety of plant types it presents, census work on breeding birds has only begun. A well-organized series of regional studies could have two goals: (1) determination of the densities of breeding birds in all the more common habitats, including their successional stages; and (2) evaluation of the fluctuations in bird life over a long period of years. It seems likely that three-year studies of tracts about 20 acres in size would give the most acceptable information for the former. As for the second goal, no one really knows how long a long-term census should be. I should like to see some worked out over a 30-year period on study areas of perhaps 30 or 40 acres. Censuses of such length very properly fall within the scope of bird clubs and institutions that can insure continuity of field research. Some of our bird clubs are already more than 50 years old, and they give every indication of continuing for many years to come. Census work could readily become an interesting and valuable part of their programs.

Some extremely worth-while census work has been completed abroad. In Germany some years ago, Gottfried Schiermann conducted the most thorough population counts ever taken along these lines. An amateur naturalist and one-time egg collector, Schiermann used 15-acre study tracts to work out the densities of swamp forest lands and Scotch pine forests. Excellent work has also been done by the Finns, who sometimes calculate their census totals by correction coefficients that are not always clear. The Finnish naturalists are the only ones so far to have censused the breeding-bird population of lakes. 'Grebe-type lakes,' according to Pontus Palmgren, vary from 0.3 to 4 birds per 10 acres; 'diving-duck lakes' range from 7.4 to 22.8. English census-takers have done their best work on heaths and moorlands and have been increasingly active in recent years.

In America, Cleveland (Ohio) bird watchers are far ahead of any other group in bird-census work. Up to the present, no study areas appear to have been censused in Nevada or Utah. Only a very few have been reported from Wyoming, Arizona, Delaware, Mississippi, Idaho, Kentucky, Oregon, South Carolina, and West Virginia. The older census tracts, as a rule, contained a mixture of too many habitats to make them comparable with modern reports, and only a few are included here. Modern census reports often distinguish between nesting birds that feed entirely on a study area, and those (like swallows and crows) that feed far outside it. This distinction eliminates spectacular densities caused by colonial nesting species (such as the purple martin) and enables us to comprehend more clearly the actual bird populations that various environments can support.

Table B will give some idea of the habitats censused on our continent up to the end of 1942. It indicates the great amount of field work that still awaits bird watchers in nearly every state. Farm censuses, not included here, have already been summarized in considerable detail by Miss May Thacher Cooke in the United States Department of Agriculture's Department Bulletin 1165.

TABLE B

SOME BREEDING-BIRD HABITATS ALREADY CENSUSED IN NORTH AMERICA

Here are summarized the results reported on study areas at least 15 acres in size. Densities are given in terms of adult birds per 10 acres. This is a fairly easy area to visualize. It is 220 yards by 220 yards; it is equivalent to two 55-yard strips on either side of a quarter mile of road; and it roughly equals the area a bird watcher checks when traversing a woodland path of that length.

Habitat	Adults per 10 acres	Place	Observer (or authority)	Size of study area in acres	Remarks
Deserts					
Sagebrush	2	Montana	(M. T. Cooke)	80	
Colorado desert of California	22.3	California	Mr. and Mrs. A. E. Hutchinson	37	2-year average; stream in study area
Chaparral					
Chamise and low chaparral	8	California	J. D. Graham, E. A. Stoner	20	Dry plateau, 1000-ft. elevation

Habitat	Adults per 10 acres	Place	Observer (or authority)	Size of study area in acres	Remarks
Foothill chaparral	56.6	California	H. L. Cogswell, J. Murdock	41	7 years after fire; other habitats nearby
Sandy Areas					
Sandy field	4	Wisconsin	J. J. Hickey	50	Abandoned farmland
Sand dunes	15.6	Ohio	M. B. Skaggs	26.4	Scattered small trees
Sandy grassland	19	Ohio	R. A. O'Reilly, Jr.	44	2 acres of old apple orchard
Pitch pine barrens	21.3	New Jersey	David Fables	76	5-year average; 4.2-acre bog
Jack pine barrens	35.6	Michigan	J. Van Tyne, F. and F. N. Hamerstrom, Jr.	16	Considerable edge
Tundra					
Tundra	2.8	Greenland	E. M. Nicholson, et al.	5100	
Grass tundra	6.1	Baffin Island	J. D. Soper	640	Careful estimates; area approximate
Grass tundra	8.5	Baffin Island	J. D. Soper	800	Careful estimates; area approximate
Salt Marshes					
Undrained salt marsh	40	New Jersey	N. J. McDonald, J. K. Potter	15	Plus 13.3 more birds breeding in area but feeding largely outside
New fill on salt marsh	0.6	New Jersey	C. A. Urner	100	Recent sand and mud from dredging
Drained marsh and fill	55.8	New York	T. and R. Imhof	20.7	Includes marsh edge; plus 10.9 birds feeding outside; 2-year average
Fresh-Water Swamps					
Cattail and reed grass	60	Ohio	J. W. Aldrich, P. N. Moulthrop	21	Water averaged 1 foot
Cattails, swamp shrubs	82.2	Ohio	J. W. Aldrich	15	3-year average (60–104)
Cattails, shrubs, trees	184.5	New York	Sialis Bird Club	40	Plus 4 more birds breeding in area but feeding largely outside; large edge effect
Cattails, hay, woods	11.3	Indiana	D. H. Boyd	19	
Cattails, wooded island	106	New York	Schenectady Bird Club	46	Plus 10 more birds breeding in area but feeding largely outside; 21 acres lightly wooded
Calamagrostis meadows	68.4	Illinois	W. J. Beecher	38.3	15-acre oak-hickory island
Bog and filled-in lake	43.6	Ohio	G. Bing	65	
Bog and Bottomland Forests					
Red maple-yellow birch	24.5	Ohio	J. W. Aldrich	23	3-year average (13.2–34.8)
Flood-plain forest	30.7	Oklahoma	Tulsa Audubon Society	34	Plus 2.2 more birds breeding in area but feeding largely outside; 3-year average
Flood-plain forest	26.8	Ohio	A. B. Williams, G. Deutschlander	45	2-year average
Open willow-mimosa shrub bottomland	115.9	Texas	L. I. Davis	15	2-year average (76–155.8)
Plains and Prairies					
Typical short-grass plains	13.1	Texas	P. F. Allen, P. R. Sime	25	3-year average; plus 4.9 birds feeding off tract
Shrubless prairie	2.0	Montana	(W. W. Cooke)	40	
Prairie	4.6	Oklahoma	J. C. Howell	35	Plus 1.1 birds feeding off tract
Native prairie	6.5	Kansas	(M. T. Cooke)	40	4-year average
Virgin prairie	11.4	Wyoming	F. W. Mickey	40	5-year average; plus .4 bird feeding off tract
Virgin palouse prairie	24	Washington	L. W. Wing	30	
Prairie pasture	8.1	Kansas	W. Goodman	50	2-year average; plus 4.4 birds feeding off tract
Prairie pasture	4.4	New Mexico	(W. W. Cooke)	80	Density on 3 tracts: 3.3; 4.3; 5.5
Prairie pasture	6.9	South Dakota	(W. W. Cooke)	40, 80	Density on 2 tracts: 6.0, 7.8
Retired prairie pasture	18.2	Iowa	S. C. Kendeigh	50	Plus 3.4 birds feeding off tract

Habitat	Adults per 10 acres	Place	Observer (or authority)	Size of study area in acres	Remarks
Swampy prairie pasture	59.1	Illinois	W. Robertson, Jr.	65.5	After one year, grazing reduced density from 97 to 21.2, plus 21.8 birds feeding off tract
Open Fields					
Prairie-type fields	20	Ohio	M. B. Walters, A. B. Williams	15	Suburban area
Prairie-type fields	21.3	Ohio	C. H. Knight	40	Suburban area
Prairie-type fields	13.1	Ohio	M. B. Skaggs	28.3	2-year average
Dry grassy upland	27.9	Ohio	R. A. O'Reilly, Jr.	40	2-year average; scattering of trees
Open field	20	Missouri	J. E. Comfort	15	Scattered elms
Open fields	34	Ohio	A. B. Fuller, B. P. Bole, Jr.	43	25 bird boxes
Fields with Brush, Brambles, Etc.					
Open and scrubby fields	29	Ohio	C. H. Knight	31	Includes 14 acres of crab apples and black cherry
Open scrubby field	27.6	Ohio	Ruth Newcomer	25	2-year average
Brushy field	38.8	Ohio	J. W. Aldrich, P. N. Moulthrop	18	Briars and shrubs
Open field, beginning of trees	30.2	Ohio	P. N. Moulthrop	42	2-year average
Open field, beginning of trees	72.8	Ohio	P. N. Moulthrop	22	Density created by new lake
Thorn scrub	10	Ohio	A. B. Fuller, B. P. Bole, Jr.	18	
Maple-Beech Woodlands					
Young maple-beech-hemlock	47.7	Ohio	P. N. Moulthrop, M. B. Walters, A. B. Williams	39	5-year average (42.6–52.3); well-developed understory
Beech-maple-hemlock	29.2	Ohio	D. R. Perry	26	Scout camp
Climax maple-beech	41.7	Ohio	A. B. Williams	65	10-year average (35–54.2)
Previously grazed maple-beech	59.3	Ohio	Ohio State University	26.8	Plus 15.9 birds feeding off the tract; 5-year average
Dense lowland maple-beech	42.7	Ohio	E. O. Mellinger	55.3	3-year average
Wet maple-beech	63.4	Ohio	M. E. Morse, V. Carrothers	30	3-year average (59.4–70)
Oak-Hickory Woodlands					
Upland oak-hickory	23.2	Ohio	A. H. Claugus	35	6-year average; scout camp
Second-growth oak-hickory	57.2	Ohio	L. E. Hicks, F. B. Chapman, D. L. Leedy	100	5-year average; clearings
Second-growth oak-hickory	45.2	Ohio	H. E. Wallin	50	
Cut-over oak-hickory	56.2	Illinois	W. Robertson, Jr.	56	2-year average; with pond; plus 10 birds feeding off tract
Other Deciduous Forests					
Oak-maple	41.4	Illinois	University of Illinois	56	2-year average
Oak-covered hills	32	California	E. A. Stoner, J. D. Graham	70	With 2-acre lake; trees 50 feet
Oak-hickory-pine	50.8	West Virginia	S. K. Dandridge	24	60-foot stand protected 60 years
Gambel oak-yellow pine	8.9	Arizona	(W. W. Cooke)	70	7100 feet elevation
Elm-ash association	105.3	Texas	L. I. Davis	15	Climax; dense undergrowth; plus 18.7 birds feeding off tract
Upland oak-poplar	58	Virginia	M. Marshall, Jr.	20	Plus 10 birds feeding off tract
Mixed hardwoods	56.2	New York	J. L. Bull, J. J. Hickey	40	5-year average (52–60.6)
Chestnut woodlot	15.6	Massachusetts	A. A. Cross	20	10-year average (9–23)

Habitat	Adults per 10 acres	Place	Observer (or authority)	Size of study area in acres	Remarks
Canyons, Creek Bottoms, Etc.					
Wooded canyon	10.6	New Mexico	J. K. Jensen	90	Aspens, virgin conifers, oaks; at elevation of 8000 feet
Wooded canyon	45	California	J. D. Graham, E. A. Stoner	40	With small mountain stream
Timbered stream-bed	26.8	Oklahoma	F. M. and A. M. Baumgartner	22	Upland oak forest; typical submarginal land
Creek bottom	27.4	Ohio	L. E. Hicks	80	10-year average (22–32)
Creek bottom	36	Montana	J. Kittredge, Jr.	40	3-year average
Maple-beech ravine	35.5	Ohio	J. Corbe	255	Stream present
Coniferous Forest Lands					
Cleared Land	41.6	New Hampshire	C. L. Whittle	78	48 acres in cultivation
Second-growth white pine	17.8	New Hampshire	C. L. Whittle	562	20 to 40-year-old stand
Open conifers, birches	50	New Hampshire	J. M. Abbott	30	30-foot stand
Conifers, hardwoods	58.4	Quebec	J. D. Cleghorn, J. H. Molson	50	⅔ climax; ⅓ shrubbery; plus 1.6 birds feeding off tract
Upland pine-hemlock-red maple	31.6	Ohio	B. P. Bole, Jr.	75	Pine canopy 100 to 200 feet high; dense understory; 3-year average
White pine-hemlock forest	35.3	Vermont	W. P. Smith	50	6-year average (30–45)
Climax red and white spruce	60	Maine	Audubon Nature Camp	30	Includes clearing; 7-year average
Modified Communities					
Country estate	123	Ohio	Baldwin Research Laboratory	15	5-year average (109–158); high degree of bird protection
Campus	45	New York	A. A. Allen *et al.*	256	Cornell University
Campus	45.7	New Mexico	J. K. Jenson	106	With irrigated farmland; 45% English sparrows
Campus	14	Massachusetts	(M. T. Cooke)	80	Wellesley College
Campus	90	California	(M. T. Cooke)	20	University of California woodland; 2-year average
Campus	54	Virginia	Martha Clark	36	Sweet Briar College
Village	143.2	Alabama	(M. T. Cooke)	25	61% English sparrows
Suburban	44	Ohio	M. M. Nice	40	4-year average (38–55)
Suburban	167	Maryland	(M. T. Cooke)	23	2-year average (140–194.8); English sparrows 'discouraged'
City park	43	New York	(M. T. Cooke)	95	5-year average
City park	202	California	(M. T. Cooke)	40	Maximum in 5 years
City park	64	Indiana	(M. T. Cooke)	44	2-year average

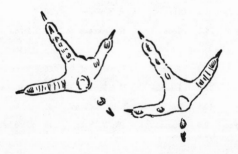

Appendix C

OUTLINE FOR A LIFE-HISTORY STUDY *

No ONE OUTLINE for a life-history study can fit all species of birds. Gallinaceous birds like the quail and the pheasant have many special problems, colonial birds like the herons and gulls have others. This outline was prepared for a songbird study—the kind that many amateur naturalists can begin in their gardens or near their homes. It does not raise all the questions, but it does show that many exist.

Although completeness is always desirable as a goal of ornithological research, its attainment may be due as much to luck as to persistence. No one need worry, then, about answering all of the questions in this outline. It is better *to work for small objectives each season,* and *to publish neatly condensed notes on those questions that have been answered.* The projects listed here tend to have a chronological order. They might be taken up at any stage of the nesting cycle. In many cases they involve simple bird watching with no other tools than a keen eye and a field notebook. In their more advanced aspects their solution depends on banding and the use of similar techniques in marking birds.

Here are studies for the old and for the young, for the agile and the convalescent, for stay-near-homes and for the active. Working out the answers is a lot of fun.

I. ARRIVAL OF MIGRANTS IN SPRING

    A. *When do the resident males arrive—all at once, or over a long period of time?*

* The items in this section of the appendix were compiled after going over Margaret M. Nice's writings on the subject. They were also compared with an excellent outline written by Dr. Eugene P. Odum for Georgia bird watchers in 1941. Many of the questions undoubtedly owe their inspiration to the recent reports of other naturalists who have engaged in life-history studies and other field investigations of birds.

1. Is there any indication that the older birds arrive first?
2. Do they at once separate themselves into territories?
3. If a common feeding area is used, how much time is first spent on the nesting territory?
4. How frequently do they sing (if at all), and at what hours?
5. Where and how early in the day do these birds roost?

B. *When do the resident females arrive—all at once or over a long period of time?*
   1. Do they move about the area freely?
   2. Do they inspect the males or their territories?
   3. Where do they roost?

C. *When do transient birds of this species pass through?*
   1. Is their song different from that of the resident males?
   2. When do they sing?
   3. How do the resident birds react to them?
   4. Are transients seemingly aware of territories already set up?
   5. How long do they stay?
   6. Do the males pass through at a somewhat different period than the females?
   7. Are they quieter than the resident birds? More inconspicuous?
   8. Do they rest more or feed more during the day than the residents?
   9. Where do these birds roost?
   10. Do they roost at the same time as resident birds?

D. *How does the arrival of each group of migrants coincide with the development of vegetation? With the budding and blooming of local trees and flowers?*
   1. How does the arrival of each migratory group coincide with weather conditions to the south?
   2. Does this species wait for good weather, or does it migrate with little regard to wind and temperature?
   3. Can a graph be drawn showing how each group of migrants built up in numbers?

II. Song

A. *How many types of song does a male of this species have?*
   1. Are these used on different occasions, or at different periods of the season?
   2. Does the male have an advertising song that is uttered from a high, somewhat conspicuous place?

3. Does this attract females or just warn other males? Or both?
4. Does the male ever sing *sotto voce* from a low perch?
5. What kind of songs are uttered by young birds in the autumn and winter?

B. *How does the frequency of song vary?*
1. With the time of year? With the nesting cycle?
2. With temperature, humidity, cloudiness?
3. With the time of day?
4. With the density of that species' population?
5. With the arrival of females?
6. With the completion of pair formation?
7. With nest building, egg laying, incubation, and other events in the nesting cycle?

C. *Are regular singing perches used?*
1. Have these any relation to
   a. The presence of near-by males?
   b. The site of last year's or this year's nest?
   c. The size and shape of the territory?
   d. The site of the male's roost?
2. Do the singing perches vary in height or type?
   a. Throughout the nesting cycle?
   b. Throughout the day?
   c. From one male to another?

D. *Do the female birds ever sing? When?*

III. TERRITORY

A. *Do the males defend individual territories? Do they also possess a common feeding area? Which of the following takes place in the territory?*
1. Formation of the pair?
2. Copulation?
3. Nesting?
4. Foraging for the young?
5. Roosting?

B. *Upon arriving do the males settle down on their territories and begin defending each territory at once? Or is defense at first restricted to only a part of each day?*

C. *Do the males have certain poses or special displays when they meet intruding birds of their own species?*
1. Are these ever performed before both males and females alike?
2. Are supplementary displays performed before females, too?

D. *What is the average size of a territory? The maximum? The minimum?*
1. Does size shrink or expand as the season advances?
2. What percentage of it is used for feeding the young?
3. Does an individual male's territory vary much from year to year in size and site?

E. *Does the female observe boundaries of the territory like the male?*
1. Does she drive off other females?
2. How does she react to intruding males?

F. *Do male and female both roost in the territory?*
1. Do they roost together?
2. Do they always roost in the same places?
3. At what hours do they roost?

IV. Pair Formation

A. *How does the male react to strange birds of its own species during the breeding season?*
1. Is its first reaction hostile or friendly?
2. Does it recognize females at once?
3. Do female birds have special behavior traits that enable males to distinguish their sex?
4. At what distances is the male at first able to recognize a female?
5. After pair formation, does he recognize his mate at longer distances? And merely by sound?
   a. How does he treat neighboring females during the nesting season?
   b. How quickly and by what means does he recognize them?
   c. How long does it take him to know the voice of his own mate?

B. *In forming a pair, does dominance enter into the relation between the male and his mate?*
1. Does this change at any time during the breeding cycle?
2. Does copulation occur as soon as the birds are paired?
   a. How frequently does it occur during the different stages of the nesting season?
   b. Does it occur only between members of a pair?
   c. Is its frequency in any way related to temperature or other elements of the weather?
   d. Does the male or female give any special signals or displays immediately prior to coition?

C. *Is there any evidence that the female selects the largest males, or the best-looking ones?*
   1. Does a particularly favorable territory give a male bird some advantage in securing a mate?
   2. Do young males obtain mates as quickly as the older birds?

V. NEST BUILDING

A. *Which sex selects the nesting site?*
   1. How long does selection of a site take?
   2. How close (if at all) is the new nest located to last year's site?
   3. How close is it to the male's singing perches?

B. *Do both sexes build the nest?*
   1. Which plays the leading part?
   2. Where are the materials obtained?
   3. About how many trips are needed to construct a nest?
   4. What materials are used to construct the nest?

C. *How is the start of nest building correlated with weather and the season's growth of vegetation?*

D. *During what hours is the nest built?*

E. *Is nest building accompanied by an increased frequency of copulation?*

F. *Do other pairs of this species build at the same time?*

G. *Do older birds appear to build better nests than the younger ones?*

H. *When second nests are built later on in the season, do the young of the first brood ever help?*

I. *In years of dense population, do prolonged territorial disputes delay nest construction and egg laying?*

VI. EGG LAYING AND INCUBATION

A. *Is the date of the first egg largely determined by the weather?*
   1. What interval of time occurs between completion of the nest and laying of the first egg?
   2. Does this interval vary among different pairs?

B. *At what hour of the day is each egg laid?*
   1. How many hours elapse between the laying of each egg?

C. *What is the average number of eggs in a clutch? The maximum? The minimum?*
   1. Does a search of the literature show that this average is constant for all latitudes?

2. Are fewer eggs laid in second layings?
3. Does the average size of clutches vary according to
   a. The age of the female?
   b. The local density of this species' population?
   c. The time of the season?
   d. Latitude?
   e. Inheritance?
   f. Precipitation or drought?
   g. Local abundance of food?

D. *How does a female bird react when (a) the eggs are taken;*
   (b) the whole nest destroyed?
   1. Does it desert the locality or does it promptly prepare
      to renest?
   2. How does this behavior vary with the progress of incuba-
      tion?
   3. How many renestings will a female bird attempt?
   4. How many eggs could she lay if her eggs were never
      permitted to accumulate past one or two?
   5. What percentage of nests with eggs are destroyed?
      a. What are the birds' enemies at this time?
      b. What percentage of nesting failures is due to each?
      c. What percentage of nesting failures is due to weather?

E. *Just when does the female begin to incubate?*
   1. With the laying of the first egg, the last egg, or at some
      later interval?

F. *Exactly how long does it take to hatch the eggs?*
   1. If the eggs are numbered with india ink, do any exhibit
      slightly different periods necessary for hatching?
   2. Does the incubation period ever vary?
      a. With unusual weather conditions?
      b. With any unusual lack of attention shown the eggs
         by one of the parents?

G. *Do both sexes brood the eggs? Or does just one sex brood*
   them?
   1. Which sex incubates at night?
   2. Does the male ever feed the female on the nest?
   3. Does the female ever call from the nest?
   4. Does the male ever call his mate back to the nest?

H. *Over a five- to eight-hour period on a given day, how much*
   time is actually spent in brooding the eggs?

    1. What is the average time spent on the nest? The maximum? The minimum? *

    2. How do these periods vary with the progress of incubation and differences in weather?

I. *If both sexes incubate, do they ever engage in a special ceremony when they change places at the nest?*

    1. Does either sex exhibit any unusual behavior when the eggs are about to hatch?

J. *Is this species able to recognize its own eggs?*

    1. Will it tolerate foreign objects in the nest?

    2. Would the birds continue to brood if an entire set of some other species' eggs was substituted for their own?

    3. Would they react in the same way if only a single egg was substituted?

    4. If the nest is on the ground, will the adults recognize their own eggs when these are conspicuously placed outside the nest?

    a. Will they endeavor to roll the eggs back?

    b. What is the maximum distance at which they will do this?

K. *How does the weight of each egg vary from day to day?*

L. *How do the weights of the parents vary at this time?*

VII. CARE AND FEEDING OF NESTLINGS

A. *What percentage of the pairs hatch their first set of eggs?*

    1. What percentage of all the eggs hatch?

    2. What is the percentage of infertility?

    3. What is the average number of young hatched in successful nests?

    4. Are old birds more successful in hatching their eggs than younger parents?

    5. What happens to the egg shells? Are they eaten by the parent birds or carried away?

* In *The Auk,* Frank A. Pitelka has recently pointed out the advantages of publishing these facts in a standard form of table, viz.

Time advance of nesting: incubation, 5th day (June 15, 1940)
Length of observation: 5 hours (8 A.M.-1 P.M.)

Incubation by both sexes:	*on nest*	*off nest*
Number of periods	7	8
Average time (minutes)	30	10.3
Extremes (minutes)	10-50	5-55
Percentage of total time	70%	30%

Similar tables can be used to show attention given the eggs by the male and female birds separately.

   B. *What is the weight of the newly hatched young?*
      1. How does this vary from day to day while they are in
         the nest?
      2. How does the size of the young increase from day to
         day?
         a. Do all parts of the body grow at the same rate?
      3. For how many days does the female continue to brood
         the young?
   C. *How many visits do the parents make to the nest each day
      to feed the young?* *
      1. How is the number of these visits related to the time of
         day, changes in the weather, the increased growth of
         the fledglings?
      2. How soon after hatching are the fledglings first fed?
         a. Do the parents ever bring food before the young birds
            have gaped (i.e. elevated their heads and opened
            their mouths for food)?
      3. Do the parents ever visit the nest and not feed the
         young? How often?
      4. About how many morsels or pieces of food are brought
         at each visit?
   D. *When does defecation by the young first occur?*
      1. Do the adults remove the fecal sacs at once?
      2. How many of these are swallowed?
      3. How far are the others carried away?
      4. Do the parents ever wait for the young to defecate?
   E. *Do the male and female have habitual ways in which they
      approach the nest?*
      1. Are the same paths used when the nest contains eggs and
         when it contains young?

* These visits obviously vary in number as the young grow older. Information reported will be clear and convenient if it is summarized in this standard
table suggested by Pitelka:

Age of nestlings: 4 days	*Number of intervals:* 6
Period of observation: 5 hours	*Average length:* 40 minutes
(8 A.M.-1 P.M.)	*Extremes:* 5-50 minutes
Number of nestlings: 3	*Number of nestlings fed per visit:*
Total number of feeding visits: 8	*Known instances:* 8
Average number per hour: 1.6	*Average number:* 2
Extremes: 1-3	*Extremes:* 1-3

Probably a five-hour period of observation would be enough for one day in
studies of smaller species. With larger birds like terns, gulls, and hawks, all-
day observation would be better. This table can be used to summarize information for both adults, for the male, and for the female. Unusual weather
conditions might also be listed in a table of this kind.

F. *What striking colors or patterns, if any, do the young exhibit inside their mouths when they gape?*
   1. What are the exact colors of the naked parts of the fledgling?
   2. Do these colors change
      a. From youth to maturity?
      b. With the seasons? With age?

G. *For how many days are the young blind?*
   1. In this early stage, what causes them to gape?
      a. Calls of the adults?
      b. Any noise?
      c. A slight jarring or tapping of the nest?
   2. Do they raise their mouths straight up at first?

H. *When they finally see, will the young gape at both moving and stationary objects? At shadows or rapid changes in light intensity at the nest?*
   1. Will they gape at cardboard outlines of their parents?
   2. At square pieces of cardboard, round pieces, triangles, large pieces, small pieces, pieces with knob-like projections (representing an adult's head)?
   3. When is gaping first directed toward the adult birds, instead of aimlessly upward?

I. *How do the parents react when their fledglings fail to gape for food?*

J. *At what age do the young*
   1. First call for food?
   2. First pay attention to noise?
   3. First react to warning cries of the adults?
   4. First react with fear
      a. To human beings?
      b. To stuffed hawks and owls?
      c. To moving cardboard outlines of hawks and owls?

K. *In what order do the feather tracts develop?*

L. *What is the minimum age for the successful banding of nestlings?*
   1. At what age will banding operations result in the young prematurely leaving the nest?
   2. What is the best age at which to place young birds in a trap and use them as bait to capture and color band the adults?

M. *What are the enemies of this species at this time?*
   1. What percentage of fledgling mortality is due to each of these?

2. What percentage of nests are broken up or destroyed?
3. Compared to the original number of eggs laid, what percentage of young successfully leave the nest?
4. What is the average number of young raised per pair that attempted to nest?
5. Does this vary from year to year? Are variations due to
   a. Fluctuations in the predator population?
   b. Differences in weather?
   c. Changes in the habitat or vegetation?
   d. Fluctuations in the availability of food?
   e. Changes in the population density of this species?
N. *Where do the parent birds now forage for food?*
   1. Does the male continue to defend his original territory?
O. *How many broods of young do pairs of this species raise in this region?*

VIII. ABANDONMENT OF THE NEST

A. *At what hours do the young leave the nest?*
   1. Are they prompted by the parents in any way? How?
B. *How far do they scatter the first day?*
   1. Is their direction due to chance?
   2. Do they continue to move each day? Or do they become relatively immobile, awaiting the development of flight?
   3. Do they spread beyond the boundaries of the adults' territory?
   4. Do they ever return to the nest?
   5. How do they signal their presence to their parents?
   6. Do they ever beg from adult birds of other species?
   7. Where and how fortuitously do they roost at first?
C. *Is their behavior now marked by changes in vocabulary or new reactions?*
   1. Do these changes appear a fixed number of days after hatching? Or are they coincident with abandonment of the nest?
D. *Does the behavior of the adult birds change as this time approaches?*
   1. What happens to the adults' weight during this period?
   2. How do the parents now share in feeding the young?
   3. Is territorial defense still maintained? When does it cease?
E. *At what age do the young birds*
   1. Begin feeding themselves?
   2. Stop begging for food?
   3. First bathe (in dust or water)?

    4. First give warning cries?

    5. First sing experimentally?

F. *What percentage of the young successfully manage to fly?*

    1. What percentages of the mortality at this time can be attributed to weather, or to predators?

G. *How long do the young birds remain in a family flock?*

    1. If colored feathers are attached (with Duco cement) to their backs, can it be determined where the young birds settle down for the summer?

H. *How long do the parents remain together? Do both spend the summer in the vicinity or do they move off once their family ties are ended?*

I. *Why do certain males remain in song very late in the season?*

    1. Are they unmated males, or are they birds involved in late renestings?

    2. Does an unusually late song season in a given locality indicate a population with an unbalanced sex ratio, or one in which many early nestings were broken up by weather?

IX. Sex Ratio

A. *What is the ratio of male to female birds?*

    1. Does this change in any way from month to month?

    2. Does it vary from year to year?

    3. Is it the same in old and young?

B. *How do unmated birds act in the breeding season?*

    1. Do they sing more and longer?

    2. Do they attempt to form polygamous or polyandrous relations with mated birds?

    3. Do their territories seem to be adequate?

    4. Do they tend to be rather old, rather young, or equally distributed in all age classes?

    5. Do they ever attempt to help other birds incubate eggs or feed young?

C. *Does an unbalanced sex ratio seriously affect the reproductive capacity of the population?*

X. Population Questions (in addition to those questions already listed for reproductive success and sex ratio, many of the following can only be answered by banding)

A. *What percentages of the breeding population can be assigned to different age classes (birds one year old, those two years old, etc.)?*

    1. How do these percentages vary from year to year?
      a. Do they reflect last year's reproductive success?
      b. Are they more dependent on migrational winter mortality?

B. *How many eggs are laid to replace one adult bird in the breeding population a year later?*
    1. At what age do most birds of this species breed for the first time?

C. *What is the life expectancy of*
    1. A young bird just hatching?
    2. A bird one year old?
    3. A bird banded in random trapping operations?

D. *How does the total population vary*
    1. From month to month?
    2. From year to year?

E. *Can these fluctuations be correlated with*
    1. Nesting success, weather, predation?
    2. Spring, migrational, or winter mortality of the adults?
    3. Balanced or unbalanced sex ratio?
    4. Changes in habitat?

F. *In multi-brooded species (robin, house wren, etc.), which brood contributes the largest percentage of one-year-old birds in next year's population?*

XI. ROOSTING

A. *How high up and in what cover does this species generally roost in this region?*

B. *How is the roost site selected?*

C. *How does the time of arrival at the roost vary with*
    1. Temperature?
    2. The amount of light each day (cloudiness, etc.)? *
    3. The time of sunset?
    4. The distance traveled from feeding grounds?
    5. Progress of the season?

D. *Will certain levels of low temperature cause the birds to roost closely together?*

E. *How many birds die or are killed at their roost sites?*
    1. What are their enemies believed to be at this time?
    2. What is the density of owls in this locality?

F. *Is the roost site changed after the nesting season?*

G. *Compared to individual roosts, do communal roosts give birds any additional protection from predators?*

---

* Excellent suggestions on the exploration of this phenomenon are contained in volume 2 of Margaret M. Nice's *Life-History Studies of the Song Sparrow.*

H. *During what seasons (if any) do these birds exercise territorial rights to their roosting perch?*
   1. How large an area do they then defend?
   2. What other species roost in the same cover?

XII. Bird Parasites

A. *Are there any ticks, mites, lice, or 'maggots' in the nest?*
B. *Are there any of these attached to the fledglings?*
   1. Are any maggots in the ears or on the necks?
   2. Are mites or lice present on the feathers?
   3. Are ticks present on the head or neck?
   4. Are tumor-like growths present on the vent? *
C. *Are flies, mosquitoes, or gnats present on the nestlings?* (They may be carriers of filarial or malarial parasites, and should be collected and preserved in alcohol.)
D. *Are any of these also found on the adults?*
E. *Are lesions, abrasions, or scabs present on the soft parts?*
F. *Are growths present on the feet?*

XIII. Flocking Habits

A. *When do flocks of this species form?*
   1. Are they composed of family groups?
B. *How does the size of the flock vary from week to week?*
   1. What are the causes of flock losses?
C. *How far does the flock forage each day?*
   1. Does it follow customary routes?
   2. Does it select foraging places with some regard to wind conditions?
   3. How is its behavior affected by the appearance of predators?
D. *What other species become a part of the flock?*
   1. Are they more alert to predators or less so than this species?
   2. Do they react to warning calls when they first join the flock, or do they learn them later?
E. *What is the age composition of the group? The sex?*
F. *Do observations on color-marked birds disclose definite relations among various individuals?*
   1. Can the individual birds be set in an order of dominance?
   2. Are these relations fixed for the season, or do they vary?

---

* Such fledglings very probably contain anal flukes, which will eventually spread to other birds. The young birds should be painlessly killed (by tightly pressing their sides together under the wings) and sent to the nearest parasitologist in a jar of rubbing alcohol.

XIV. General Questions

A. *How much of a bird's day is spent in foraging for food? In preening? In resting?*
  1. Over how large an area does this species forage in each season?
  2. How do these activities vary from one season to another?
  3. How are they related to territorialism?
B. *How often do birds bathe? How often do they drink?*
C. *How many different call notes are used by each sex?*
  1. Under what conditions is each call used?
  2. Can these calls be broken down into alarm notes, warning notes, scolding notes, location ('here I am') notes?
D. *What animals invoke fear reactions in this species?*
  1. Are these reactions all innate or are some of them learned?
E. *Over how long a period does molting take place?*
  1. In what order are the various feathers replaced?
  2. How much time is required to replace important feather tracts like those of the primary feathers?
  3. How is this time affected by weather conditions?
  4. Do the birds spend more time feeding during this period?
  5. What factors inhibit molt? Which ones stimulate it?
F. *Can very slight differences in the shape (or tips) of feathers be used to distinguish between sexes, or between old and young birds?*
  1. Can wing and tail measurements also be used to distinguish between males and females that are thought to look alike?
G. *How do the adults' weights vary, with the time of day, with temperature, with the season, according to sex, during the molt?*
H. *How does the departure of migrants take place?*
  1. Which leave first—the adults or the young?
  2. What are the dates of departure? Is there a peak?
  3. How is departure affected?
    a. By temperature?
    b. By wind?
    c. By cloudy and clear nights?
    d. By available food supplies?
  4. When do migrants from more northern regions pass through?
    a. Do these differ in size or weight from resident birds?
    b. How long do individual birds stay locally?

c. When is their peak? How is this correlated with weather conditions to the north?
5. Are late fall stragglers resident birds or individuals from a more northern latitude?
6. How closely does the peak of departure by summer residents coincide with the peak of numbers of birds migrating through?

Appendix D

AN ANNOTATED LIST OF BIRD BOOKS

1. Colored portraits of birds
2. Field identification guides
3. Regional works
4. Bird songs
5. Bird watching (general)
6. Bird behavior
7. Birds and their environment
8. Bird migration
9. Life-history studies
   a. Books for general readers
   b. Books for bird watchers
   c. Technical dissertations
10. General reference books
11. Bird biology
12. Miscellaneous
13. Bird conservation
14. Biographical works

BIRD BOOKS are here grouped according to the special needs and requirements of bird watchers. The list is fairly extensive (although by no means complete). Books that are out of print can often be purchased from second-hand dealers, who advertise in periodicals such as *The Auk* or *Audubon Magazine*. The newer volumes can be ordered through one's local book dealer, or from the National Audubon Society (except in the case of state and federal publications).

In starting the study of birds, the novice naturalist will require two or three books in the first three categories listed here. He will so frequently consult them when first learning to identify birds that they should be purchased as soon as possible. Books in the remaining groups are occasionally found in public libraries, although seldom in any number.

Reading bird books is a good deal of fun. Through them the amateur naturalist can pursue his hobby on many occasions when field work is impossible—in the evenings, on railroad trains, and during periods of convalescence. One ardent bird watcher is said to have read over 30 volumes of the periodical *British Birds* while riding subway trains back and forth from work. His field work inevitably was enriched by new points of view and by a knowledge of the many ways others have explored the mysteries of bird life.

1. COLORED PORTRAITS OF BIRDS

A good set of colored plates is the first requirement of most novice bird students. Occasionally such plates are found in state bird books (see regional works), but for the most part these are out of print or are about to become so.

The Book of Birds. Edited by Gilbert Grosvenor and Alexander Wetmore, etc. 1937. National Geographic Society, Washington, D.C., Vol. 1, viii + 357 pp.; vol. 2, 374 pp. 204 color plates, 228 photographs.

Recommended to all beginners who do not find colored plates in their regional bird books. These two volumes bring together the well-known articles on birds written for the *National Geographic Magazine* by leading ornithologists. Short biographies cover 633 species, giving their approximate length, range, behavior high lights, and subspecies. Chapters on bird banding, an eagle's eyrie, and photographic adventures are included. The chief value of the book is its extensive series of excellent color plates (mostly by Major Allan Brooks, the noted Canadian illustrator); these cover about 500 species (over 950 portraits). There is also a fine series of bird photographs. The book can be used anywhere in the United States or Canada, and must be ordered directly from the publisher.

The Hawks of North America. By John B. May. 1935. National Association of Audubon Societies (now National Audubon Society), New York. ix + 140 pp. 41 plates, 33 maps.

Largely limited to the identification of various hawks and a comprehensive summary of their food habits. Four plates in black and white by Roger T. Peterson give the flight outlines of hawks, and a list shows the state laws protecting them (as of March 1, 1935). There are 37 color plates by Major Brooks, especially pleasing because the figures are not crowded. Maps show the distribution of each species. Order directly from the publisher.

The Ducks, Geese, and Swans of North America. By Francis H. Kortright. 1942. American Wildlife Institute, Washington, D.C. viii + 476 pp. 36 color plates, 57 text figures, 59 maps, 158 drawings in black and white.

Parts of this waterfowl handbook duplicate the material found in Bent's life histories (now rare and very expensive). Information on 62 species and subspecies is summarized under: scientific names (each being fully explained), colloquial names, descriptions, specimen identification, field marks (on the water, in flight, and voice), and life story. To beginners, the many illustrations will undoubtedly be instructive, although T. M. Shortt's fine drawings are marred by being printed on a cheap paper. Nine methods for sex and age determinations, now commonly used by experts in game research, are described. The 282 informative color illustrations include 8 hybrids and albinos, 44 birds in the downy stage, and a number of others in interesting stages of molt. There are good maps of the summer and winter range of each species but, beyond a general description by F. C. Lincoln, there is no information on waterfowl banding.

Bird Portraits in Color. By Thomas S. Roberts. 1934. University of Minnesota Press, Minneapolis, Minn.

Plates from the Minnesota state bird book, covering 295 species and supplemented by a brief text. Recommended to bird students in the Middle West and central Canada.

2. FIELD IDENTIFICATION GUIDES

Field guides provide helpful short cuts to the identification of birds at a distance. They can be carried in the pocket to settle problems in the field. Even experienced naturalists find them useful. Most of the birds are drawn without color—the way they usually appear in the field.

A Field Guide to the Birds. By Roger T. Peterson. 1939, rev. ed. Houghton Mifflin Co., Boston, Mass. xx + 180 pp. 4 color plates, 36 plates in black and white, 24 text figures.

A helpful book for the beginner, brief and telegraphic in style. For each species there is a short description of the field marks, voice, and range. The plates are diagrammatic and emphasize diagnostic marks. The book covers the area from the Dakotas and east Texas to the Atlantic coast. The author is a staff member of the National Audubon Society and a contributing editor to *Audubon Magazine*.

A Field Guide to Western Birds. By Roger T. Peterson. 1941. Houghton Mifflin Co., Boston, Mass. xviii + 240 pp. 46 plates (5 in color), 40 text figures.

An excellent counterpart of the author's much-used guide for eastern birds (see above). Covers Oregon, California, Nevada, Idaho, Utah, Washington, Montana, Wyoming, Colorado, Arizona, New Mexico, and the western part of Texas. It is both up to date and competent.

3. REGIONAL WORKS

Every student who attempts to identify birds in the field will save himself much trouble by obtaining the best available list of birds known to occur in his region. In this section, the emphasis has been placed on state publications. For more local lists, which are often more up to date, consult an officer of the nearest bird club.

Birds of Alabama. By Arthur H. Howell. 1928, 2nd ed. Dept. of Game and Fisheries, Montgomery, Ala. 384 pp. 7 plates in black and white, 31 text figures.

A report of 314 kinds of birds, together with a list of references. Treats of state records, general habits, and food habits.

A Distributional List of the Birds of Arizona. By H. S. Swarth. 1914. Cooper Ornithological Club. Pacific Coast Avifauna No. 10. 133 pp. 1 map.

Status of birds in the state, with a bibliography of papers relating to Arizona ornithology. Now somewhat dated. See also *Birds of New Mexico.*

Birds of Arkansas. By W. J. Baerg. 1931. University of Arkansas Experiment Station, Fayetteville, Ark. Bull. 258. 197 pp.

A brief description of the range of 312 species and subspecies, with a short account of the habits of the better-known species. Contains a number of half-tone illustrations.

The Birds of California. By William L. Dawson. 1923. Distributed by W. L. Chambers, Topanga, Calif. 4 vols. 2121 pp. 30 photogravures, 120 full-page duotone plates, 44 drawings, 110 full-page color plates, over 1100 photographs.

Popular accounts of 580 species and subspecies, with brief summaries of the birds' synonyms, descriptions, field marks, nesting, general range, and distribution in California. These sumptuous volumes are noted for their many photographs (nests and habitats) and their color plates. Under each species is a useful list of references. There are several editions of these volumes, all differently priced. A number of excellent regional studies have subsequently been published: Yosemite, 1924; San Francisco Bay region, 1927; northern California, 1930; and southwestern California, 1933.

A Guide to Colorado Birds. By W. H. Bergtold, 1928. Smith-Brooks Printing Co., Denver, Colo. 207 pp.

Not examined. A more recent publication, *The Birds of Denver and Mountain Parks* by R. J. Niedrach and R. B. Rockwell, was issued in 1939 by the Colorado Museum of Natural History, Denver, Colo.

The Birds of Connecticut. By John Hall Sage and Louis B. Bishop. 1913. State Geological and Natural History Survey, Bull. No. 20. 370 pp.

The status of 329 kinds of birds occurring in Connecticut, together with arrival and departure dates, nest dates, and egg dates. This state is now adequately covered by Forbush's *Birds of Massachusetts* and Cruickshank's *Birds around New York City*.

Florida Bird Life. By Arthur H. Howell. 1932. Florida Department of Game and Fresh Water Fish and Bureau of Biological Survey, U.S.D.A. Distributed by National Audubon Society, New York. xxiv + 579 pp. 37 plates (35 in color), 36 photographs, 73 maps.

Distribution of birds in the state with emphasis on life zones. Illustrations of 173 birds in color by F. L. Jaques. The introductory chapters include a history of Florida ornithology, a history of legislative attempts to protect birds in the state, and a discussion of the physiographic regions of Florida.

Birds of the Atlanta, Georgia, Area. By Earle R. Greene. 1933. Bull. No. 2, Georgia Society of Naturalists, Atlanta, Ga. 46 pp. 3 plates, 2 maps.

No state list of birds for Georgia is now available. This list, the one following, and *Florida Bird Life* will give some idea of what can be expected.

Observations on the Bird Life of the Middle Savannah Valley, 1890-1937. By Eugene Edmund Murphey. 1937. Charleston Museum, Charleston, S.C. Contribution No. 9. 61 pp. Frontispiece, 1 map.

A briefly annotated list of birds occurring along the 'fall line' between Georgia and South Carolina, based on observations covering a span of 40 years.

Birds of the Chicago Region. By Edward Ford, Colin C. Sanford, and C. Blair Coursen. 1934. Chicago Academy of Sciences, Chicago, Ill. Vol. v, Nos. 2 and 3.

A list of 371 species and subspecies, giving the status and migration dates of each.

The Birds of Indiana. By Amos W. Butler, 1898. Prepared for the Indiana Horticultural Society and originally published in its Transactions for 1890. Pp. 515-1197. 102 figures, 5 plates in black and white.

A description of 321 kinds of birds known to occur within the state up to the time of publication. Aside from more local lists in the periodical literature, there is no modern list covering the entire state. General statements on bird distribution can, of course, be found in the A.O.U. *Check-List* and in Peterson's field guides. Dates for representative parts of the country are available in Chapman's handbook.

A Revised List of the Birds of Iowa. By Philip A. Dumont. 1934. University of Iowa, Iowa City, Iowa. University of Iowa Studies in Natural History, Vol. xv (No. 5). 171 pp. 1 map.

Status and distribution of birds in the state up to 1933.

History of the Birds of Kansas. By N. G. Goss. 1891. George W. Crane and Co., Topeka, Kans. 692 pp. 35 plates in black and white.

A detailed description of Kansas birds known in the nineteenth century.

Notes on the Birds of Kentucky. By Alexander Wetmore. 1940. Proceedings of the United States National Museum, Washington, D.C. Vol. 88, No. 3089. Pp. 529-74.

Distributional notes on 167 kinds of birds reported by field parties from the National Museum. There is no list of birds for this state.

The Bird Life of Louisiana. By Harry C. Oberholser. 1938. Department of Conservation, New Orleans, La. Bull. No. 28. xii + 834 pp. 8 color plates, 37 photographs.

Annotated list of 429 forms reported within the state, with a comprehensive bibliography and a good index. Not all the kinds of birds mentioned are as yet recognized by scientists. The excellent photographs are by A. M. Bailey and F. R. Dickinson.

The Birds of Maine. By Ora Willis Knight. 1908. Published by the author, Bangor, Me. 693 pp. 30 illustrations.

An account of 327 species and subspecies, their distribution and migration, their abundance in the various counties, and something of their life histories. Although this material has been brought more up to date in Forbush's *Birds of Massachusetts,* Knight's volume still remains the only publication devoted exclusively to birds of Maine.

The Birds of Massachusetts and Other New England States. By Edward Howe Forbush. 1925-9. Massachusetts Department of Agriculture, Boston, Mass. Vol. 1, xxxi + 481 pp.; vol. 2, 1 + 461 pp.; vol. 3, xlviii + 466 pp. 93 color plates, 98 photographs, 123 line cuts, 37 maps.

Of great use to students in all northeastern states. Describes the known plumages in great detail; includes measurements, molts, field marks, voice, number and size of eggs, dates of laying and periods of incubation, range in the world, distribution in New England, and 'season' in Massachusetts. This material is set off by headings and can be quickly consulted.

The remaining text is given over to popularly written life-history accounts, compiled from the literature and from the author's extensive correspondence. The color plates, by Louis A. Fuertes, American portrait painter of birds, and by Major Brooks, Canadian illustrator, were made when both men were at the peak of their powers.

Volume 2 (gallinaceous birds, hawks, owls, woodpeckers, flycatchers, blackbirds) is out of print, other volumes are still available (1943) from the Secretary of the Commonwealth, State House, Boston, Mass.

Birds of the Connecticut Valley in Massachusetts. By Aaron C. Bagg and Samuel A. Eliot, Jr. 1937. The Hampshire Bookshop, Northampton, Mass. lxxiv + (20) + 813 pp.

A systematic list of the distribution of over 300 species, giving local occurrence according to various towns. Comparisons with distribution in near-by regions are also given.

Check List of the Birds of Michigan. By Josselyn Van Tyne. 1938. University of Michigan, Ann Arbor, Mich. Museum of Zoölogy, Occasional Papers, No. 379. 44 pp. 1 map.

The first complete state list since 1912 when *Michigan Bird Life* by W. B. Barrows was published by the Michigan Agricultural College.

The Birds of Minnesota. By Thomas S. Roberts. 1937, 2nd rev. ed. University of Minnesota Press, Minneapolis, Minn. Vol. 1, xxii + 691 pp.; vol. 2, xv + 821 pp. 92 plates in color, 606 figures, 5 maps.

For the Middlewest and Manitoba. In the introduction, the geography of Minnesota and its bird life are discussed at length. The birds are then systematically described: general range, Minnesota range, Minnesota migration dates, Minnesota nesting, nest, food, and field marks. Miscellaneous details concerning life history are scattered in accounts under each species. The splendid color portraits by Brooks, Sutton, Weber, Jaques, and Fuertes cover 295 species and subspecies. There is a detailed key, useful in identifying dead birds.

The author has studied the ornithology of the state for over half a century; he has been a long-time compiler of 'The Season' (in Minnesota) for *Bird-Lore* and *Audubon Magazine,* and is director of the University of Minnesota's Museum of Natural History.

Check-List of the Birds of Missouri. By Rudolf Bennitt. 1932. University of Missouri Studies VII, No. 3. 81 pp. 1 map.

The first state list since 1907; gives the status in Missouri of 296 species and subspecies.

A Distributional List of the Birds of Montana. By Aretas A. Saunders. 1921. Pacific Coast Avifauna No. 14. Cooper Ornithological Club. 194 pp. 1 map, 35 photographs.

Describes the status in Montana of 332 kinds of birds, giving migratory or resident status and nesting dates. There is a discussion of the state's distributional areas, which the author classifies under faunal, zonal, and associational. Contains a bibliography of 10 pages.

The Birds of Nevada. By Jean M. Linsdale. 1936. Pacific Coast Avifauna No. 23. Cooper Ornithological Club. 145 pp.

A summary of all that is known (to 1936) about the birds occurring in Nevada; treats of 338 species and subspecies.

Bird Studies at Old Cape May. By Witmer Stone. 1937. Delaware Valley Ornithological Club. Vol. 1, xv + 520 pp; vol. 2, 420 pp. 239 photographs, 2 plates in color, 270 text figures.

An authoritative ornithology of southern New Jersey, notable for its descriptions of the great fall migrations at Cape May Point. Beautifully printed, illustrated, and bound, the work is a memorial to the late Dr. Stone, founder of the club and long-time editor of *The Auk.*

Birds of New Mexico. By Florence Merriam Bailey. 1928. New Mexico Department of Game and Fish (in co-operation with the State Game Protective Association and the Bureau of Biological Survey), Santa Fe, N.M. xxiv + 807 pp. 80 plates, 136 figures, 60 maps, 2 diagrams.

The best book for birds of the Southwest; with descriptions of each species and subspecies, their several plumages, general range, local distribution, nests, eggs, and food. There are 59 species illustrated in color on 24 full-page plates (mostly by Major Allan Brooks), 53 more are in full-page half-tones (mostly drawings by Louis A. Fuertes). The author is an authority on western birds.

Birds of New York. By Elon Howard Eaton. 1923, 2nd ed. New York State Museum, Albany, N.Y., Memoir 12. Vol. 1, 501, pp; vol. 2, 719 pp. 106 color plates.

First of the more impressive state bird books, these two volumes, describing 411 kinds of birds known to occur in New York, are outstanding for their fine plates by Louis A. Fuertes. Introductory material includes lists of permanent residents, summer residents, transients, and winter, summer, and accidental visitants, a discussion of the state's life zones, and lengthy tables showing the status of each species in various counties and towns (as of 1910 and 1914, when this work was first published). Now more-or-less outmoded by Forbush's *Birds of Massachusetts*, with its more complete details and essays on the various species. Abundantly illustrated with maps, line drawings, and photographs.

Birds around New York City. By Allan D. Cruickshank. 1942. American Museum of Natural History, New York. Handbook Series No. 13. xvii + 489 pp. 35 plates, 1 map.

Covers the distribution and status of birds in northern New Jersey, the lower Hudson River valley, and all of Long Island; with superb photographs of birds by the author, and an interesting discussion of local bird life in relation to major ecological blocks.

Birds of North Carolina. By T. Gilbert Pearson and C. S. and H. H. Brimley. 1942. State Museum Division, North Carolina Department of Agriculture, Raleigh, N.C. xxxii + 416 pp. 40 plates (20 in color), 141 text figures.

In this greatly revised edition of an earlier work, the distribution of 396 species and subspecies is given, along with a general statement of habits, vernacular names, and dates of occurrence. There are a number of plates by Roger T. Peterson similar to those in his *A Field Guide to the Birds*.

A Preliminary Survey of the Bird Life of North Dakota. By Norman A. Wood. 1923. University of Michigan, Ann Arbor, Mich. Museum of Zoölogy, Pub. No. 10. 97 pp. 17 photographs, 1 map.

The occurrence of 321 kinds of birds within the state, together with a discussion of the three main geographical areas, and an extensive list of references.

Distribution of the Breeding Birds of Ohio. By Lawrence E. Hicks. 1936. Ohio State University, Columbus, Ohio. 65 pp.

An important state list of breeding birds, with a discussion of the exact status of each species. Compiled from the literature, museum collections, extensive field work by the author, and many contributions from Ohio bird watchers.

The Birds of Buckeye Lake, Ohio. By Milton B. Trautman. 1940. University of Michigan, Ann Arbor, Mich. Museum of Zoölogy, Misc. Pub. No. 44. 466 pp. 15 plates, 2 maps.

This volume, concerning an area of some 44 square miles, is generally recognized as the best regional study so far produced in this country.

The Birds of Oklahoma. By Margaret Morse Nice. 1931, rev. ed. Publication of the University of Oklahoma, Vol. ɪɪɪ (No. 1). 224 pp. 2 maps, 1 diagram.

A systematic list of 385 species and subspecies, together with notes on their status within the state. Introductory pages deal with the state's faunal areas, recent changes in its bird life, the economic value of birds, methods for their attraction and protection, and notes on field workers in Oklahoma from 1719 to 1929.

Birds of Oregon. By Ira N. Gabrielson and Stanley C. Jewett. 1940. Oregon State College, Corvallis, Ore. xxx + 650 pp. 1 color plate, 166 photographs, 21 maps.

An indispensable book for bird students in the Northwest, emphasizing the distribution of birds in Oregon. It also contains a brief account of the plumages of each species, the size of the birds, their nests and eggs. The photographs were taken largely by William L. Finley and H. T. Bohlman, two of the foremost bird photographers in the country.

Birds of Western Pennsylvania. By W. E. Clyde Todd. 1940. University of Pittsburgh Press, Pittsburgh, Pa. xv + 710 pp. 23 plates, 41 maps.

A standard work of reference for western Pennsylvania and near-by regions. Good summaries of each species' plumage, detailed accounts of their range and distribution, and brief descriptions of their habits. There are small but beautiful color portraits by George Miksch Sutton of 118 species. Local distribution of 39 species is mapped. The introduction includes a discussion of the problems of local distribution, and the text closes with an extensive bibliography of the ornithology of western Pennsylvania. Introduced birds like the starling and English sparrow are not considered in this book. The most recent volume covering the entire state was B. H. Warren's *Birds of Pennsylvania,* printed in 1890.

The Birds of Rhode Island. By Reginald Heber Howe, Jr., and Edward Sturtevant. 1899. Published by the authors. 111 pp. 6 photographs.

A list of 290 species and subspecies recorded in the state up to 1899. The same authors published a 24-page supplement in 1903. Now replaced by Forbush's *Birds of Massachusetts.*

Birds of South Carolina. By A. T. Wayne. 1910. Charleston Museum, Charleston, S.C. xvi + 254 pp.

An annotated list of 309 species of coastal South Carolina, together with a list of 28 species from the interior, and 22 hypothetical species.

A second supplement to this work, published as a contribution from the Charleston Museum (vi) in 1931 by Alexander Sprunt, Jr., and E. B. Chamberlain, contains notes on 197 kinds of birds. For the fauna along the Georgia-South Carolina boundary, see Dr. E. E. Murphey's *Observations on the Bird Life of the Middle Savannah Valley*, on page 212.

Birds of South Dakota. By William H. Over and Craig S. Thomas. 1920. Bulletin of the University of South Dakota, Vermillion, S.D. Series xxi, No. 9. 142 pp. 50 photographs.

Distribution of 322 species and subspecies, a short discussion of bird study, and a bibliography.

A Distributional List of the Birds of Tennessee. By Albert F. Ganier. 1933. Tennessee Ornithological Society, Nashville, Tenn. Tennessee Avifauna No. 1. 64 pp. 1 map.

A briefly annotated list of 293 species and subspecies, and a discussion of the state's distinctive physiographic features as they relate to bird distribution.

A state book on the birds of *Texas* has long been in preparation by Dr. Harry C. Oberholser. Good regional lists are: *Birds of the Austin Region* by George Finlay Simmons (1925, University of Texas); *The Birds of Brewster County, Texas*, by Josselyn Van Tyne and George M. Sutton (1938, University of Michigan Press, Ann Arbor, Mich.); and *Check List of Birds of Dallas County, Texas*, by Jerry E. Stillwell (1939, Dallas Ornithological Society).

A List of Vermont Birds. By H. C. Fortner, Wendell P. Smith, and E. J. Dole. 1933. Vermont Department of Agriculture, Montpelier, Vt. Bull. No. 41. 54 pp.

Supplements the material in Forbush's *Birds of Massachusetts*. A list of 298 species and subspecies.

The Birds of Virginia. By Harold H. Bailey. 1913. J. P. Bell Co., Lynchburg, Va. 362 pp. 14 color plates, 1 map, 108 photographs.

An account of the range and status of all birds known by the author to breed in the state, together with a 'hypothetical' list of species that should breed in Virginia, but for which the author was unable to find any evidence.

Distributional Check-List of the Birds of Washington. By E. A. Kitchin. 1934. Pacific Northwest Bird and Mammal Society, Seattle, Wash. Northwest Fauna Series No. 1. 28 pp.

A list of 389 kinds of birds, with a brief statement of the status of each in the state and some details of distribution; also contains a list of 39 other species that may be expected to occur in Washington.

List of the Birds of West Virginia, in *The West Virginia Encyclopedia.* By Earle A. Brooks. 1929. West Virginia Publishing Co., Charleston, W.Va. Pp. 60-74.

An annotated list of 268 kinds of birds found in the state, with short notes on the character of their occurrence, and a number of half-tone illustrations.

Wisconsin Birds. By N. R. Barger, *et al.* 1942. Wisconsin Society of Ornithology. Distributed by E. L. Loyster, Conservation Department, Madison, Wis. 32 pp.

A check list giving the general status of all birds known to occur in this state, together with a handy chart showing the periods when migratory species may be expected.

Wyoming Bird Life. By Otto McCreary. 1937. University of Wyoming, Laramie, Wyo.

Not examined.

Natural History of the Birds of Eastern and Central North America. By E. H. Forbush. Revised and abridged by John B. May. 1939. Houghton Mifflin Co., Boston, Mass. xxvi + 554 pp. 97 color plates.

An abridged edition of the *Birds of Massachusetts,* the second volume of which is out of print. Contains brief remarks on identification, calls, breeding, and range; also short accounts of each species' haunts and habits. Illustrated in color are 375 kinds of birds. This book can be used as a companion to Peterson's field guide (east of the Mississippi). Somewhat similar in scope to *The Book of Birds,* it lacks the remarkable photographs of that work, but compensates somewhat by its abstracts of Mr. Forbush's delightful essays on each species.

Birds of the Pacific States. By Ralph Hoffmann. 1927. Houghton Mifflin Co., Boston, Mass. xix + 353 pp. 10 color plates, 200 illustrations in black and white.

One of the most useful bird books for the Pacific Coast states. Emphasis is placed on the field identification of some 400 kinds of birds described. For each species there is a description of its occurrence, typical habits, song, measurements, a concise statement of diagnostic field characters, and distribution in California, Oregon, and Washington. Color plates and line drawings are by Major Allan Brooks.

Birds of Canada. By P. A. Taverner. 1938. David McKay Co., 604 South Washington Square, Philadelphia, Pa. 455 pp. 173 small plates in color, 488 figures in black and white.

The bird book for a Canadian, this contains excellent color plates and brief descriptions of all Canadian birds. The French names of birds will be of some help to Americans visiting Quebec. There is also a good list of books dealing with provincial birds and special geographic regions. The present volume was first issued by the National Museum of Canada in 1934.

The Distribution of Breeding Birds in Ontario. By James L. Baillie, Jr., and Paul Harrington. 1937. Royal Ontario Museum of Zoölogy, Toronto. Contribution No. 8. 283 pp. 1 map.

An accurate account of the nesting birds of this province. Treats of 210 species, and contains a list of 225 references.

The Birds of Newfoundland Labrador. By Oliver L. Austin, Jr. 1932. Memoirs of the Nuttall Ornithological Club, No. vii. i + 229 pp.

A good summary of what is known of the distribution of birds in this little-studied region.

Birds of the Ocean. By W. B. Alexander. 1928. G. W. Putnam's Sons, New York and London. xx + 428 pp. 140 illustrations.

A handbook for voyagers, covering 294 species that are scattered over the several oceans. The habits and characters of each family are described, and for each species there are brief descriptions, measurements, ranges, egg dates, and field marks. Faunal lists are given for different seasons to aid the traveler in identifying birds on the ocean.

Identifying sea birds is not an easy task. There is no book with the charts of field marks used by Peterson in his field guides.

On the Habits and Distribution of Birds in the North Atlantic. By V. C. Wynne-Edwards. 1935. Proceedings of the Boston Society of Natural History, Vol. 40 (No. 4). Pp. 233-346, pl. 3-5.

More detailed information on distribution than Alexander's *Birds of the Ocean.*

The Birds of the West Indies. By James Bond. 1935. Academy of Natural Sciences, Philadelphia, Pa. xxv + 455 pp. 1 map, 1 color plate, 158 text figures.

The best combined field guide and reference book for this area. It contains descriptions of each species and detailed accounts of their range. Illustrated by Earle L. Poole. A briefer (184 pp.) check-list of the birds of the West Indies by the same author was published in 1940 by the Academy of Natural Sciences, adding 6 more species and much additional information on distribution.

4. BIRD SONGS

American Bird Songs. Recorded by the Albert R. Brand Bird Song Foundation (Laboratory of Ornithology, Cornell University). Comstock Publishing Co., Ithaca, N.Y. 1942. 6 double-disc records.

The perfect way to learn bird songs in our country. 72 are recorded here from nature. According to Roger T. Peterson, to listeners in the next room the songs sound exactly as they do out-of-doors; when one is close to the phonograph, the mechanical sounds of the recording are somewhat evident. Single records are as follows:

Nos. 1 A-B. *Birds of the Northwoods*
Nos. 2 A-B. *Birds of Northern Gardens and Shade Trees*
Nos. 3 A-B. *Birds of Southern Woods and Gardens*
Nos. 4 A-B. *Birds of the Fields and Prairies*
Nos. 5 A-B. *North American Game Birds*
Nos. 6 A-B. *Birds of Western North America*

A Guide to Bird Songs. By Aretas A. Saunders. 1935. D. Appleton-Century Co., New York, N.Y. xvii + 285 pp. 163 figures.

Descriptions of the songs and singing habits of 109 land birds of the northeastern states, diagrammed and presented in clear fashion. Nearly all of these birds can also be heard in the Middlewest. A good book for beginners, it is most useful when studied in the field and supplemented by the students' own notes.

5. BIRD WATCHING (GENERAL)

Bird watching, as a subject, has received much more attention abroad than in our country. The following volumes are arranged according to the levels of experience or maturity which they require of their readers. Fisher's *Watching Birds,* printed on cheap pulp paper, is unattractive in appearance, but by far the best buy for the money. Some excellent examples of successful bird watching may also be found in the sections on bird behavior and life-history studies.

Many American bird students have contented themselves with a field guide and a handbook. Such books are scarcely more than a prelude to the real fun in bird watching. Many other works, much less expensive, tell how birds live, and how interesting field studies have been used to explore the secrets still surrounding them.

The Book of Bird Life. By Arthur A. Allen. 1930. D. Van Nostrand Co., New York. xix + 426 pp.

Designed for young students, about one-half of the book is devoted to how birds live. Chapters include history, classification, distribution, communities, migration, courtship, home life, adaptation, coloration, and economics. The second half describes methods of studying birds: bird walks, calendars, banding, bird nests, attracting birds, observation blinds, bird photography, bird song, and bird pets. The author, long a professor of ornithology at Cornell University, is one of America's best bird photographers. In this volume, technical subjects are discussed with simplicity and naturalness.

Watching Birds. By James Fisher. 1940. Penguin Books, Inc., New York. 192 pp. 53 figures.

This inexpensive little book is well written and full of facts. Pocket-sized and written for British bird students, it will reward American bird watchers by its fresh and stimulating point of view and its fund of up-to-date information.

The Art of Bird Watching. By E. M. Nicholson. 1932. Charles Scribner's Sons, New York. 218 pp. 7 photographs, 14 text figures.

A lively British book on how to study birds, with a good chapter on bird-census methods. Many of its excellent ideas can be applied to bird watching in the United States. The author is an officer of the British Trust for Ornithology, a private institution that sponsors the bird-banding program of the British Isles and seeks to co-ordinate bird watching by amateur naturalists.

Birds as Animals. By James Fisher. 1939. Heinemann, London and Toronto. xviii + 281 pp. 2 maps, 2 photographs, 5 charts, 1 figure.

Designed chiefly for amateur naturalists in the British Isles, this book is especially notable for its wealth of documentation (802 references are cited) and may be regarded as a bibliographic introduction to bird watching. The author, an assistant curator at the Zoölogical Society of London, discusses adaptation and habitat selection, variation and distribution, environment, habitats, numbers, migration, colors and display, territory, and reproduction as they play a part in bird life.

Bird Watching. By Edmund Selous. 1901. J. M. Dent and Son, London. xi + 347 pp. 14 drawings. Out of print.

Observations on plovers, stock-doves, wood-pigeons, ravens, curlews, eider ducks, cormorants, rooks, blackbirds, nightingales, and many other British birds. Selous was a distinguished bird watcher of considerable originality. Of his several books, this is perhaps his best. Another excellent volume is *A Bird Watcher in the Shetlands.*

Publications of the British Trust for Ornithology. Vol. 1 (1935-9).
Edward Gray Institute of Field Ornithology, Oxford, England. 338
pp. 18 photographs, 8 maps, 6 charts and graphs.
Examples of co-operative bird watching abroad, which will interest
experienced students in this country and those intent on regional studies.
The present volume covers censuses, habitat surveys, food studies, and
population counts that were reported originally in British periodicals.

6. Bird Behavior

Simple introductions to bird behavior can be found in James
Fisher's books on bird watching, in which a chapter or two is devoted to courtship and territory. The most comprehensive survey
of the field is contained in Nice's study of the song sparrow (volume
2), which is described under life-history studies. Behavior studies
can often be roughly divided into two groups—those on land birds,
and those on sea birds. More accurately, these are described by
naturalists as territorial birds and colonial birds. Good examples
of the first type are the works of Nice, Tinbergen, and Kendeigh;
examples of the second are those of Kirkman, Darling, and Palmer.

Wild Birds at Home. By Francis H. Herrick. 1935. D. Appleton-Century
Co., Inc., New York. xxii + 345 pp.
A study by a keen-eyed observer, this is a classic American example
of how interesting birds can be studied without going far from home.

Courtship and Display among Birds. By C. R. Stoner. 1940. Country
Life, Ltd., London. xvi + 144 pp. 57 plates.
Written for the 'non-specialist interested in natural history and for
ornithologists who have not had the time to go deeply into this branch
of their subject.' There are minute descriptions of many spectacular and
typical displays used in courtship and in combat, and a discussion of
the principles involved. Illustrated by a remarkable series of photographs
taken at the famous Zoölogical Gardens at Whipsnade, England.

The Behavior of the Snow Bunting in Spring. By Nicholas Tinbergen.
1939. Transactions of the Linnaean Society of New York, Vol. 5.
95 pp. 15 text figures, 4 photographs, 1 map.
An interesting description of this bird's breeding behavior in Greenland, with a stimulating discussion of fighting, territory, and song in
bird life. The volume is rich in its examples and well worth the attention of students interested in nesting studies. Written by a well-known

animal psychologist of the University of Leyden, the text is free of technical verbosity and represents alert bird watching at its best.

Territorial and Mating Behavior of the House Wren. By S. Charles Kendeigh. 1941. University of Illinois Press, Urbana, Ill. Illinois Biological Monographs, 18, No. 3. 120 pp. 2 photographs, 30 maps and diagrams.

A well-ordered summary of a 19-year behavior study in northern Ohio —the longest ever made of a limited population of birds. The interesting territorial relations of 142 males and 147 females are described, together with an account of their arrival in spring, their mating activities, and their reproductive vigor. The second half of the report, giving the history of individual birds and individual territories, is somewhat technical and rather hard to read. It is illustrated, however, by 26 maps showing how the size, shape, and position of territories varied from year to year and during each half of the breeding season. Long connected with the famous Baldwin research station on the outskirts of Cleveland, Ohio, Dr. Kendeigh now teaches at the University of Illinois.

Bird Behaviour. By F. B. Kirkman. 1937. T. Nelson & Sons, New York. 232 pp. 38 photographs, 6 diagrams.

An interesting study of the black-headed gull in England. Half of the book describes the sequence of events at the birds' nesting colonies; the other half covers the author's many experiments with eggs and nests (one photograph shows a gull brooding a gilt tin box in place of its eggs) and his analyses of the birds' reactions. A stimulating book for bird students in any country.

A Behavior Study of the Common Tern. By Ralph S. Palmer. 1941. Proceedings of the Boston Society of Natural History, Vol. 42. 119 pp. 2 charts, 14 plates.

A report on a 2-year study of the birds breeding on the coast of Maine; offers a useful model for students who would like to study the behavior of sea birds. The behavior of terns is also given in the Marples' book, described under life-history studies.

Bird Flocks and the Breeding Cycle. By F. Fraser Darling. 1938. Cambridge University Press; Macmillan Co., New York. x + 124 pp. 1 photograph, 1 chart.

An oft-quoted and well-written little book that will interest students of bird behavior and those in contact with bird colonies. Observations on sea birds breeding off the coast of Scotland are recounted: the herring gull, the lesser black-backed gull, eider ducks, black guillemots, razor-billed auks, and fulmars. The few biological terms that crop up are deftly handled. Recommended to those who want to pick up new ideas in bird watching.

An Introduction to Bird Behaviour. By H. Eliot Howard. 1929. Cambridge University Press; Macmillan Co., New York. 136 pp.

A mistitled and ornately printed work which discusses the author's own observations. Written by a careful and original observer of birds, it is primarily for advanced students in bird behavior.

The Nature of a Bird's World. By H. Eliot Howard. 1935. Cambridge University Press; Macmillan Co., New York, N.Y. 102 pp.

A thought-provoking book written by one of the most resolute thinkers on bird behavior in our generation.

A Waterhen's Worlds. By H. Eliot Howard. 1940. Cambridge University Press; Macmillan Co., New York. ix + 84 pp. 2 plates.

An analytical discussion of the breeding behavior of a gallinule, which is only superficially different from our American form. As nearly as anyone, Howard succeeds in penetrating the mysteries of a bird's mind. His essays, however, are exercises in thinking and will not interest those who wish to race in their reading.

7. BIRDS AND THEIR ENVIRONMENT

Studies of the mutual relationship of birds and their environment are often grouped together under the title of bird ecology. Regional books and life-history monographs also consider the subject in varying detail. (Some emphasize climates and life zones; others stress the classification of birds according to vegetational blocks.) Other books analyze the effects of environment on bird mortality and reproduction. At the moment, plant ecologists appear to be far ahead of animal ecologists in their studies. There are several periodicals now devoting themselves exclusively to this subject. For the most part, these attract college professors, graduate students, and the like.

In America, *Ecology,* a quarterly journal of the Ecological Society of America, published by the Brooklyn Botanic Garden (Brooklyn, N.Y.), covers all forms of life. *Ecological Monographs,* published by Duke University Press, is a quarterly devoted to longer papers in the same broad field.

In England, *The Journal of Animal Ecology,* published twice a year by the Cambridge University Press for the British Ecological Society, often contains papers on birds.

Interesting papers on bird ecology can also be found from time to time in *The Journal of Wildlife Management,* a quarterly devoted to professional game management and research, published by the Wildlife Society. Subscriptions to this periodical ($3 a year) should be sent to the Society's secretary, Frank C. Edminster, Soil Conservation Service, Upper Darby, Pa.

Many other periodicals of course carry the results of bird watching in this field. The importance of ecology is now so great that the periodical literature is constantly expanding, and special abstracting services now endeavor to publish summaries of the many papers that are written (see p. 242).

Ecology of the Birds of Quaker Run Valley. By Aretas A. Saunders. 1936. New York State Museum, Albany, N.Y. Handbook No. 16. 174 pp. 2 charts, 2 maps, 64 photographs. Stiff paper.

A study of the distribution of breeding birds in Alleghany State Park, New York, based on counts, estimates, and cross-country cruises. This is the best systematic attempt by an American to calculate the actual density of birds in a fairly large area. Although the method of counting is not clearly defined in the report, this study points the way to the regional bird books of the future, when the local density of every species will be set forth for each kind of habitat. An inexpensive but important book for students undertaking regional studies of birds. Mr. Saunders, a Connecticut high-school teacher, has written a number of valuable bird books (*Birds of Montana, A Guide to Bird Songs,* etc.).

Nesting Birds and the Vegetation Substrate. By William J. Beecher. 1942. Chicago Ornithological Society, Chicago, Ill. 69 pp. 1 photograph, 10 figures.

An interesting discussion of factors that the author believes affect the density of birds in a small region, together with an account of over 1200 nests in a 482-acre upland marsh in northern Illinois.

Game Management. By Aldo Leopold. 1933. Charles Scribner's Sons, New York. xxi + 481 pp. 35 charts, graphs, and diagrams.

Game research in America now exceeds in both extent and intensity that of all other countries combined. The present distinguished volume summarizes its progress up to 1932, and describes 'the art of cropping land for game.' It is notable for its accumulation of facts, and for its clear style and thoughtful assimilation of a complex subject in terms that both bird student and sportsman can understand. There are excellent discussions of the properties of game populations, game-census methods, and the measurement of productivity. Illustrated with pleasing line drawings in black and white by Allan Brooks, and buttressed by a useful 22½-page index. The author, for many years a forester and now professor of game management at the University of Wisconsin, has written many articles on game research, land use, and conservation.

Animal Ecology. By Charles Elton. 1927. Cambridge University Press; Macmillan Co., New York. xx + 207 pp. 13 photographs, 13 diagrams.

The sociology and economics of animal life related with an emphasis on principles, an excellent choice of examples, and a freedom from wordiness. This book will interest bird watchers in parallel studies being carried out in other fields of natural history. The author, an authority on wildlife cycles in North America, has more recently had published a noteworthy volume, *Voles, Mice, and Lemmings.* He is now director of the Bureau of Animal Population at Oxford University.

8. Bird Migration

Bird migration has been studied so long and by so many people that it is now virtually impossible for authors to write books that are both original and yet comprehensive. Hence, there is much duplication of material.

There are no periodicals in English devoted exclusively to bird migration. *Audubon Magazine* contains interesting summaries of the high lights of bird migration in the United States. *Bird-Banding* carries important results of American banding work as well as pertinent abstracts of important papers scattered among various periodicals and in many languages.

The Migration of American Birds. By Frederick C. Lincoln. 1939. Doubleday, Doran & Co., New York. xii + 189 pp. 12 color plates, 22 maps.

Written by an official of the United States Fish and Wildlife Service, who for many years has been in charge of the bird-banding program in this country, the book includes two excellent chapters summarizing the more important discoveries made by banders of North American migrants. The color plates (now somewhat worn) originally appeared in *Birds of New York.* An excellent condensation of this volume is available in United States Department of Agriculture Circular No. 363, a 72-page paper illustrated with 20 maps, and sold by the Superintendent of Documents at the Government Printing Office, Washington, D.C., for 10¢.

The Migrations of Birds. By Alexander Wetmore. 1926 (3rd printing 1930). Harvard University Press, Cambridge, Mass. viii + 225 pp. 2 figures, 5 maps.

Particularly interesting to North American readers for references to the habits and occurrence of our birds in South America. The author is assistant secretary of the Smithsonian Institution, and one of America's foremost ornithologists.

Bird Migration. By A. Landsborough Thomson. 1942, 2nd rev. ed. H. F. and G. Witherby, London. 192 pp. 7 photographs, 13 maps.

A short account of our present knowledge of bird migration written for the general reader by the leading British author in this field.

The Problems of Bird Migration. By A. Landsborough Thomson. 1926. Houghton Mifflin Co., Boston, Mass. xvi + 350 pp. 2 diagrams, 10 maps.

A British book for advanced students and specialists; the most comprehensive treatise on bird migration now available. Contains an account of the results of European banding, but does not cover the more recent experimental work on homing and physiology. (For an early popular account of the latter, see Professor Rowan's volume, which follows.)

The Riddle of Migration. By William Rowan. 1931. Williams and Wilkins Co., Baltimore, Md. xiv + 151 pp.

A popular presentation of the author's pioneering experiments in bird migration. (Caged juncos, crows, etc., were exposed to varying amounts of light and then liberated in winter to see whether they would go north or south.) Professor Rowan, who teaches at the University of Alberta, writes easily and not without humor on a technical subject.

9. LIFE-HISTORY STUDIES

Comparatively few naturalists have, up to the present, concentrated their field work on a single species and published their observations as life-history studies. Some of these authors are bird watchers, others are wildlife photographers, still others are professional research men or college professors. An increasing number are graduate students. From the pens of such writers, a wide diversity of books and reports have emanated, appealing to varying levels of reader interest and experience. I have tried here to classify these books according to the amount of technical background they seem to require of their readers. The arrangement is by no means entirely satisfactory, but it will, I think, help readers find the books that will most interest them.

As time goes on, life-history reports are certain to become collectors' items. Paper-covered volumes, upon being purchased, should therefore be bound in cloth or buckram at some bindery. This adds but little to their cost as a rule, and their value is sure to increase with the passage of time.

A. Books for the General Reader

Although popular books, these volumes are full of observations that will interest all bird watchers.

The American Eagle. By Francis H. Herrick. 1934. D. Appleton-Century Co., Inc., New York. xx + 267 pp. 66 photographs, 28 text figures.

The only available nesting study of our national bird. Most of the narrative concerns the story of several nests in northern Ohio, which were observed over a 7-year period. There is also an account of the eagle's place in American history, as well as many fine photographs. The author was for many years professor of biology at Western Reserve University.

The Island of Penguins. By Cherry Kearton. 1931. Robert M. McBride & Co., New York. xviii + 248 pp. 70 illustrations, 1 map.

A popular and very readable account of the life history of the black-footed penguin. The author spent five months off the Cape of Good Hope on an island where some five million of these birds breed.

Shearwaters. By R. M. Lockley. 1942. J. M. Dent & Sons, Ltd., London. xii + 238 pp. 31 photographs, 4 figures, 4 maps. (Distributed in this country by William Salloch, New York.)

The delightful story of Manx shearwaters nesting on an island off the Welsh coast, where 12 pairs of these strange birds were banded and closely watched. Told by a skillful writer, this is good bird watching and excellent reading.

B. Books for Bird Watchers

These volumes are factual and require no background other than an absorbing interest in birds. Only *Sea Terns* and *The Cowbirds* in this list are bound in cloth. Bird watchers will also find good reading in the works described in sections A and C.

Sea Terns or Sea Swallows. By George and Anne Marples. 1934. Country Life, London. xii + 228 pp. 25 diagrams, 7 maps and drawings, 113 photographs.

Among the five species studied were three (common, Arctic, and roseate) that breed in America. Bird students in this country will be interested especially in those chapters on courtship, nests, eggs, and young; food and feeding; attacks and defense; and population fluctuations. Data on 8696 nests are given. A unique chapter on footprints in the sand describes methods by which tracks can be used to reconstruct activities. The authors list 73 banding records and describe 34 experiments involving eggs and nests. Well indexed.

For tern behavior in this country, the reader should also read Ralph S. Palmer's report listed under 'Bird Behavior.' A great deal of noteworthy information on terns is to be found in the pages of *Bird-Banding*, where Dr. O. L. Austin, Sr., and his son publish from time to time the results of their extensive banding on Cape Cod.

The Passenger Pigeon in Ontario. By Margaret H. Mitchell. 1935. University of Toronto Press, Toronto, Ont. Royal Ontario Museum of Zoölogy, Contribution No. 7. 181 pp. 1 plate, 5 maps, 2 diagrams, 6 figures.

An interesting account of this extinct species in Ontario, originally begun with a questionnaire to persons who remembered the bird. This report is the best life history of the wild pigeon now compiled. It is an excellent example of how bird lore can be collected from many sources.

The Prairie Horned Lark. By Gayle B. Pickwell. 1931. Transactions of the St. Louis Academy of Sciences, Vol. 27. 153 pp. 6 maps, 3 drawings, 11 graphs, 87 photographs.

A 2-year study in which 33 nests were watched in Illinois and New York. The distribution of this species is given in detail, its life history throughout the year described, and a useful account given of other species sharing the prairie horned lark's ecological niche.

Studies in the Life History of the Song Sparrow. By Margaret M. Nice. 1939-43. Vol. 1: A Population Study of the Song Sparrow. vi + 247 pp. 1 colored plate, 4 photographs, 14 maps, 18 charts and diagrams. Vol. 2, on the behavior of passerine birds with special reference to the song sparrow, was in press when this appendix was written. Transactions of the Linnaean Society of New York (c/o American Museum of Natural History, New York), Vol. 4 and 6.

Commonly regarded as an indispensable reference work for bird watchers and ornithologists interested in field studies of passerine birds. Volume 1 emphasizes statistics and compares the author's 8-year research on the song sparrow with the results obtained by other investigators of environment, weights, territory, nests, eggs, incubation, nesting succession, survival, and similar subjects. Volume 2 covers the behavior of song birds in the field and adds in detail many observations on the song sparrow. Conveniently summarized and adequately indexed for quick reference. Of the 870 birds banded the territorial relationships of 336 were studied in detail. No other life-history study combines such rich scholarship with such keen field work.

The Cowbirds. By Herbert Friedmann. 1929. C. C. Thomas, Springfield, Ill., and Baltimore, Md. xvii + 421 pp. 73 photographs, 9 maps, 4 graphs. Out of print.

An unusual book showing how life histories differ among various species in the same family. The author studied 7 species of cowbirds in New York state, on the Texas-Mexican border, and in the Argentine. His interesting comparisons are concluded by two stimulating chapters on the evolution of this group and their parasitic habits. Written by one of America's most distinguished ornithologists, now curator of birds at the National Museum, Washington, D.C. Shorter cowbird studies have also been written by Hann and Nice.

C. *Technical Dissertations*

Life-history studies often form an important part of monographs on a single species. Very often these are produced by graduate students working for doctorate degrees, and engaged in problems of distribution, taxonomy, physiology, wildlife management, and conservation. The degree of consideration given to these other problems varies widely. Distribution seems to be a favorite and often dominates the opening sections of a monograph.

The life-history work likewise varies widely in character and value. The freedom of observation found in a field investigation of a common bird like the song sparrow is greatly restricted in studies of rare species like the spoonbill, shy and retiring birds like the woodcock and Bicknell's thrush, and in nearly extinct species like the ivory-billed woodpecker. A good clue to the extent of the difficulties encountered by investigators is the number of nests they discovered.

Only the first three books in this group are cloth bound.

The Bobwhite Quail. By Herbert L. Stoddard. 1931. Charles Scribner's Sons, New York. xxix + 559 pp. 5 color plates, 32 text figures, 33 diagrams and graphs, 135 photographs. Out of print.

One of the great monographs on a North American bird, this work is based on a 5-year study of quail in Georgia and Florida. A total of 602 nests were studied. Principal subjects included are: (1) the bird's life history, with the emphasis on ecology; (2) parasites and diseases, which will interest bird banders; and (3) management of quail preserves. Mr. Stoddard is a professional consultant on quail management and the leading authority on this much-studied species.

The Blue-winged Teal. By Logan J. Bennett. 1938. Collegiate Press, Inc., Ames, Iowa. xiv + 144 pp. 1 color plate, 31 photographs, 6 maps.

Brief and to the point, abounding in facts that will interest all bird students: Range, distribution, and migration; life-history findings; various aspects of the bird's ecology and management. The best study now available on an American duck, this book is the result of 4½ years of research, principally in Iowa, where 250 nests were found. Supplementary observations were conducted from Manitoba to Mexico. The author is now on the faculty of Pennsylvania State College.

The American Woodcock. By Olin Sewall Pettingill, Jr. 1936. Memoirs of the Boston Society of Natural History, Vol. 9, No. 2. Pp. 167-391. 1 color plate, 7 diagrams, 14 drawings, 48 photographs.

Discussions of taxonomy, plumages, pterylosis, and osteology; range and distribution; food and feeding habits; and life history. A total of 16 nests were studied. Dr. Pettingill is a well-known wildlife photographer and lecturer, now on the faculty of Carleton College in Minnesota.

Bicknell's Thrush, Its Taxonomy, Distribution, and Life History. By George J. Wallace. 1939. Proceedings of the Boston Society of Natural History, Vol. 41. Pp. 211-402. 2 graphs, 1 text figure.

A three-year study which included two summers of observation of the nesting habits of this retiring bird. The complete history of 13 nests was studied and additional notes were made on others. The discussion covers taxonomic problems, distributional and migrational records, and reproductive habits.

The Ivory-billed Woodpecker. By James T. Tanner. 1942. National Audubon Society, New York, N.Y. Research Report No. 1. xii + 111 pp. 1 color plate, 19 photographs, 4 diagrams, 18 maps.

In this quiet report lies the dramatic story of a magnificent species doomed to extinction. The book contains a detailed history of its former distribution and gradual disappearance, a description of its ecology and its life history, and a discussion of a possible conservation program. Well illustrated with photographs, the book is the result of a field study undertaken by a Cornell University graduate student for the National Audubon Society.

The Roseate Spoonbill. By Robert P. Allen. 1942. National Audubon Society, New York. Research Report No. 2. xviii + 142 pp. 1 color plate, 8 maps, 16 charts and diagrams, 20 line drawings, 20 photographs.

This well-illustrated study represents 16 months of field work on the wild coasts of Florida and Texas, and 9 months of follow-up research in museum and library. The first fifth of the book describes the spoonbill's changing numbers in the United States, and its migrations and postnuptial wanderings. The major part summarizes the ecological problems: the factors affecting its population, its food and feeding habits. An interesting and valuable chapter on breeding-cycle behavior is illustrated with sketches made by the author in the field. Written by the former director of sanctuaries for the National Audubon Society, this volume covers problems in bird watching and conservation.

Systematic Revision and Natural History of the American Shrikes (Lanius). By Alden H. Miller. 1931. University of California Publications in Zoölogy, Vol. 38, No. 2. Pp. 11-242. 65 text figures.

This monograph falls into two distinct parts. In the first, taxonomic problems occupy a prominent place, plumages are described in detail, and geographic variation is discussed. Of particular interest is the analysis of factors affecting the birds' distribution. In the second half, aspects of natural history are grouped together: migration, habitats, territory, courtship, nests, mortality, etc. The discussions are based on an extensive review of the literature, field studies of about 10 pairs, and the interesting reactions of several caged birds. Written by a leading western ornithologist, now editor of *The Condor,* this book is essentially an inquiry into species and a consideration of the normal activities of these birds throughout the year.

The White-crowned Sparrows of the Pacific Seaboard: Environment and Annual Cycle. By Barbara D. Blanchard. 1941. University of California Publications in Zoölogy, Vol. 46. 176 pp. 4 maps, 26 charts, 6 photographs, 31 microphotographs.

An interesting comparison of two closely related races, one migratory, the other resident. Observations on breeding-bird behavior made over a four-year period are described and correlated with physiological studies.

The Natural History of Magpies. By Jean M. Linsdale. 1937. Cooper
Ornithological Club, c/o W. L. Chambers, Robinson Road, Topanga,
Calif. Pacific Coast Avifauna No. 25. 234 pp. 1 color plate, 4 maps,
9 charts and diagrams, 43 photographs.

This volume brings together material from many sources: field work
by the author in western states (extensive rather than intensive), over
600 references in the literature, museum materials, and observations on
several caged birds. Distribution, habitats, nesting, general habits, plumages and anatomy, and relations to other animals are some of the subjects considered.

10. GENERAL REFERENCE BOOKS

Books that treat of a large number of species and summarize
their habits are included here. Bent's volumes are noted for their
extensiveness, the British handbook for its modernity, and Chapman's for its introduction and bibliographies. Some regional books
are also of the general reference type—Hoffmann's *Birds of the
Pacific States* and Forbush's *Birds of Massachusetts* are best re-
spectively for the western and eastern halves of the country.

Life Histories of North American Birds. By Arthur Cleveland Bent.
United States National Museum, Washington, D.C.

These volumes are the products of a great co-operative project undertaken in 1919 and now approaching completion. The plan involves the
compilation of life-history notes scattered in the literature and in the
notebooks of naturalists for every species and subspecies recorded in
North America. The habits of each are described; sections are devoted to
courtship, nesting, eggs, young, plumages, food, behavior, and enemies.
The data on distribution, taken from the extensive files of the Fish and
Wildlife Service, are given in great detail. Egg dates are summarized
to show the earliest and latest dates in various parts of the country, and
the height of the season. Plumage descriptions enable the reader, for
the most part, to trace the sequence of molts from birth to maturity.
More complete descriptions of adult plumages have been deliberately
left to other manuals. These volumes rapidly go out of print. Each
contains its own index and a good list of references. As issued by the
Government Printing Office, they sell at prices ranging from 50¢ to $1.25.
Complete sets are usually found only in the larger libraries. The photographs, on the whole, are good. The text is easy to read and interesting
to both beginners and experienced students.

Bent's sketches summarize for the student what is already known and
offer him a firm foundation upon which he can begin an intensive life-

history study of his own. The author is a distinguished former president of the American Ornithologists' Union.

Life Histories of North American Diving Birds. Order Pygopodes. 1919. Bull. 107. xiii + 245 pp. 55 plates (12 in color).

Life Histories of North American Gulls and Terns. Order Longipennes. 1921. Bull. 113. x + 345 pp. 93 plates (16 in color, showing eggs).

Life Histories of North American Petrels, Pelicans, and Their Allies. Order Tubinares and Steganopodes. 1922. Bull. 121. xii + 343 pp. 69 plates.

Life Histories of North American Wild Fowl. Order Anseres. Part 1. 1925. Bull. 126. ix + 250 pp. 46 plates.

Life Histories of North American Wild Fowl. Order Anseres. Part 2. 1925. Bull. 130. x + 376 pp. 60 plates.

Life Histories of North American Marsh Birds. Order Odontoglossae, Herodiones, and Paludicolae. 1926 (1927). Bull. 135. xi + 490 pp. 98 plates.

Life Histories of North American Shore Birds. Order Limicolae. Part 1. 1927. Bull. 142. ix + 420 pp. 55 plates.

Life Histories of North American Shore Birds. Order Limicolae. Part 2. 1929. Bull. 146. ix + 412 pp. 66 plates.

Life Histories of North American Gallinaceous Birds. Order Galliformes and Columbiformes. 1932. Bull. 162. xi + 490 pp. 93 plates.

Life Histories of North American Birds of Prey. Order Falconiformes. Part 1. 1937. Bull. 167. viii + 409 pp. 102 plates.

Life Histories of North American Birds of Prey. Order Falconiformes and Strigiformes. Part 2. 1938. Bull. 170. viii + 482 pp. 92 plates.

Life Histories of North American Woodpeckers. Order Piciformes. 1939. Bull. 174. viii + 334 pp. 39 plates.

Life Histories of North American Cuckoos, Goatsuckers, Hummingbirds, and Their Allies. Order Psittaciformes, Cuculiformes, Trogoniformes, Coraciiformes, Caprimulgiformes, and Micropodiiformes. 1940. Bull. 176. viii + 506 pp. 75 plates.

Life Histories of North American Flycatchers, Larks, Swallows, and Their Allies. Order Passeriformes. 1942. Bull. 179. xi + 555 pp. 70 plates.

Handbook of Birds of Eastern North America. By Frank M. Chapman. 1932, 2nd rev. ed. D. Appleton-Century Co., New York, N.Y. xxxvi + 581 pp. 29 plates, 166 text figures.

For 40 years this was an indispensable book for bird students in the East. Spanning the field ornithology of the nineteenth century and bird watching in the twentieth, it is still a useful volume. Its introduction, running to 124 pages, contains a fine color chart, a good historical review, a description of how birds are named by scientists, directions on making bird skins, a good chapter on bird migration, and an excellent account of how birds live. The major part of the book is given over to a discussion of those birds that occur east of the 93rd meridian (plumage descriptions, ranges, and nests). The bulk of these latter details are repeated or amplified in the larger state books; condensed versions are also found in the field guides. Under each species the more important papers written before 1933 are cited. The appendix contains a complete bibliography of local lists for all of the eastern states and Canadian provinces.

The Handbook of British Birds. By H. F. Witherby, F. C. R. Jourdain, N. F. Ticehurst, and B. W. Tucker. 1938-41. H. F. and G. Witherby, London. Vol. 1; Crows to Flycatchers; xl + 326 pp; 33 plates. Vol. 2; Warblers to Owls; xiii + 352 pp.; 30 plates, 41 figures. Vol. 3; Hawks to Ducks; x + 387 pp.; 39 plates, 46 figures, 7 maps. Vol. 4; Cormorants to Cranes; xiv + 461 pp.; 32 plates, 46 figures. Vol. 5; Terns to Gamebirds; xii + 356 pp.; 22 plates, 62 figures, map.

The best work of general reference on the birds of western Europe. The information on living birds is far more detailed than in American texts. It includes summaries for each species on habitats, field characters, general habits, voice, displays, breeding habits (nest site, construction of nest, the number, size, and color of eggs, incubation, and fledgling periods), food, distribution, plumages, molts, and measurements. For the most part, the illustrations are designed to show essential details of birds' plumage.

About 170 birds included on the North American list are treated here, together with 30 other closely related subspecies. The book is therefore a quick compendium of information; its price is, however, more than the average student can afford.

11. Bird Biology

Background information about birds, written in nontechnical style for amateur naturalists, is best found in Dr. Allen's book described below. Books on this subject generally treat birds along with numerous other classes in the animal kingdom. Dr. H. B. Cott's's interesting *Adaptive Coloration in Animals* is an example. More general books on biology can be found in practically any public library.

Birds and Their Attributes. By Glover M. Allen. 1926. Marshall Jones Co., Boston. xiv + 338 pp. 1 color plate, 50 drawings and photographs.

The best available American book on the general biology of birds, this was originally written as a series of lectures, delivered in 1924 under the auspices of the Northeastern Bird Banding Association. The chapters deal with a history of ornithology; feathers; colors; bills, feet, wings, and bones; food; origin and distribution; ecological relations;

eggs and nests; parasitic habits; senses and behavior; flight and song; birds at rest; migration; nomenclature and classification.

Dr. Allen, a curator at the Harvard Museum of Comparative Zoölogy, was one of America's leading ornithologists and mammalogists. His volume is now somewhat dated, but it should be read by every student who would like to acquire some background of bird biology.

12. MISCELLANEOUS

Key to North American Birds. By Elliott Coues. 1927, 6th rev. ed. Dana Estes & Co., Boston. 2 vol. xli + 1152 pp. 747 figures.

This is the classic North American Ornithology of the nineteenth century. Birds are here described in great detail, since the student is presumed to have a skin in hand as he reads. Included is a manual of instruction for collecting, preparing, and preserving birds, discussions of structure, classification, and anatomy. Especially interesting is Dr. Coues' brief history of ornithology and his pointed advice on how to take up field ornithology. The author, now long deceased, was a United States Army surgeon, a famous editor, and one of the most brilliant ornithologists America has ever produced.

Check-List of North American Birds. 1931. 4th ed. American Ornithologists' Union, Philadelphia, Pa. xix + 526 pp.

This is the official list of all North American birds, divided into various classes, orders, families, and the like. In no other bird book are the ranges of all the species and subspecies given. To bird students it offers an authoritative spelling of birds' names, as well as the correct order of listing species in breeding-bird censuses, Christmas bird counts, and similar reports. Records of the occurrence of rarities are usually checked against this list. If they are thus found to change the status of a bird, they should be published in some ornithological periodical like *The Auk.* The check-list also mentions where each species and subspecies were first found. To many students this constitutes the best reading in the book (the ring-necked duck was first discovered in Leadanhall market, London!). Work on a fifth (and revised) edition is now in progress.

Abridged Check-List of North American Birds. 1935. American Ornithologists' Union, Philadelphia, Pa. 177 pp.

From the fourth edition of the American Ornithologists' Union's *Check-List,* this gives the popular and scientific names of all North American birds in their official order. The left-hand pages are all left blank and can be used for brief notations.

Fifty Years' Progress of American Ornithology, 1883-1933. American Ornithologists' Union, Philadelphia, Pa. 249 pp. (Paper cover.)

An excellent historical review with chapters by leading ornithologists on: the American Ornithologists' Union, American ornithological literature, bird migration, bird banding, the theory of territorialism, life-history work, economic ornithology, collections of birds in the United States and Canada, bird photography in America, American bird art, bird protection, ornithological education in America, and fossil birds.

A Dictionary of Birds. By Alfred Newton, *et al.* 1893-6. Adam & Charles Black, London. xii + 1088 pp. 700 text figures, 1 map. Out of print.

One of the great reference works of nineteenth-century ornithology, explaining all terms then in use in the study of birds. An abridged second edition was issued in 1899.

Measurements of Birds. By S. Prentiss Baldwin, Harry C. Oberholser, and Leonard G. Worley. 1931. Cleveland Museum of Natural History, Cleveland, Ohio. Scientific Publication, II. ix + 165 pp. 151 figures.

A standard system of measurements worked out in detail by the authors as a guide for all those working with either live or dead birds.

13. BIRD CONSERVATION

Conservation problems receive varying degrees of attention in bird books. Attention to the problem usually is given over to the result of some trend—the destruction of a local swamp, or the extinction or extirpation of a vanishing bird. R. P. Allen's *The Roseate Spoonbill* and J. T. Tanner's *The Ivory-billed Woodpecker* have already been described. More general books follow.

Adventures in Bird Protection. By T. Gilbert Pearson. 1935. D. Appleton-Century Co., New York. xiv + 459 pp. 11 photographs.

An autobiography of the leading figure in the Audubon society movement, and a record of great achievements in bird conservation, this striking chronicle has much of the matchless zeal of its author.

Fading Trails. By Daniel B. Beard, *et al.* 1942. The Macmillan Co., New York. xv + 279 pp. 4 color plates, 16 half-tone plates, 12 drawings in black and white.

Interesting accounts of how various forms of wildlife have been nearing the brink of extinction; prepared by well-informed members of the National Park Service and the Fish and Wildlife Service. Special chapters on 13 species of birds, now rapidly vanishing in the United States and its territories. Illustrated with fine paintings and drawings by Walter A. Weber.

Wildlife Conservation. By Ira N. Gabrielson. 1941. The Macmillan Co., New York. xv + 250 pp. 32 photographs, 5 diagrams, 19 maps.
Generalized discussions of many problems connected with the subject. The last chapter should be read by every American. Written by the Chief of the Department of the Interior's Fish and Wildlife Service.

14. BIOGRAPHICAL WORKS

Only relatively complete biographies are listed here. Many famous naturalists have also written travelogues which make excellent reading. Among them are F. M. Chapman (*Camps and Cruises of an Ornithologist, My Tropical Air Castle,* and *Life in an Air Castle*), G. M. Sutton (*Eskimo Year, Birds in the Wilderness*), Fraser Darling (*Island Years, A Naturalist on Rona*), and R. M. Lockley (*I Know an Island, Dream Island*).

Audubon the Naturalist. By Francis H. Herrick. 1917. D. Appleton-Century Co., New York. Vol. 1, xl + 451 pp.; vol. 2, xiii + 494 pp.
The standard biography with an extensive bibliography, copious notes on early American naturalists, and an appendix of useful Auduboniana reference material. A one-volume edition of this work was published in 1938, with considerable new material.

Autobiography of a Bird Lover. By Frank M. Chapman. 1933. D. Appleton-Century Co., Inc., New York. xiii + 420 pp. 6 plates (3 in color), 81 photographs.
The life story of one of America's most famous ornithologists, well told and well illustrated. Spanning almost a half century of bird study, the book is also a rich travelogue of Central and South America seen through the eyes of a sensitive naturalist.

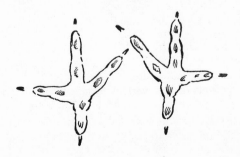

Index

A CATALOGUE OF SELECTED DOVER BOOKS
IN ALL FIELDS OF INTEREST

A CATALOGUE OF SELECTED DOVER
BOOKS IN ALL FIELDS OF INTEREST

CELESTIAL OBJECTS FOR COMMON TELESCOPES, T. W. Webb. The most used book in amateur astronomy: inestimable aid for locating and identifying nearly 4,000 celestial objects. Edited, updated by Margaret W. Mayall. 77 illustrations. Total of 645pp. 5⅜ x 8½.
20917-2, 20918-0 Pa., Two-vol. set $9.00

HISTORICAL STUDIES IN THE LANGUAGE OF CHEMISTRY, M. P. Crosland. The important part language has played in the development of chemistry from the symbolism of alchemy to the adoption of systematic nomenclature in 1892. ". . . wholeheartedly recommended,"—Science. 15 illustrations. 416pp. of text. 5⅝ x 8¼.
63702-6 Pa. $6.00

BURNHAM'S CELESTIAL HANDBOOK, Robert Burnham, Jr. Thorough, readable guide to the stars beyond our solar system. Exhaustive treatment, fully illustrated. Breakdown is alphabetical by constellation: Andromeda to Cetus in Vol. 1; Chamaeleon to Orion in Vol. 2; and Pavo to Vulpecula in Vol. 3. Hundreds of illustrations. Total of about 2000pp. 6⅛ x 9¼.
23567-X, 23568-8, 23673-0 Pa., Three-vol. set $26.85

THEORY OF WING SECTIONS: INCLUDING A SUMMARY OF AIR-FOIL DATA, Ira H. Abbott and A. E. von Doenhoff. Concise compilation of subatomic aerodynamic characteristics of modern NASA wing sections, plus description of theory. 350pp. of tables. 693pp. 5⅜ x 8½.
60586-8 Pa. $7.00

DE RE METALLICA, Georgius Agricola. Translated by Herbert C. Hoover and Lou H. Hoover. The famous Hoover translation of greatest treatise on technological chemistry, engineering, geology, mining of early modern times (1556). All 289 original woodcuts. 638pp. 6¾ x 11.
60006-8 Clothbd. $17.95

THE ORIGIN OF CONTINENTS AND OCEANS, Alfred Wegener. One of the most influential, most controversial books in science, the classic statement for continental drift. Full 1966 translation of Wegener's final (1929) version. 64 illustrations. 246pp. 5⅜ x 8½. 61708-4 Pa. $4.50

THE PRINCIPLES OF PSYCHOLOGY, William James. Famous long course complete, unabridged. Stream of thought, time perception, memory, experimental methods; great work decades ahead of its time. Still valid, useful; read in many classes. 94 figures. Total of 1391pp. 5⅜ x 8½.
20381-6, 20382-4 Pa., Two-vol. set $13.00

CATALOGUE OF DOVER BOOKS

AMERICAN BIRD ENGRAVINGS, Alexander Wilson et al. All 76 plates. from Wilson's *American Ornithology* (1808-14), most important ornithological work before Audubon, plus 27 plates from the supplement (1825-33) by Charles Bonaparte. Over 250 birds portrayed. 8 plates also reproduced in full color. 111pp. 9⅜ x 12½. 23195-X Pa. $6.00

CRUICKSHANK'S PHOTOGRAPHS OF BIRDS OF AMERICA, Allan D. Cruickshank. Great ornithologist, photographer presents 177 closeups, groupings, panoramas, flightings, etc., of about 150 different birds. Expanded *Wings in the Wilderness*. Introduction by Helen G. Cruickshank. 191pp. 8¼ x 11. 23497-5 Pa. $6.00

AMERICAN WILDLIFE AND PLANTS, A. C. Martin, et al. Describes food habits of more than 1000 species of mammals, birds, fish. Special treatment of important food plants. Over 300 illustrations. 500pp. 5⅜ x 8½. 20793-5 Pa. $4.95

THE PEOPLE CALLED SHAKERS, Edward D. Andrews. Lifetime of research, definitive study of Shakers: origins, beliefs, practices, dances, social organization, furniture and crafts, impact on 19th-century USA, present heritage. Indispensable to student of American history, collector. 33 illustrations. 351pp. 5⅜ x 8½. 21081-2 Pa. $4.00

OLD NEW YORK IN EARLY PHOTOGRAPHS, Mary Black. New York City as it was in 1853-1901, through 196 wonderful photographs from N.-Y. Historical Society. Great Blizzard, Lincoln's funeral procession, great buildings. 228pp. 9 x 12. 22907-6 Pa. $7.95

MR. LINCOLN'S CAMERA MAN: MATHEW BRADY, Roy Meredith. Over 300 Brady photos reproduced directly from original negatives, photos. Jackson, Webster, Grant, Lee, Carnegie, Barnum; Lincoln; Battle Smoke, Death of Rebel Sniper, Atlanta Just After Capture. Lively commentary. 368pp. 8⅜ x 11¼. 23021-X Pa. $8.95

TRAVELS OF WILLIAM BARTRAM, William Bartram. From 1773-8, Bartram explored Northern Florida, Georgia, Carolinas, and reported on wild life, plants, Indians, early settlers. Basic account for period, entertaining reading. Edited by Mark Van Doren. 13 illustrations. 141pp. 5⅜ x 8½. 20013-2 Pa. $4.50

THE GENTLEMAN AND CABINET MAKER'S DIRECTOR, Thomas Chippendale. Full reprint, 1762 style book, most influential of all time; chairs, tables, sofas, mirrors, cabinets, etc. 200 plates, plus 24 photographs of surviving pieces. 249pp. 9⅞ x 12¾. 21601-2 Pa. $6.50

AMERICAN CARRIAGES, SLEIGHS, SULKIES AND CARTS, edited by Don H. Berkebile. 168 Victorian illustrations from catalogues, trade journals, fully captioned. Useful for artists. Author is Assoc. Curator, Div. of Transportation of Smithsonian Institution. 168pp. 8½ x 9½. 23328-6 Pa. $5.00

THE CURVES OF LIFE, Theodore A. Cook. Examination of shells, leaves, horns, human body, art, etc., in *"the* classic reference on how the golden ratio applies to spirals and helices in nature . . . . "—Martin Gardner. 426 illustrations. Total of 512pp. 5⅜ x 8½.   23701-X Pa. $5.95

AN ILLUSTRATED FLORA OF THE NORTHERN UNITED STATES AND CANADA, Nathaniel L. Britton, Addison Brown. Encyclopedic work covers 4666 species, ferns on up. Everything. Full botanical information, illustration for each. This earlier edition is preferred · by many to more recent revisions. 1913 edition. Over 4000 illustrations, total of 2087pp. 6⅛ x 9¼.   22642-5, 22643-3, 22644-1 Pa., Three-vol. set $24.00

MANUAL OF THE GRASSES OF THE UNITED STATES, A. S. Hitchcock, U.S. Dept. of Agriculture. The basic study of American grasses, both indigenous and escapes, cultivated and wild. Over 1400 species. Full descriptions, information. Over 1100 maps, illustrations. Total of 1051pp. 5⅜ x 8½.   22717-0, 22718-9 Pa., Two-vol. set $15.00

THE CACTACEAE,, Nathaniel L. Britton, John N. Rose. Exhaustive, definitive. Every cactus in the world. Full botanical descriptions. Thorough statement of nomenclatures, habitat, detailed finding keys. The one book needed by every cactus enthusiast. Over 1275 illustrations. Total of 1080pp. 8 x 10¼.   21191-6, 21192-4 Clothbd., Two-vol. set $35.00

AMERICAN MEDICINAL PLANTS, Charles F. Millspaugh. Full descriptions, 180 plants covered: history; physical description; methods of preparation with all chemical constituents extracted; all claimed curative or adverse effects. 180 full-page plates. Classification table. 804pp. 6½ x 9¼.
23034-1 Pa. $10.00

A MODERN HERBAL, Margaret Grieve. Much the fullest, most exact, most useful compilation of herbal material. Gigantic alphabetical encyclopedia, from aconite to zedoary, gives botanical information, medical properties, folklore, economic uses, and much else. Indispensable to serious reader. 161 illustrations. 888pp. 6½ x 9¼. (Available in U.S. only)
22798-7, 22799-5 Pa., Two-vol. set $12.00

THE HERBAL or GENERAL HISTORY OF PLANTS, John Gerard. The 1633 edition revised and enlarged by Thomas Johnson. Containing almost 2850 plant descriptions and 2705 superb illustrations, Gerard's *Herbal* is a monumental work, the book all modern English herbals are derived from, the one herbal every serious enthusiast should have in its entirety. Original editions are worth perhaps $750. 1678pp. 8½ x 12¼.
23147-X Clothbd. $50.00

MANUAL OF THE TREES OF NORTH AMERICA, Charles S. Sargent. The basic survey of every native tree and tree-like shrub, 717 species in all. Extremely full descriptions, information on habitat, growth, locales, economics, etc. Necessary to every serious tree lover. Over 100 finding keys. 783 illustrations. Total of 986pp. 5⅜ x 8½.
20277-1, 20278-X Pa., Two-vol. set $10.00

AMERICAN ANTIQUE FURNITURE, Edgar G. Miller, Jr. The basic coverage of all American furniture before 1840: chapters per item chronologically cover all types of furniture, with more than 2100 photos. Total of 1106pp. 7⅞ x 10¾. 21599-7, 21600-4 Pa., Two-vol. set $17.90

ILLUSTRATED GUIDE TO SHAKER FURNITURE, Robert Meader. Director, Shaker Museum, Old Chatham, presents up-to-date coverage of all furniture and appurtenances, with much on local styles not available elsewhere. 235 photos. 146pp. 9 x 12. 22819-3 Pa. $5.00

ORIENTAL RUGS, ANTIQUE AND MODERN, Walter A. Hawley. Persia, Turkey, Caucasus, Central Asia, China, other traditions. Best general survey of all aspects: styles and periods, manufacture, uses, symbols and their interpretation, and identification. 96 illustrations, 11 in color. 320pp. 6⅛ x 9¼. 22366-3 Pa. $6.95

CHINESE POTTERY AND PORCELAIN, R. L. Hobson. Detailed descriptions and analyses by former Keeper of the Department of Oriental Antiquities and Ethnography at the British Museum. Covers hundreds of pieces from primitive times to 1915. Still the standard text for most periods. 136 plates, 40 in full color. Total of 750pp. 5⅜ x 8½. 23253-0 Pa. $10.00

THE WARES OF THE MING DYNASTY, R. L. Hobson. Foremost scholar examines and illustrates many varieties of Ming (1368-1644). Famous blue and white, polychrome, lesser-known styles and shapes. 117 illustrations, 9 full color, of outstanding pieces. Total of 263pp. 6⅛ x 9¼. (Available in U.S. only) 23652-8 Pa. $6.00

Prices subject to change without notice.

Available at your book dealer or write for free catalogue to Dept. GI, Dover Publications, Inc., 180 Varick St., N.Y., N.Y. 10014. Dover publishes more than 175 books each year on science, elementary and advanced mathematics, biology, music, art, literary history, social sciences and other areas.